61

WITHDRAWN

WITHDRAWN

HOMELESS CHILDREN
AND YOUTH

HOMELESS CHILDREN AND YOUTH

A New American Dilemma

Edited by

Julee H. Kryder-Coe, Lester M. Salamon,
and Janice M. Molnar

with a foreword by
Congressman George Miller

Transaction Publishers
New Brunswick (U.S.A.) and London (U.K.)

Second Printing, 1992

Copyright © 1991 by Transaction Publishers
New Brunswick, New Jersey 08903

All rights reserved under International and Pan-American Copyright
Conventions. No part of this book may be reproduced or transmitted in any
form or by any means, electronic or mechanical, including photocopy,
recording, or any information storage and retrieval system, without prior
permission from the publisher. All inquiries should be addressed to
Transaction Publishers, Rutgers-The State University, New Brunswick, New
Jersey 08903.

Library of Congress Catalogue Number: 90-42495
ISBN: 0-88738-386-6
Printed in the United States of America

Library of Congress Cataloging-in-Publication Data

Homeless children and youth: a new American dilemma / edited by Julee H.
    Kryder-Coe, Lester M. Salamon, and Janice M. Molnar; with a foreword
    by George Miller.
        p.   cm.
    Includes bibliographical references and index.
    ISBN 0-88738-386-6
    1. Homeless children – United States. 2. Homeless youth – United
States. I. Kryder-Coe, Julee H. II. Salamon, Lester M. III. Molnar,
Janice Marie, 1954-
HV4505.H6515 1990
362.7'08'6942–dc20
                                                                                90-42495
                                                                                    CIP

This book is based on papers commissioned for the national conference,
"Homeless Children and Youth: Coping with a National Tragedy," held in
Washington, D.C. from April 25-28, 1989 and sponsored by the Johns
Hopkins Institute for Policy Studies.

Contents

Preface
Lester M. Salamon   vii

Foreword
George Miller   xi

Part I. The Scope of Child and Youth Homelessness

1. Introduction
   Janice M. Molnar   3

2. Beyond the Numbers: Homeless Families with Children
   Lisa Mihaly   11

3. Homeless Youth: An Overview of Recent Literature
   Marjorie J. Robertson   33

Part II. The Impact of Child and Youth Homelessness

4. Poverty, Homelessness, Health, Nutrition, and Children
   James D. Wright   71

5. Developmental and Educational Consequences of Homelessness on
   Children and Youth
   Yvonne Rafferty   105

Part III. The Causes of Child and Youth Homelessness

6. Macroeconomic Issues in Poverty: Implications for Child and Youth
   Homelessness
   Kay Young McChesney   143

7. What is Wrong with the Housing Market
   Chester Hartman and Barry Zigas   175

Part IV. The Response to the Crisis – Housing, Welfare, and Child Welfare Policy: Part of the Solution or Part of the Problem?

8. What is Wrong with Our Housing Programs
    Chester Hartman and Barry Zigas   197

9. Remedies for Homelessness: An Analysis of Potential
    Housing Policy and Program Responses
    Michael A. Stegman   225

10. The Welfare System's Response to Homelessness
    Linda A. Wolf   271

11. Child Welfare Services and Homelessness: Issues in
    Policy, Philosophy, and Programs
    Carol W. Williams   285

Contributors   301
Name Index   303
Subject Index   315

Preface

In 1987, several Baltimore community leaders, concerned about reports of growing numbers of "street children" in Baltimore and other cities across the United States, asked the Johns Hopkins Institute for Policy Studies to look into this issue and see what is known. With support from the Baltimore-based Abell Foundation, we conducted an initial inquiry and concluded that homelessness was indeed becoming a widespread reality in the United States not only for adults, but for large numbers of children and adolescents as well. Preliminary indications were that at least one-third of the homeless in the country were families with children and that additional children were homeless on their own. Children, it turned out, have become the most rapidly growing segment of the homeless population, changing the face of homelessness dramatically and alarmingly. At the same time, we discovered that the existing base of knowledge about the scope, causes, and consequences of this phenomenon was limited and diffuse at best, with little effort to date to pull together what is known and decide what should be done.

At the urging of a number of national organizations active in this field, we set out to fill at least part of this gap by convening a national conference designed to focus national attention on this alarming problem, to assemble what is known about it, and to decide what can be done. Support for this conference was secured from the Carnegie Corporation of New York, the Edna McConnell Clark Foundation, the Foundation for Child Development, and the Mailman Foundation. The conference took place in Washington in April 1989.

As background for the conference, we commissioned twelve expert papers designed to examine different facets of homelessness among both young children in families and adolescents on their own. Underlying both the conference and the papers was the conviction, grounded in our early investigation, that homelessness among children and youth was not just a housing problem. Rather, it reflected strains or breakdowns in a variety of other social support systems as well, ranging from welfare to foster care. An approach to the problem of homelessness that failed to address these broader problems thus seemed doomed to ineffectiveness. In addition, we concluded early on that the problems facing adolescents on their own differed significantly from those of young children "on the road" with their parents.

Accordingly, papers were commissioned on the scope and consequences of homelessness both among adolescents on their own and among younger children in families. We also commissioned special studies of the varied social support systems thought to be relevant to the problem, including housing policy, child welfare policy, and income assistance policy. The result is the most current summary of the state of knowledge on homelessness among children and youth that has been assembled to date.

The purpose of this book is to make this timely collection of materials available to a wider audience. The book contains most of the papers originally prepared for our conference, revised where appropriate to take account of conference discussions.

Numerous people assisted in the development of this book and the conference out of which it grows. Lee Tawney and Ross Pologe first alerted us to the problem of growing child homelessness. An outstanding advisory committee chaired by James Rouse and including June Bucy, Ann Dalton, Harriett Goldman, Chester Hartman, Pat Langley, Kay Young McChesney, Lisa Mihaly, Janice Molnar, David Paige, Ross Pologe, Marilyn Rocky, Anthony Russo, Lee Tawney, Laura Waxman, and Barry Zigas assisted with the design and organization of our national conference. Our conference also benefited from the encouragement of several co-sponsors or cooperating organizations, including The Johns Hopkins School of Hygiene and Public Health, CHILDHOPE, Family Service America, The Association of Junior Leagues, and the U.S. Committee for UNICEF. We are also grateful to the many participants in the conference, as well as the special speakers – Congressman George Miller (D. Ca.), chairman of the House Select Committee on Children and Youth; Jonathan Kozol, author of *Rachel and Her Children: Homeless Families in America;* and Marian Wright Edelman, president of the Children's Defense Fund. A debt of gratitude is owed as well to the funders of this effort noted above, to Janice Molnar and Bill Rath for help in editing the manuscripts; to Dee Sullivan, Marie Butler, Jackie Perry, and Jean

Biddinger for help with conference planning and arrangements; and to Jean Derby, Rose Livingston, Katharine Rylaarsdam, and Susan Mitchell for invaluable help in preparing the manuscript. Finally, I want to express special appreciation to Ms. Julee Kryder-Coe, who had principal responsibility for organizing the conference, for recruiting the paper authors and speakers, and for assembling the materials presented here. Her insight, dedication, and drive were crucial to this whole effort.

Homelessness among children and youth is too serious a problem to be ignored in our national social policy. Both for its immediate effects on those who are homeless, and for the inadequacies it reveals in our social support systems, homelessness among children and youth has truly become a national tragedy. If this book helps to bring this problem to national attention, to document its scope and consequences, and to point the way toward possible solutions, it will have amply served its purpose.

LESTER M. SALAMON
Director
Johns Hopkins Institute for Policy Studies

Foreword

We have always taken for granted in this country that all Americans, no matter how affluent or impoverished, have a right to a roof over their heads.

In America today, however, that is simply not the case. Over the past few years, we have been confronted by the fact that millions of our citizens lack basic shelter. The earliest assumption we made – that homelessness would be a temporary emergency situation – is quickly fading. For both our cities and our suburbs, homeless populations are becoming a permanent fact of life.

Slowly, too, we have begun to debunk the myth that the only ones who are homeless are middle-aged men and women, displaced by institutions or ravaged by chronic alcoholism. Whether resulting from the scarcity of affordable housing, or the inadequacy of public benefits, or a lack of jobs, or an increase in family crises – or any combination of these – the reality is that a significant portion of this nation's homeless population is families with children. The Department of Housing and Urban Development estimates that families comprise 40 percent of the homeless population in shelters. The U.S. Conference of Mayors reports that in cities like Detroit, New York, Norfolk, Portland and Trenton, families with children account for *more than half* of the homeless. The fact is, families with children are the fastest growing group of homeless Americans.

Contrary to common perceptions, homelessness among families knows no geographic boundaries; it is not limited to inner cities, or to one region of the country. In a recent hearing, the Select Committee on Children, Youth, and Families heard from a rural Michigan family forced to live in an 8 by 10 feet camper when they lost their farm and 42 landlords turned them down because their income was insufficient. In my own high-growth suburban community in California, as many as 70 percent of the homeless may be families with children.

Despite the painful fact that families with children comprise a significant portion of the nation's homeless, many homeless families *still* cannot find temporary shelter even for a single night. In two-thirds of cities surveyed by the Conference of Mayors, emergency shelters report they must turn families away because they lack the space to house them. All too often these families find themselves with nowhere to live but cars or campers, abandoned buildings, or on the street. In communities where jobs are scarce, families have begun to split up in order to find work, creating a new class of migrant workers camping in the streets and parks of America.

All too often, we ask them to give up what little they own or what self-esteem they have left before they can qualify for assistance. One mother, fleeing an abusive situation, testified to our Committee that she was forced to quit her job of 17 years and go on welfare before she could qualify for shelter.

Most distressing are the growing number of families who wind up homeless after leaving behind only slightly better situations – perilous living conditions in long-neglected and run-down substandard housing, often in the poorest, most crime-ridden, drug-infested neighborhoods. Many are evicted from overcrowded, stressed living quarters where families double or triple up in an apartment. Or, like the New York City mother I just mentioned – a woman victimized by spousal abuse – many are families forced to escape their own homes to protect themselves and their children.

The most striking and catastrophic example of the system's failure to respond can be seen in the child welfare system. The Select Committee has evidence that when all else fails, families resort to placing their children in foster care, often with little chance of reunification. Congress intended the foster care system to protect children from harm in dysfunctional families, not to house homeless children who come from families whose only "crime" is that they have no place to live.

At the other end of the child welfare system are the teenagers who have languished for years in foster care, unattended and ignored, who age out of the system only to join a new generation of youth on the street – homeless, at risk of drug abuse, prostitution, crime and now AIDS.

Effects of Homelessness/Shelter Living

Daily life for children who must wander the streets with their parents or are housed "temporarily" in some makeshift shelter is precarious at best. But more often it is harrowing and high risk, far from the "sugar and spice and everything nice" that childhood is supposed to be made of. In and around the few shelters, hotels or temporary facilities available for homeless families, drug abuse, crime and prostitution are everyday occurrences. Unsafe and crowded living conditions are the norm – families with three and four children frequently share one small room. Rarely are these rooms equipped with kitchen facilities, and even hot plates to warm food are prohibited.

In 1983, when the Select Committee first walked through the Martinique Hotel in New York City as part of our exploration of the living conditions homeless families are forced into, the fear, the desperation, the sense of hopelessness were unmistakable. When we knocked on their doors, we could hear families scramble to hide their hot plates for fear of eviction.

In our own backyard, 700 homeless children sheltered at the Capitol City Inn in Washington, D.C. have no place to play except for the train tracks behind the shelter. In 1988, two infants died at the hotel within two days of each other, and two disabled children ages four and eight were killed by their father, who then tried to kill himself.

Homeless shelter children have told the committee that the most difficult task for them is to find a quiet place to do their homework, if they are able to get to school at all. In Atlanta, the only transportation for children from shelter to school has been police vans. Tragically, these are the places which we have asked families with children to call "home" – some for months or even years at a time.

The federal government recently threatened to cut off federal emergency aid to homeless families in welfare hotels. This threat has sent cities scrambling to find alternative housing. The good news is that many welfare hotels have been closed down.

Housing/Income Crunch

The danger all along has been accepting shelters as a long-term solution, when in effect, they provide only a ragged Band-aid on a massive hemorrhage. Closing down welfare hotels is certainly a step in the right direction. But too many communities still maintain homeless families with children in squalid and unacceptable conditions. For the past decade, this government has engaged in a deliberate program of cutting federal housing subsidies for the poor at the same time housing costs have been soaring. As a result, there is a shortage of almost 4 million low-cost housing units, according to the National Low-Income Housing Coalition.

The bottom line is that families can't pay the rent. Incomes for the lowest income families and for young families dropped by about a quarter in the 70's and 80's. Now more than two-thirds of the nation's poor renters spend more than half their incomes for a place to live (The Center on Budget and Policy Priorities, The Low-Income Housing Service).

While the common denominator among homeless families is that they can't afford a place to live, we now know that having a job is no protection against homelessness. Nearly 20 million American families work but are still poor, an increase of 40 percent since 1979. For them, minor incidents like the car breaking down or failed child care arrangements can mean lost work days, lost wages, and lost jobs. When all supports fail, these are the very conditions that can lead to homelessness.

Without a long-term policy for safe and adequate housing together with the comprehensive, on-going services – financial and otherwise – necessary for families to remain together and stable, we will continue to foster homelessness rather than eliminate it.

There have been some recent innovations to help families cope with shelter living. In New York, Dr. Irwin Redlener delivers health care to families from a mobile van. One elementary school in New York provides a special after-school program just so kids will have quiet time to unwind and do their homework and perhaps even receive a hot meal. These and other model programs around the country strive to provide support to keep these families on an even keel, despite the terrible odds.

What is so frustrating for all of us is that there are not enough innovations available to families *before* they become homeless. Many of the supports that are available to families *after* they've reached the breaking point are often just the same supports or guidance that if offered earlier might have prevented homelessness from occurring in the first place.

Young Children At Risk

In the past decade alone, most of the indicators of children's well-being have taken a turn for the worse. We have left millions of children vulnerable to hunger, abuse, illness and illiteracy, as well as homelessness. Poverty has taken nearly 13 million children into its grip – some 3 million more than in 1979, according to the U.S. Census Bureau.

Young children are medically homeless when they have no health care. Twelve million children have no health insurance and almost 40,000 infants die before their first birthday. In some homeless shelters, the infant mortality rate rivals that of Third World nations.

Young children are educationally homeless when 80 percent of low-income preschoolers are denied Head Start services or other early childhood educational experiences that could prevent the need for more costly special education later.

Young children are nutritionally homeless when 50 percent of those who are eligible are denied the benefits of high protein foods available through the Special Supplemental Food Program for Women, Infants and Children. For children in shelters, where cooking is forbidden and restaurant allowances are sufficient only to pay for fast food, the risk of malnutrition and anemia is escalated.

Cost to Society

When we wait for these children, many of whom are already at great risk, to become homeless, they become the nation's most expensive children. Everyone says the budget deficit is the reason we can't correct these inequities. What we have failed to recognize is that when children start out with health, social, and educational deficits, they will be contributing to the federal deficit every day of their lives. We have failed to recognize that we have created not only a permanent class of homeless individuals, but candidates for our child welfare system, for our public assistance rolls, and for our courts and jails.

Government Role

In my view, our government should be ensuring that our children are not "homeless" in any sense. They need fundamental services that are comprehensive and intensive. We have made the case that proven effective preventive programs such as prenatal care, early intervention, and immunization save from $3 to $10 for every $1 invested, and offer basic supports to high-risk families to ease their burden.

That is why I have spearheaded a major legislative initiative that will guarantee vulnerable young children will not be denied the opportunity for good health, full mental and emotional development and educational readiness. "The Child Investment and Security Act," which I authored, is a multi-year, comprehensive, cross-program strategy to expand health care and nutritional supports to more low-income pregnant women, infants and young children, and to expand greater early childhood educational experiences to more at-risk young children. While such an effort doesn't pretend to solve the problem of homelessness, it may be a first step in preventing some of the most debilitating effects of poverty.

What Is Needed to Secure a Better Future

Fortunately, a growing concern and awareness about children among policymakers, corporate leaders and the public is helping to turn the tide – from empty rhetoric to positive action. While this is exciting news, it does not mean our work is over. We need to continue work together to ensure that the growing consensus about investing in children includes what homeless children need most – a home and a stable family. And it must not neglect the needs of over a million homeless youth who left home to escape physical or sexual abuse or the ravages of alcoholism or family dysfunction, or who were victims of a failed child welfare system.

We must find ways to make it up to these children – if it is possible at all – for their lost childhoods, for missed school days, for their growing inability to trust or to dream. The challenge is to develop the best strategies to remedy and prevent the tragedy of homelessness – and this must include shaping a new national housing policy. But this policy must also address the fragility, the complexity, the myriad problems a growing number of at-risk families now face which can lead to homelessness at the drop of a hat.

Forging a homelessness/housing/income support measure, which takes into account both *family needs* for economic independence and *children's health and development,* and which can find the money to pay for it will remain a major challenge – substantively and politically.

The stakes are very high. If we *don't* confront the need to invest significantly in housing opportunities – and in health care, nutrition and education for our children – we risk creating a permanent class of poor and homeless in this country and recreating the poorhouses of a century ago.

The Bush Administration has called for full funding of the Stewart McKinney Act in FY1990. Unfortunately, it appears that the funds to pay for it are to come from freezing or cutting other domestic discretionary programs, including those that could prevent homelessness in the first place. And while Secretary of Housing and Urban Development Jack Kemp expresses compassion for the homeless, a dramatic change from the previous Administration, his actions have only begun to match his rhetoric.

Homeless children and youth don't vote or contribute to political action committees. They need to have many tenacious voices emanating from every sector of society – from corporate leaders to church leaders, from academics to advocates – to represent their interests in Congress and in municipal and state governments.

The conference sponsored by the Johns Hopkins Institute for Policy Studies is a first step in the right direction. The leadership of the conference's honorary Chairman, Jim Rouse, is greatly appreciated as is the dedication of the many scholars, advocates and public officials who have shone a spotlight on a side of America that has breached the threshold of civility we hold so dear.

For all homeless children and their families to whom we owe dignity, decency and opportunity and a home they can call their own, we need to be bold, forthright and be visionary.

HONORABLE GEORGE MILLER
Chairman, House Select Committee on Children,
Youth and Families

(This foreword was adapted from remarks made before the Johns Hopkins University Institute for Policy Studies Conference, "Homeless Children and Youth: Coping with a National Tragedy," 25 April 1989.)

PART I

The Scope of Child and Youth Homelessness

1

Introduction

Janice M. Molnar

There is little need to add to the foregoing remarks by Lester Salamon and Congressman Miller. The following pages illustrate all too clearly that the plight of homeless children and youth is, indeed, a national tragedy, one which, as Congressman Miller movingly observes, we can ill afford, either morally or economically, to tolerate any longer. Technically speaking, this book is a compilation of literature reviews, policy and systems analyses, and reports of original research; but from a larger perspective it can be viewed as a kind of collective witness – witness to a phenomenon that threatens some of our most cherished assumptions about the character and mindset of this country.

The chapters of the first section provide an overview of homelessness, its recent history, and demographic profile. The second section is devoted to a close examination of the impact of homelessness on children, specifically in the areas of health, development, and education. Part 3's two chapters explore the root causes of homelessness in terms of macroeconomic issues and U.S. housing policy. The final group of four chapters focuses on the government's programmatic and policy responses to homelessness, with a particular emphasis on how they affect children and youth, and suggested policy alternatives.

Part 1: The Scope of the Problem

The second chapter, authored by Lisa Mihaly, reports the current estimates of homeless children and their families. While describing the

3

diversity of these families, she also highlights those factors that place certain families at higher risk of homelessness than others. The options of homeless families are limited. Mihaly shows us why the emergency shelter system is viewed as a last resort for most, and how shelter restrictions and procedures can themselves create barriers to re-establishing permanent housing.

Marjorie Robertson addresses some of the same issues as they relate to homeless youth. In keeping with Mihaly's observations, she finds there is no typical profile of a homeless adolescent. Rather, the stereotype of the adventure-seeking teenage runaway is just that – a stereotype. Furthermore, Robertson presents a taxonomy of the pathways to homelessness among youth, which clusters into three categories: family issues, residential instability, and socioeconomic pressure. The special problems experienced by homeless young people are of grave concern. Robertson reviews existing research, summarizing the survival needs and behavioral responses of homeless youth, and their serious physical and mental health problems. She concludes with recommendations for subsequent policy and research initiatives, focusing in particular on the kinds of comprehensive, tailored services that are most essential to meeting the special needs of homeless youth.

Part 2: The Impact of Homelessness on Children and Youth

The evidence is clear: rootlessness, chaos, no place – literally – to call home; these conditions are inimical to healthy child development. Together, the next two papers address the health, developmental, and educational consequences of homelessness on children and youth. Each reviews the relevant literature and then reports on original research. Because health is the non-negotiable bottom-line of human development, the section opens with James Wright's review. As he points out, poverty is a well-documented risk factor for poor health. Many of the health and nutritional problems of homeless children and youth are directly attributable to the abject conditions in which they live and the paucity of adequate health services. Nonetheless, based on data gathered by the National Health Care for the Homeless Project, Wright states that the chronic poor health of homeless children and youth "is not just a simple consequence of their impoverished circumstances.

Homelessness is an independent and quite consequential 'risk factor' in its own right."

Yvonne Rafferty broadens the focus to consideration of developmental and educational progress. Her review of the cognitive and psychological damage observed among young homeless children should concern us deeply. Quite simply, a shelter, alleyway, or car is a developmentally inappropriate environment for young children. Both the physical aspects of such settings and the emotional trauma they engender significantly compromise the growth and development of young children. Older children, too, are deeply affected. Rafferty reports the findings of her recently completed research which compares reading and math performance, grade retention, and attendance of school-aged homeless children to students systemwide in the New York City public schools. On all counts, homeless children fared worse.

Part 3: The Causes of Child and Youth Homelessness

How did all this come about? The next two chapters demonstrate that the swelling numbers of homeless children and families are the predictable outcome of intentional housing and family support policies. In the first, Kay Young McChesney illustrates how "homelessness is the result of the imbalance between the number of households living in poverty and the amount of low-income housing available – the low-income housing ratio." Taking into account macroeconomic factors (i.e., the business cycle, deindustrialization and the global economy), social factors (especially sex and racial discrimination) and policy factors (the inadequacy of safety net programs), McChesney presents a model of family poverty grounded in both economic and sociological theory. Key to it all is the availability of work at a living wage. But, while macroeconomic factors determine the number and type of jobs available, McChesney notes that it is demographic variables which determine "who gets those jobs and how much they are paid." She presents disturbing statistics pointing to the huge disparities between blacks and whites, men and women, and single-parent and two-parent families, and gives special attention to the vulnerability of single-mother families to poverty. She concludes with policy recommendations that link industrial and economic policy to necessary changes in those welfare policies that most affect families.

Following McChesney's argument about the relationship between poverty and housing availability, Chester Hartman and Barry Zigas address the history of low-income housing policy in the U.S. During the last 20 years, they argue, the nation's housing crisis has been transformed from a crisis of quality to a problem of affordability. An analysis of private market forces (gentrification, urban renewal, undermaintenance and abandonment, and lowered production levels in response to high interest rates) supports the chapter's main thesis that the housing market does not meet the most basic housing needs of many families. Since the 1970s, there has been a growing gap between what housing costs and what families can afford to pay. In particular, the authors cite the failure of neo-classical economic theory, which would predict a re-alignment of affordability and availability in a situation of short supply and rising prices. It simply hasn't happened. In conclusion, they argue that an alternative production, delivery, and operation system must be developed.

Part 4: The System's Response

The remaining four chapters illustrate how the problem of child and youth homelessness, along with the larger issues of poverty and housing, have been inadequately addressed by existing governmental programs and policies. These have been characterized largely by stop-gap, emergency measures that do little if anything to attack more systemic issues that are at the root of the problem. As the first two chapters in this section suggest, the main missing ingredient for effecting change is political will.

The one thing that all homeless people have in common is their lack of housing. Elaborating on a theme introduced in their earlier chapter, Chester Hartman and Barry Zigas illustrate the unevenness of federal housing policy across income levels. For the middle class, the message is a positive one. Homeownership – at middle- and upper-income levels – is encouraged through generous incentives like tax deductions and government support of the mortgage market. Renters – who tend to be lower income – do not benefit from these deductions. For them, especially the lowest income households, the federal housing message is ambivalent, if not actually exclusionary. Hartman and Zigas argue that the transition of the federal role from its 50-year commitment to direct development and management of housing to tenant-based subsidies only aggravates the problem, in that it does nothing to increase the supply of housing. Moreover, as the authors enumerate, threats to the existing stock of public housing are numerous – leaving low-income households with few if any options. The authors conclude with recommendations as to how best to reactivate the goal of the National Housing Act of 1949: "a decent home and suitable living environment for every American family."

Michael Stegman speculates on the future and what we might expect from Congress and the Bush administration. Following a brief review of assisted housing budgets under the Reagan administration, the bulk of this chapter is devoted to description and analysis of six major legislative proposals currently before the 101st Congress. These proposals are selected and rank-ordered both in terms of their potential for adding to the supply of permanent housing for homeless families and the political feasibility of their passage. Considering the risk of homelessness faced by many precariously housed low-income households, Stegman speculates as to why there is such scant attention in these six bills to rental assistance measures, or, more broadly, to significant welfare reform. He identifies three tendencies in the distribution of housing benefits that produce significant inequities in the availability of housing to homeless families as compared to other household groups. Although it did not realize the hopes of many housing advocates, Stegman also summarizes those relevant low- and middle-income housing provisions of the Savings & Loan Bailout Law. He concludes with a call for planning imperatives that he deems essential to curbing the rise in homelessness.

As the final two chapters show, responsibility for caring for the homeless often lands at the feet of those systems least able to take on new burdens. Linda Wolf essentially argues that the welfare system is caught between a rock and a hard place, for it cannot effect change in regard to either of the systemic roots of homelessness. "Welfare benefits," she writes, "are not high enough to make poor people true competitors in the limited low-income housing market and welfare agencies cannot create new housing." The chapter also provides an overview of the key programs that comprise the welfare system. Wolf points out that, with too few exceptions, service delivery mechanisms are not adapted to make access to services easier or more appropriate for homeless families. She illustrates the irony of labeling funding for homeless families "special" or "emergency" as the problems they are designed to address become more and more widespread. Summarizing policy recommendations devised by the American Public Welfare Association, she highlights the importance of acknowledging the interrelationship between self-sufficiency and housing in crafting welfare system reform, specifically, by overcoming parochial boundaries and developing operational relationships among welfare and housing agencies.

Like Wolf, Carol Williams in her chapter argues that the child welfare system is inappropriately being asked to respond to crises related to low family income and inadequate housing. Yet, she states, current child welfare policies may actually compound those problems. Williams' central thesis is that "the philosophy, decisionmaking and operations of the child welfare system may have the unintended consequence of promoting homelessness among families and children." In particular, she describes the problems of the tight interrelationship between housing and income supports and family size, and their relationship to family homelessness in the case of child placement in foster care. She also presents the central features of the debate about whether or not homelessness is in itself evidence of child neglect, and thus cause for child placement. Finally, she shows that the very unity of families is threatened by housing instability and homelessness. The chapter concludes with recommendations for comprehensive, coordinated actions that cut across governmental levels and service systems.

*   *   *

Three years ago, a noted criminologist remarked that second only to the threat of nuclear war, chronic poverty and a "locked-in underclass" represent the greatest problems this country faces (Morris 1987, in Schorr 1988, 22). In light of recent events that have transformed the communist world and a rapidly diminishing possibility of nuclear conflict, the crisis depicted in this book looms now as the greatest challenge that confronts America's future. The central purpose of this book has been to impress upon the reader – through close examination of the relationship between chronic poverty and homelessness, and the injury both conditions inflict upon children – the urgency of that challenge. There is a danger, however, that upon finishing this volume, the reader may simply feel overwhelmed by the sheer size and scope of the dynamics that give rise to homelessness and the historical inability or willingness of our socio-political institutions to address them.

These problems should not be minimized. They are grave, indeed, but they are not without solution, even within the framework of those circumstances which have spawned them. Stegman, and Hartman and Zigas, for example, offer suggestions for reforms in housing policies and programs that would substantially alleviate current housing shortages. McChesney's chapter concludes with a whole set of recommendations for restructuring macroeconomic policy in a way that would directly affect the cycle of poverty. Outside this book, recent works by Lisbeth Schorr (1988) and Marian Wright Edelman (1987) and a major report published by the Ford Foundation (1989) all propose fundamental reallocations of our national resources in a wholesale assault on poverty and the plight of the children of poverty. Significantly, all agree that the means are currently available to substantially – if not wholly – reverse the tides of poverty and homelessness; what has been lacking thus far has been the social and political will, the commitment of resources, but most importantly, a real understanding of the profound threat that chronic poverty/homelessness poses for our nation. That, then, is the real purpose of this book, to help the reader come to such an understanding through a comprehensive review of the facts. Ultimately, we hope, that understanding will bring with it a deep feeling of injustice and outrage on behalf of all of America's poor and homeless children and youth. In the most concrete sense, they hold the key to America's future. It is up to us now to ensure that future.

References

Edelman, M. W. 1987. *Families in Peril*. Cambridge: Harvard University Press.

Ford Foundation Project on Social Welfare and the American Future. 1989. *The Common Good: Social Welfare and the American Future*. New York: Ford Foundation.

Schorr, L. B. 1988. *Within Our Reach*. New York: Anchor Press.

2

Beyond the Numbers: Homeless Families with Children

Lisa Mihaly

Bernice A. worked for seven years as a government clerk but lost her job after unreliable child care for her three- and five-year-old children made her late for work too often. She applied for Aid to Families with Dependent Children (AFDC), but was denied help because the computer showed that she still was employed. She could not pay her rent and was evicted. Now she lives with her two children in a gymnasium. The family is awakened at 5:30 each morning when shelter staff bang on the side of the thin partition that gives Bernice and her children their only privacy. They take a bus across town to another shelter for breakfast. Then Bernice, who is now five months pregnant, spends her day on the bus taking her older child, James, to Head Start, returning to the shelter for lunch, and then going back again to pick up James. All the while, she has three-year-old Denise in tow. Denise has no place to nap and little space to play. After dinner, the family returns to the gymnasium. Bernice cannot find a minute to look for a job or new housing.

John and Sheila T. moved to Washington, D.C., from New Jersey because John had heard there was work in construction. When they arrived, they slept on the couch in a friend's apartment, with their two-year-old daughter, Tia. When the landlord found out, he threatened to evict their friend, so the family sought help from the social services agency. Tia and Sheila, who was pregnant, were given a room at one of the homeless shelters. John could not join them because he could not document that he was married to Sheila or that he was Tia's father. Instead, he slept in the family's truck outside the shelter, despite subfreezing temperatures. During the day, his wife and daughter joined him in the truck, because the shelter let them stay inside only between 7:00 P.M. and 7:00 A.M. Tia resisted toilet training

© *1990 Children's Defense Fund*

1 1

in the unfamiliar and unstable setting and developed a bad case of bronchitis.

These two families are typical of the growing numbers of homeless families in cities and towns across the country. Images of families living in campgrounds and sleeping on cots in crowded shelters are joining those of disheveled men sleeping on park benches and women pushing their belongings through bus stations in shopping carts.

Throughout the country, families are the fastest growing segment of the homeless population. Because counting the homeless is difficult and has become highly politicized there is no single, accepted count of homeless families. There is virtual unanimity, however, that the 1980s have produced a homeless population – and a rate of homelessness among families – far larger than at any other time since the Great Depression of the 1930s. Estimates of the total number of homeless persons range from 250,000 to 3 million; it is generally thought that members of homeless families with children make up about one-third of this population. Every night, according to a 1988 estimate by the Institute of Medicine, 100,000 American children go to sleep homeless.

Families are homeless today primarily because there is a shortage of affordable housing. The number of homeless families will continue to grow unless the country addresses the pressures that are forcing more and more families out of their homes. By the year 2000, if current trends continue, millions of American children will have spent at least a part of their childhoods without a place to call home. Throughout their lives, these youngsters will bear the physical, educational, and emotional scars that result from a childhood punctuated by cold, hunger, sporadic schooling, and frequent moves among temporary shelters and "welfare hotels" riddled with violence and drugs.

This chapter will discuss homeless families and their children: how many there are and the limitations of these numbers; what is known about the faces behind the numbers; and where most of these families reside.

What Do the Numbers Mean?

Counting homeless people is very difficult. Normal methods of enumeration, such as knocking on doors, cannot be used to count a very fluid, sometimes hidden, and often mistrustful and frightened population. Ensuring an accurate count of homeless families with children is even more problematic.

Numerous efforts have been made to count homeless Americans, all with significant limitations. Estimates of the number of homeless families, with one or more parents or caretakers and children, have been derived from these national counts.

How Many Homeless Americans Are There?

Current counts of the number of homeless Americans range from 250,000 to 350,000, reported by the U.S. Department of Housing and Urban Development (HUD) in 1984, to an estimated 3 million people reported homeless that same year by the National Coalition for the Homeless. The divergence in these estimates has created a battleground for many political disputes about the severity and causes of homelessness. These disputes often have taken place between those who see homelessness as a problem linked to individual shortcomings or problems (i.e., mental illness, substance abuse) and those who see it as an extreme outcome of poverty and a shortage of affordable low-income housing. The numbers are used to argue for different levels of national investment to address the problems.

Generally, counts of homeless people have been derived through indirect estimation. Agencies that serve homeless people, including shelters, are asked to report how many clients they serve. These figures then are added to produce an estimate of the total homeless population in a given community or area. Attempts often are made to adjust for the additional number of so-called "invisible" or "hidden" homeless people residing in the area.

The shortcomings of indirect estimation are numerous: some providers may be missed and their clients not counted; the rural and suburban homeless may be excluded; other adjustments for regional variations also may be omitted; and daily counts may be combined with counts of homeless persons over a longer period of time (Cowan, Breakey, and Fisher 1988). When some of those shortcomings are addressed, the estimates change significantly. For example, the National Alliance to End Homelessness reworked HUD's 1984 data, adjusting for the difference between urban and suburban homelessness, the invisible homeless, and the growth in homelessness between 1984 and

1988. The Alliance then estimated that 736,000 people were homeless on any given night, and that more than 2 million would be homeless during the course of 1988 (National Alliance to End Homelessness 1988).

Other national estimates have been based on censuses of homeless people in a predetermined area at a particular time. Shelters, streets, and other places to which homeless persons are known to go are surveyed during a given period. Some surveys then add an estimate of the number of people who were missed because they were not seen or did not identify themselves as homeless. This method, as well, has produced a variety of numbers, ranging from 350,000 homeless persons nationwide in 1986, based on a survey of 500 homeless people in New York City (Freeman and Hall 1986), to 600,000, based on interviews with 1,700 homeless individuals nationwide (Burt and Cohen 1988).

In 1990, for the first time, the federal decennial Census of Population attempted to count "selected components" of the homeless population during a designated 24-hour period. Census takers surveyed homeless people found in shelters, on the streets, and living in abandoned buildings, all locations provided to them by local governments.

Although a first step, even the 1990 census data dramatically undercounted the homeless population, and no adjustment will be prepared. Census officials and advocates alike caution that the count is not complete because it excluded those homeless people staying in nontraditional shelter (i.e., cars), those in shelters not identified by local officials, those on the street who were not visibly identifiable as homeless, and those residing in abandoned buildings who did not emerge during the count period (census workers did not actually enter the buildings).

How Many Homeless Families with Children Are There?

Whatever the method, counts of homeless families with children often are hindered further by some of the special characteristics of this population. First, afraid that they will be charged as neglectful parents and their children taken from them, parents are often particularly hesitant to identify themselves as homeless. Second, families in unconventional forms of shelter, such as campgrounds and cars, may not be counted.

Third, families that have been separated by homelessness are not likely to be captured in surveys. They may have members in different shelters, some with friends or relatives, or children in foster care.

Perhaps the most complete pictures of the homeless family population to date have come from the annual surveys conducted by the U.S. Conference of Mayors. The surveys, conducted since 1982, collect information about the number and characteristics of homeless persons served in approximately 28 cities around the country. Since 1986, the reports have estimated that, on average, one-third of the homeless population nationwide are parents and children. This proportion has been rising steadily. In 1985, homeless families were about one-fourth of the homeless population (Reyes and Waxman 1986). In the 1989 report, families were estimated to comprise 36 percent of the homeless population in the sites studied (Reyes and Waxman 1989b). Other reports have confirmed these findings. For example, one-third of the homeless population in Delaware shelters in 1988 were members of families with children, as were 26 percent of those in Colorado shelters that same year (Peuquet and Leland 1988; Parvensky and Krasniewski 1988).

Based on such findings, national estimates of the number of homeless persons in families most often are calculated as one-third of various national estimates of the total homeless population. To obtain counts of homeless children, further manipulations are necessary. It generally is assumed that the average homeless family includes one parent and one or two children. Thus, children are estimated to make up between one-third and one-half of the members of homeless families. Using estimates of homeless persons ranging from 250,000 to 3 million, the Children's Defense Fund estimated that between 50,000 and 500,000 children were homeless in 1988 (1988). A 1988 study by the Institute of Medicine, which used other figures, estimated that a minimum of 100,000 children are homeless on any given night.

In 1988, the General Accounting Office (GAO), using indirect estimates, conducted the first national study of the number of homeless children. The GAO first surveyed shelters and hotels in forty randomly selected urban counties; it counted all the children under age sixteen who were residing there with their families. To those counts were added the estimated numbers of homeless families presumed not sheltered and those living in suburban and rural communities. It finally estimated that

68,000 children were homeless on any given night in 1988 and that an estimated 310,000 children were served by homeless shelters during the course of that year (GAO 1989).

It is agreed widely that families with children currently make up the fastest-growing segment of the homeless population. Cities surveyed by the Conference of Mayors have had greater increases in requests for shelter by families than by individuals for the past several years. For example, in 1987, cities surveyed reported an average 32 percent increase in shelter requests by families, while overall requests (including families) rose only 21 percent. In 1988, family requests for shelter rose 22 percent while requests by all homeless persons rose 13 percent (Reyes and Waxman 1989a). Some local sources have confirmed particularly dramatic growth. Washington, D.C., experienced a 500 percent increase in the number of sheltered families during 1986 (Rowe 1986). Charleston, West Virginia, reported a 144 percent increase during that same period (Reyes and Waxman 1989a).

Homelessness plagues rural areas and smaller cities as well as large cities. Campgrounds and state parks in many rural areas report homeless families living in them (Patton 1988). Reports to the Federal Department of Education on the number of homeless school-age children provide some interesting statistics on homeless families outside of the largest cities. For example, Oklahoma City reported more than 2,500 homeless children (Status Report: Oklahoma 1988). Montana reported 1,600 homeless children (Status Report: Montana 1988). Arkansas reported 800 homeless children outside of Little Rock (Status Report: Arkansas 1988).

The Need to Include Hidden Homeless Families

Because the numbers of homeless families are used as a backdrop for discussions about the problems they face and the services they need, families who are among the "hidden homeless" also should be counted and considered. Hidden homeless families include families living "doubled up" or "camped out" with friends and family because they have no home of their own, those living in cars and other unconventional settings, and families in which parents and children have been separated due to homelessness.

Many homeless families are hidden in doubled-up households, where two or more families share housing intended for only one. This is not the same as shared housing, in which two or more families choose to share adequate living space and utility expenses, and often help each other with child care and other needs.

Doubled-up families often suffer many of the consequences of homelessness, such as lack of privacy, instability, and overcrowding. In many communities today, there are almost as many doubled-up families as there are other homeless families. The 1988 GAO national study estimated that on any given night, while there are 68,000 homeless children, there are 186,000 precariously housed, as defined by shelter providers (GAO 1989). In 1988, over 5 million children lived doubled up in the homes of friends or family, a 36 percent increase since 1980. Although not all of those children are in overcrowded or precarious housing, this dramatic rise is an indication of the growing inability of many families to find affordable housing of their own.

To avoid going to emergency shelter when they lose their own homes, families often first choose to move in with family or friends. In fact, research by Kay Young McChesney indicates that the lack of family or friends with whom to stay may be a key factor in determining which poor families become homeless (1988a).

Doubling up is a precarious housing alternative, as illustrated by the significant proportion of homeless families that come to shelters from friends' or families' homes: 27 percent of the families in Alameda County shelters (Emergency Services Network 1988), 30 percent of the shelter families interviewed by the Philadelphia Committee for Children and Youth, and 71 percent of the families applying for shelter in a New York City study (Knickman and Weitzman 1989).

Homeless families also may be hidden because they are not in traditional shelters. These are usually families that either have chosen not to approach a shelter or have been turned away for lack of space. Families may choose not to seek formal shelter for a variety of reasons. There may be no facilities that can accommodate two-parent families or teen-age parents with children. Parents also may fear that the shelter will report them to city child-protection officials as neglectful, and that their children will be taken from them and placed in foster care. Others may be concerned that conditions in the local shelters are unsafe for women and children or fear that an abusive spouse will be able to find them.

They may be forced to seek shelter instead in cars, vans, abandoned buildings, public parks, and campgrounds.

Also among the hidden homeless are families whose members have been separated from each other by homelessness. In 62 percent of the cities surveyed by the Conference of Mayors, families sometimes must be separated to find shelter (Reyes and Waxman 1989b). In some cases, shelters cannot house two-parent families at all, or will do so only if the parents provide a marriage license or birth certificates. Many shelters cannot accommodate boys over the age of ten, so that a mother may go to one shelter, while men and older boys go to another. Sometimes parents, anticipating separation, may send their children to stay with friends or relatives. In some cases, homelessness may result, directly or indirectly, in the placement of children in foster care.

Some communities report substantial numbers of children placed in foster care solely because of housing problems. A New Jersey study reported that homelessness was the primary cause of placement in 19 percent of the placements studied and a contributing factor in an additional 40 percent (Tomaszewicz 1985). Similarly, a 1989 report issued by the National Black Child Development Institute found that housing problems, including homelessness, were a significant and contributing factor in placement in 38 percent of the cases they reviewed in six major cities (National Black Child Development Institute 1989). Often, housing problems exacerbate other family problems, such as child abuse, which then may precipitate the placement of children in care.

Who Are the Homeless Families?

Homeless families are a diverse population. No systematic national research describes them. What is known about them comes primarily from surveys and studies of families using services in specific communities. The findings from these studies have limited general applicability because they usually include only families that seek help (and often a fairly small number). They do, however, provide some useful information. Not surprisingly, the studies report that the families most likely to be homeless look very much like families most likely to be poor. They also describe several problems, in addition to poverty, that seem to put families at increased risk of homelessness.

Most Are Single-Parent Families

Single-parent families, most often headed by women, represent almost four-fifths of all homeless families nationwide, according to the U.S. Conference of Mayors (Reyes and Waxman 1989b). In Pennsylvania, for example, 90 percent of all homeless families are headed by single women (Ryan, Goldstein, and Bartelt 1989). This phenomenon, however, is not universal. In the West, for example, about 25 percent of the homeless families in cities such as Denver, Portland, and Seattle are two-parent families (Reyes and Waxman 1989b). Two-parent families are also the majority of homeless families in some rural areas (Patton 1988).

Female-headed families are often at increased risk of homelessness because they are more likely to be poor. They lack a second wage earner, and women's wages are generally lower than men's. In addition, those who become single parents as adolescents often have limited education and job skills. Those who become single through divorce may experience a very sudden decline in family resources.

Many Are Headed by Young Parents and Have Young Children

Young families, those headed by parents under thirty, also are heavily represented among the homeless. In Delaware, for example, in 30 percent of the homeless, female-headed families the mother was between twenty and twenty-nine years old and another 8 percent were under twenty (Peuquet and Leland 1988). Among single-parent homeless families in Pennsylvania, 13 percent of the parents were between sixteen and twenty, 30 percent were between twenty-one and twenty-five, and another 29 percent were between twenty-six and thirty (Ryan, Goldstein, and Bartelt 1989).

Young families have been hit very hard by the economic changes of the past fifteen years. Their earnings declined by an average of 39 percent between 1973 and 1986. Not surprisingly, the poverty rate among young families almost doubled, from 12 percent to 24 percent, in that same period, increasing their risk of homelessness (Johnson, Sum, and Weill 1988).

Young parents tend to have young children, who also often make up a significant proportion of the homeless-shelter residents. In Alameda County, California, 21 percent of the children in shelters in 1987 were younger than five (Emergency Services Network 1988). In Colorado, 35 percent of the children in shelters in 1988 were younger than three (Parvensky and Krasniewski 1988). It is possible that the predominance of young children is due in part to regulations in some shelters that exclude older children, especially males. Parents also may be more reluctant to send young children off alone to family or friends, which they may do with older children to spare them the horror of shelter life and the disruption of schooling.

Most Lack Resources to Afford Permanent Housing

Most homeless families lack the resources to afford available housing. A severe shortage of affordable housing, a dramatic decrease in federal housing funds, an increase in the number of poor families, and the stagnation of poor families' incomes have converged to create the current crisis.

Between 1980 and 1988, federal funding for low-income housing dropped more than 80 percent in real dollars. The number of new units for which funding was reserved dropped from an average of 261,000 a year to about 85,000 a year during that period (Low Income Housing Information Service 1988).

At the same time, the numbers of households in need of low-cost housing have risen significantly. Between 1980 and 1988, the number of poor families with children increased from less than 3.9 million to 5.5 million, a 40 percent increase. Federal housing assistance has fallen far behind the growing need because of inadequate funding. Fewer than one-third of all poor households received federal housing assistance in 1987 (Leonard, Dolbeare, and Lazere 1989). Even among families receiving aid for dependent children (AFDC), only about one-fifth receive any federal housing assistance (Newman and Schnare 1987). More than 1 million households are on waiting lists for public housing around the country (National Housing Task Force 1988). In virtually every large city, the waits are years long, and the lists often are larger than the total number of housing units available.

Low-income families with children and without housing assistance often live on a precarious edge, spending far more than the recommended 30 percent of their income for housing. In 1985, more than half of all poor renter households spent over 70 percent of their incomes for housing, as did close to one-third of low-income homeowners (Leonard, Dolbeare, and Lazere 1989). Thirty-five percent of all female-headed families with young children spent more than 75 percent of their incomes for rent in 1983 (Brown and Yinger 1986).

Housing experts explain that housing is not like other commodities. Unlike meals which can be skipped or medical bills that can be paid off slowly, housing must be paid for every month and in full. Families spending most of their income for housing often are left with little to pay for food, clothing, and other necessities. They have virtually no cushion if their income drops or their housing costs increase. Many families have no alternatives other than turning to emergency shelter. The struggles of families receiving AFDC and those earning the minimum wage dramatize the impossible choices many families are forced to make to both house and feed their families.

For families who must depend on AFDC, even for a short period of time, the problems are especially intense because the benefits are rarely enough to afford decent housing. AFDC benefits in a number of states include a shelter component, theoretically intended to cover the cost of housing. In no state, however, does the shelter component come close to enabling the family to pay for housing without using other parts of the grant intended to pay for food, clothes, and other necessities. In fact, in 35 states the entire AFDC grant for a family of three is less than the fair market rent (FMR, a measure established by HUD and adjusted every year) for a low-cost, two-bedroom apartment. Many families receiving AFDC spend as much as 60 percent to 80 percent of their income for housing.

It is not surprising, then, that significant proportions of the homeless population consist of families receiving AFDC. Forty-three percent of the homeless women with children surveyed in Minnesota's Twin Cities received AFDC (Owen and Williams 1988), as did 64 percent of the homeless families in Atlanta in 1987, where the maximum AFDC grant was $263 a month and the FMR was $504 a month (Atlanta Task Force for the Homeless 1987).

In addition to low benefits, bureaucratic snafus resulting in termination or interruption of AFDC benefits can push families living on the edge into homelessness. In one New York City shelter, 44 percent of the families had their AFDC grants cut off during the previous year. In a cruel twist, an additional 16 percent lost their benefits while they were homeless because they did not respond to a questionnaire sent to the homes in which they no longer were living (Citizen's Committee for Children 1988).

Many Have Completed High School

The educational attainment of homeless parents reflects the declining earning power of high school graduates. A high school diploma no longer guarantees a stable and self-sufficient life. In 1986, the average high school graduate reported annual income of $13,600, down from $19,736 in 1973. Many homeless parents have completed high school or even some college, but still cannot maintain a home. Thirty-six percent of the homeless Minnesota women interviewed in 1988 (of whom one-half had children with them) had high school diplomas; an additional 25 percent had gone beyond high school (Owen and Williams 1988). Among homeless mothers in one Massachusetts study, 37 percent had either a high school diploma or a GED and an additional 22 percent had some college education as well (Bassuk, Rubin, and Lauriat 1986).

Most Are Residents of the Area in Which They Seek Shelter

In virtually every community with a homeless population, some residents assert that the homeless have come from elsewhere – in search of better weather, jobs, or welfare benefits. On the contrary, available data show that although some homeless families are recent arrivals, often coming in search of jobs, the vast majority are long-time residents of the community in which they are sheltered, if not always the immediate neighborhood. For example, 84 percent of the Alameda County shelter clients were from that county or neighboring ones; 37 percent of the families in Minnesota shelters had lived in the state for over twenty years, and another 11 percent had been there between eleven and twenty years (Emergency Services Network 1988;

Minnesota Coalition for the Homeless 1988). Many homeless families simply no longer can afford homes in their own communities.

They Often Lack Strong Personal Support Networks

Families without strong support systems are at especially high risk of homelessness. Without family and friends on whom to rely for temporary housing, financial assistance, information about jobs and housing, and moral support, families in transition or crisis are much more likely to become homeless. In a study of homeless mothers in Los Angeles between 1985 and 1986, McChesney reported that many described a striking lack of friends or family to whom they could turn. One-third did not have a living mother, one-third did not have a living father, and about one-sixth were orphans. Many had family members far away or were estranged from their relatives, frequently because of physical or sexual abuse they had experienced as children (McChesney 1988a).

A study comparing housed poor and homeless families in Boston found that the strength of the support system was the critical difference between the two groups (Bassuk and Rosenberg 1988). When asked about their personal support system, 31 percent of the homeless mothers named a minor child as their only support, compared with 4 percent of the housed mothers. Similarly, 74 percent of the housed mothers said they had three close adult friends or relatives, compared with only 26 percent of the homeless mothers.

Even when families have personal supports, they often exhaust these resources and then are forced to seek shelter. An already tenuous support system is likely to be damaged further by the experience of homelessness itself. Many homeless families are sheltered in environments that make contact with friends and family very difficult. Shelters frequently prohibit visitors and may have only one phone for several hundred people. The shelter may be located far from a family's original neighborhood, which offered informal support systems and friendly institutions, including churches and shared child care. Frequently, shelters are not convenient to public transportation and, when available, transportation may be costly. One study of homeless families in New York City found that only 28 percent were sheltered in the borough in which they previously had lived – in a city where each subway ride costs a dollar (Citizen's Committee for Children 1988). Such isolation also makes it more difficult for homeless families to restabilize, because neighbors and acquaintances are often the best sources of information about available housing and employment.

Some Have Experienced Family Violence or Have Other Serious Problems

Some studies also have reported high rates of family violence among families in homeless shelters, involving mothers, children, or both. Thirty percent of the homeless families in New York state reported that family violence was the primary cause of their homelessness (Status Report: New York 1988). Twenty-nine of eighty homeless mothers interviewed in Boston in 1985 reported that they had been in an abusive relationship (Bassuk, Rubin, and Lauriat 1986). These figures may understate the problem because families in battered women's shelters often are not counted as homeless, although many may become so. Parents fleeing abusive homes often leave very quickly, without time, emotional strength, or financial resources to find a new place to live. The continuing threat of family violence also complicates life for homeless children. Homeless mothers who have been battered may be afraid to send their children to school, fearing that their husbands or boyfriends will either abduct and abuse the children or use the children to find them.

Although substance abuse and mental illness are believed to account for homelessness among many single adults, less is known about the extent of these problems among homeless families. Certainly, any fragile parent beset with substance abuse or emotional problems and unable to cope with parenting or household crises may be at especially high risk of homelessness. Some studies have reported histories of childhood abuse among the parents studied. One-third of the homeless mothers interviewed in Boston in 1985 by Dr. Ellen Bassuk reported that they had been physically abused as children (Bassuk, Rubin, and Lauriat 1986). In a study of homeless families in Los Angeles, mothers who had been homeless as teen-agers reported histories of abuse, failed foster placements, little education, no work experience, and no families to which they could turn (McChesney 1988b).

Where Do Homeless Families Go?

Barbara called a shelter in her suburban Northeastern home, asking for beds for herself and her five-year-old son, Michael. The shelter was full, so they slept in their car. The next morning, Barbara took Michael to his first day of kindergarten, still wearing the clothes he had slept in, and without breakfast.

Doug and Sheila M. owned a modest house in Montana. When Doug lost his job because of the farm crisis, they lost the house and moved east with their five children to be with Doug's mother. For a while the seven of them lived in a basement. One of the youngest children died of crib death. Eventually, they moved into their own apartment, but the rent was too high for their unsteady jobs. Finally they moved into a Salvation Army shelter, the only one in the city that would take the whole family. Sheila caught a male shelter resident watching her 10-year-old daughter shower one day. The family got up every morning at 6:00 A.M. so Doug could get to work and the children to school on time. The children missed breakfast every day until the shelter gave them cereal to take with them. (U.S. House 1987)

When all other options have been exhausted, emergency shelter is a last resort for families in crisis. Few go directly from their own homes to shelter. Many have doubled up with friends or family until the host family risked eviction or the overcrowding became unbearable; some have paid for hotel rooms and depleted their savings; others have lived in cars or campgrounds until the weather got too cold. Finally, they may approach the emergency shelter system, seeking a safe place to sleep and help to get back on their feet.

The specific needs of homeless families vary tremendously with the circumstances of the individual families. All need affordable housing, many need help finding it, and some need additional support services, as well. However, despite the best efforts of staff, volunteers, and agencies in many communities, these vulnerable families often find a system that is unsuited to meet their needs. First, most communities do not have adequate family-shelter space. Second, the conditions in many shelters are damaging to families and children. Third, once in shelters, families often are faced with serious barriers to re-establishing themselves in permanent and stable housing.

The rapid growth of the homeless-family population has left many communities incapable of sheltering all those in need. In 1988, 68 percent of the twenty-nine major cities surveyed by the U.S. Conference of Mayors reported turning away families. They were unable to meet an average of 23 percent of the families' requests for shelter. Overall, 88 percent of the cities reported that families were the most underserved group of homeless persons in their community.

The only significant federal response to the needs of homeless families over the past decade has been the provision of emergency shelter. The Stewart B. McKinney Homeless Assistance Act, enacted in 1987, consists of over a dozen programs, primarily focused on the provision of emergency food and shelter, as well as critical services such as health care, job training, and the education of homeless children. Funds provided under the act have helped some communities strengthen their emergency services, but funds have been very limited. Total funding for the programs has never exceeded $650 million, a meager investment compared to the federal government's biggest housing program – homeowner tax deductions, which cost over $50 billion a year.

Some communities have no family shelters at all, and others have shelters with very limited space. Fully 62 percent of the cities surveyed by the U.S. Conference of Mayors reported that families must be separated in order to be sheltered because of limited space or a range of rules and restrictions (Reyes and Waxman 1989b). Many shelters will not take male children over a certain age, sometimes as young as seven years old, although age limits of ten or twelve years are more common. In all these cases, fathers and boys must either go alone to adult shelters or sleep elsewhere. Norfolk reported in 1988 that in one shelter boys older than seven must stay in an all-male ward, away from their mothers. Sometimes, male children are placed alone in foster care.

Once in shelter, families often receive minimal services and support. Although exceptional programs do exist, shelters are almost always very harsh environments for children. Today, most homeless families are sheltered in fairly large emergency settings. These include barracks-style shelters (including converted armories and school gyms), motels, and hotels. Barracks-style settings have become the predominant source of shelter in many communities primarily because they are convenient to use and can be expanded quickly to meet increased demand. Large public buildings may be available rent-free. Hotels and motels, on the other hand, are a very expensive way to shelter families. Costs can run over $3,000 a month to shelter and feed a family, many times more than the costs of permanent housing for that same family. Some cities, however, use matching federal funds to soften the fiscal burden.

Emergency shelters generally provide families with little more than a place to sleep, although some do provide meals. Because of very tight housing markets and limited services to help families leave emergency shelter, families often stay months in shelter intended for very short-term use. In Washington, D.C., about 450 homeless families a night were sheltered in welfare hotels in 1988, and fewer than 100 families were in transitional housing. The average stay in emergency shelter was ninety days. Philadelphia shelters about 2,240 parents and children every night. Almost 2,200 are in emergency shelter, more than 1,600 of them are in shelters for more than 100 people, and about seventy beds are available in transitional housing. Some communities have developed smaller programs. For example, of the 1,200 homeless families in Massachusetts on any given night, fully 500 of them are in family shelters, most of which house fewer than ten families each; the remaining 700 are in hotels and motels (personal communications, 1989).

Families in shelters have virtually no privacy. In hotels, an entire family often shares one room, with three or four children in one bed and parents and children in the same room. Families in barracks shelters, which house dozens or hundreds of people, generally live in one large room that may be shared by single men and women. Sheets between the beds often provide the only privacy. Bathroom facilities in these congregate settings sometimes lack doors on toilet stalls and showers.

Shelter routines often deprive parents of many of their parenting roles, and their dignity as well. The staff decide when the lights go on and off, when meals will be served, what children will eat, and where and when children can play. Research has shown that this usurpation of parental roles is depressing and confusing both to parents and children, and may have effects that last far beyond the episode of homelessness itself (Boxill and Beaty). Fathers excluded from shelters often feel guilty and inadequate, and lasting damage may be done to their relationships with their partners and their children.

Congregate living has been found to endanger the health and safety of children and parents. Conditions in many of the large shelters are frighteningly bad. Homeless families may share space with drug dealers and prostitutes. Theft, assault, and rape are not uncommon. Many parents are afraid to let their children out of their rooms unaccompanied.

The health of homeless children and their parents also is compromised. At one of the large hotel shelters in Washington, D.C., plumbing regularly backs up into the rooms and days pass before it is cleaned up. Many shelters are not properly heated in the winter, and some families sleep fully clothed. Insect and rodent infestation is common. Meals, if served, may not meet the special nutritional requirements of young children or pregnant women. Rigid scheduling for meals may mean that school-aged children must choose between missing breakfast and being late for school. Facilities to refrigerate formula and other special foods are often unavailable. Disease spreads easily in overcrowded, unsanitary conditions.

Shelter life can intensify the disruption in a child's education caused by homelessness. For children in hotels, overcrowding may mean that they must do homework on a sibling's bed. For those in barracks, the total lack of privacy may make studying impossible. In addition, many shelters limit the amount of time a family can stay, forcing families to move several times before they find new housing and, in turn, forcing children to move from school to school.

Families in shelters with minimal services also experience a number of barriers to re-establishing themselves in permanent housing. Many shelters lack such basics as working telephones to help families find new homes. Social services and other staff often have hundreds of parents and children in their caseloads. Families frequently are placed in shelters far from their own neighborhoods, where most will want to find housing, and public transportation is often not available. Shelters frequently have no facilities for the storage of furniture or personal effects, so families leaving the shelter often must spend money to replace their lost or stolen belongings.

Finding a job or a home is almost impossible because of the daily routine in many shelters. Families often are required to leave the shelter early in the morning (7:00 A.M. is common) and are not allowed to return until after dinner. They frequently eat and sleep in different locations. Few shelters help families find child care, and most will not allow parents to leave their children with other families in the shelter. Thus, parents must take their children everywhere with them, a drain of time, energy, and often resources. In some communities, families sleep and eat in different locations, and may spend the whole day on the bus going from one place to another.

Although such shelters serve most homeless families, a growing number of programs are emerging around the country which are better suited to meeting their needs and helping them restabilize as quickly as possible. Our House in Atlanta is a drop-in center that provides child care to homeless children while their parents look for employment and housing. The ConServe program in Washington, D.C., serves the ongoing needs of some homeless families by helping them move from emergency shelter to permanent housing, and by then providing them with services and assistance in their new homes. In Missouri, Grace Hill Consolidated Services shelters homeless families in a converted gymnasium and provides intensive housing-search assistance, child care, and parenting education.

As advocates struggle to address the problems facing homeless families and children and try to spare more families the horror of homelessness, debates over current numbers must not be allowed to obscure the faces of the families. Whether there are 50,000 or 1 million homeless families, there are too many for a nation that clings to the belief that every child deserves a place to call home. The challenge is to move beyond the numbers to prevent family homelessness, to provide support services for those families who need them, and to help all homeless families find a new home. At the same time, the major problems which beset so many families – poverty and an inadequate supply of low-income housing – must be addressed.

References

Atlanta Task Force for the Homeless. 1987. *Homelessness in Metro Atlanta: A Working Paper and Recommendations.* Atlanta: By the author.

Bassuk, E., and L. Rosenberg. 1988. *"Why Does Family Homelessness Occur? A Case Control Study."* American Journal of Public Health 78, no. 7: 783-788.

Bassuk, E., L. Rubin, and A. Lauriat. 1986. *"Characteristics of Sheltered Homeless Families."* American Journal of Public Health 76, no. 9: 1097-1101.

Boxill, N., and A. Beaty. n.d. *An Exploration of Mother/Child Interaction Among Homeless Women and Their Children Using a Public Night Shelter in Atlanta, Georgia.* Atlanta: Atlanta Task Force for the Homeless.

Brown, J. H., and J. Yinger. 1986. *Home Ownership and Housing Affordability in the United States: 1963-1985.* Cambridge: Joint Center for Housing Studies of the Massachusetts Institute of Technology and Harvard University.

Burt, M., and B. Cohen. 1988. *Feeding the Homeless: Does the Prepared Meals Provision Work?* Washington, DC: Urban Institute Press.

Children's Defense Fund. 1988. *A Children's Defense Budget. FY 1989: An Analysis of Our Nation's Investment in Children.* Washington, DC: By the author.

Children's Defense Fund. 1989. *A Vision for America's Future. An Agenda for the 1990's: A Children's Defense Budget.* Washington, DC: By the author.

Citizen's Committee for the Children of New York. 1988. *Children in Storage: Families in New York City's Barracks-Style Shelters.* New York: By the author.

Cowan, C. D., W. R. Breakey, and P. J. Fisher. 1988. "The Methodology of Counting the Homeless." In *Homelessness, Health and Human Needs.* Washington, DC: National Academy Press.

Emergency Services Network. 1988. *Homelessness in Alameda County: 1988 Composite Profile and Unduplicated Count.* Alameda County, CA: By the author.

Freeman, R. B., and B. Hall. 1986. *Permanent Homeless in America?* National Bureau of Economic Research: By the author.

General Accounting Office. 1989. *Children and Youths: About 68,000 Homeless and 186,000 in Shared Housing at Any Given Time.* Washington, DC: By the author.

Institute of Medicine. 1988. *Homelessness, Health and Human Needs.* Washington, DC: National Academy Press.

Johnson, C. M., A. M. Sum, and J. D. Weill. 1988. *Vanishing Dreams: The Growing Economic Plight of America's Young Families.* Washington, DC: Children's Defense Fund.

Knickman, J. R., and B. C. Weitzman. 1989. *Homeless Families in New York City: An Assessment of Factors That Increase Risk of Shelter Use.* New York: Urban Research Center, NYU.

Leonard, P. A., C. N. Dolbeare, and E. B. Lazere. 1989. *A Place to Call Home: The Crisis in Housing for the Poor.* Washington, DC: Center on Budget and Policy Priorities.

Low Income Housing Information Service. 1989. *Low Income Housing and Homelessness: Facts and Myths.* Washington, DC: By the author.

McChesney, K. Y. 1988a. *Absence of a Family Safety Net for Homeless Families.* Paper submitted to Sociology of Family Session, American Sociological Association.

—1988b. *Homeless Families, Homeless Children: How Family Poverty Leads to Homelessness.* Presented at the Society for the Study of Social Problems.

Minnesota Coalition for the Homeless. 1988, Fall. "The Homeless Report." Newsletter of the Minnesota Coalition for the Homeless.

National Alliance to End Homelessness. 1988. *Housing and Homelessness: A Report of the National Alliance to End Homelessness.* Washington, DC: By the author.

National Black Child Development Institute, Inc. 1989. *Who Will Care When Parents Can't? A Study of Black Children in Foster Care.* New York: Urban Research Center, NYU.

National Housing Task Force. 1988. *A Decent Place to Live: The Report of the National Housing Task Force.* Washington, DC: By the author.

Newman, S.J., and A. Schnare. 1987. *Integrating Housing and Welfare Assistance.* Cambridge, MA: Massachusetts Institute of Technology Center for Real Estate Development.

Owen, G., and J. A. Williams. 1988. *Results of the Twin City Survey of Emergency Shelter Residents, February 25, 1988.* Minnesota: Wilder Research Center.

Parvensky, J., and D. Krasniewski. 1988. *In Search of a Place to Call Home: A Profile of Homelessness in Colorado.* Denver, Colorado: Colorado Coalition for the Homeless.

Patton, L. T. 1988. "The Rural Homeless." In *Homelessness, Health and Human Needs.* Washington, DC: National Academy Press.

Peuquet, S., and P. Leland. 1988. *Homelessness in Delaware.* Newark: University f Delaware.

Reyes, L. M., and L. D. Waxman. 1986. *The Continued Growth of Hunger, Homelessness and Poverty in America's Cities: 1986.* Washington, DC: U.S. Conference of Mayors.

—1987. *The Continuing Growth of Hunger, Homelessness and Poverty in America's Cities: 1987.* Washington, DC: U.S. Conference of Mayors.

—1989a. *A Status Report on Hunger and Homelessness in America's Cities: 1988.* Washington, DC: U.S. Conference of Mayors.

—1989b. *A Status Report on Hunger and Homelessness in America's Cities,1989: A 27-City Survey.* Washington, DC: U.S. Conference of Mayors.

Rowe, A. 1986. *Comprehensive Plan for Homeless Families.* Washington, DC: District of Columbia Government Department of Human Services, Commission on Social Services.

Ryan, P., I. Goldstein, and D. Bartelt. 1989. *Homelessness in Pennsylvania: How Can This Be?* Philadelphia: Coalition on the Homeless in Pennsylvania (CHIP) and the Institute for Public Policy Studies of Temple University.

Status Report – Education of Homeless Children and Youth Under the Stewart B. McKinney Homeless Assistance Act, New York State. 1988. Washington, DC: Department of Education.

—*Montana.* 1988. Washington, DC: Department of Education.

—*Arkansas.* 1988. Washington, DC: Department of Education.

—*Oklahoma.* 1988. Washington, DC: Department of Education.

Tomaszewicz, M. 1985. *Children Entering Foster Care: Factors Leading to Placement.* New Jersey Division of Youth and Family Services.

U.S. Congress. House. Select Committee on Children, Youth and Families. 1987. *The Crisis in Homelessness: Effects on Children and Families.* Hearing. Washington, DC: Government Printing Office.

3

Homeless Youth: An Overview of Recent Literature

Marjorie J. Robertson

> We must accurately perceive the root causes of youth homelessness and not solely attack the symptoms or coping mechanisms of these victimized youth. Importantly, we must view youth homelessness as a social problem, not as an individual problem presented by a number of troubled youth. (Chicago Coalition for the Homeless 1985, 12)

Homelessness among young people in the United States is a serious and complex problem. The number of youth who run away from home or who experience homelessness in the course of a year is unknown, and any estimate of their population size is considered highly problematic (Rothman and David 1985). There has been a great deal of media interest in runaway and homeless youth (Hevesi 1988; Sullivan 1988); however, only limited information is available, much of which is impressionistic.

Despite their apparent large numbers, runaway and homeless youth are considered the most understudied subgroup among the contemporary homeless population (Institute of Medicine 1988). Only limited empirical information is available, and most of it is based on data from client samples from shelters (Shaffer and Caton 1984), health clinics (Yates et al. 1988), or institutions (Mundy et al. 1989) which likely misrepresent the larger homeless youth population. Despite its limitations,[1] recent literature suggests that runaway and homeless youth may constitute a large and very special population that urgently requires the attention of policy makers (Solarz 1988).

This chapter was designed to provide a broad overview of information on the contemporary population of homeless adolescents. The discussion will address the prevalence of homelessness among youth, their characteristics and special problems, the causes of their homelessness, and major gaps in services.

Definition of Terms

Previous literature on runaway and homeless youth has failed to produce a consensus definition (Brennan, Huizinga, and Elliot 1979; Greater Boston 1985). Hence, a variety of terms has been used to refer to the population of young people in unstable living situations, including "homeless," "runaways," "throwaways," "push-outs," "system kids," "street kids," "unaccompanied youth," "damaged teens," "outcasts," and "hard-to-serve youth" (Adams, Gulatta, and Clancy 1985; Chelimsky 1982; Greater Boston 1985; National Network 1985). Often terms represent overlapping categories, and at times the terms "homeless" and "runaway" are used interchangeably, especially in media reports (e.g., Hevesi 1988).

Apparently, however, the terms "runaway" and "homeless" have distinctive meanings in the current literature. For example, the National Network of Runaway and Youth Services defines the terms as follows:

> Runaways are children and youth who are away from home at least overnight without parental or caretaker permission. Homeless are youth who have no parental, substitute, foster, or institutional home. Often, these youth have left, or been urged to leave with the full knowledge or approval of legal guardians and have no alternative home. (1985, 1)

Similarly, in a report to the United States Senate, homeless youth were distinguished from runaways as "youths who had been 'thrown out,' 'pushed out,' 'out of the house by mutual consent with parents' (or) those who for one reason or another could not go home again" (U.S. Congress, Senate 1980, 13-14).

The fundamental distinctions between the terms rest on presumptions of choice, access, and time away from home. Runaways presumably have chosen to leave a home to which they can return. Homeless youth, on the other hand, are perceived to lack access to either their original or an alternative home, and they may not have chosen to leave in the first place.

The term "runaway" more usually refers to a shorter time away from home, whereas "homeless" designates longer periods of time and perhaps more definite separation.

A more literal meaning of the terms raises another issue. "Running away" would seem to describe the act of separation. Youth who leave their family homes or institutional placements (Miller et al. 1980) may not actually go to a shelter or "the streets." They may go to the homes of friends or family and still refer to themselves as having run away. On the other hand, the term "homeless" seems to describe one outcome of separation from a traditional or institutional dwelling.

Such definitions are problematic, however, since they require assumptions about the youths' motives and the degree of access youths may have to homes. For the present discussion, therefore, homeless youth were conceptualized as a special subgroup of homeless persons. This perspective led to an adaptation of definitions used in studies of homeless adults, which also vary widely. However, these definitions usually involve a description of behavior or physical circumstances, and do not depend on motives. The term "homeless" will be used as a generic term to refer to persons who have spent at least one night either in an emergency shelter, in improvised shelter (including abandoned buildings, vehicles, public places, or other somewhat protective sites not normally considered conventional dwelling places), or on the streets (i.e., in outdoor areas such as parks or beaches). Of greatest interest are those under age eighteen, since that age is a common delimiter in empirical studies of homeless populations, and since the legal status of minors often distinguishes them from older homeless persons in terms of access to services, employment, and many other resources. In sum, homeless youth are conceptualized as unaccompanied minors who have spent at least one night either in a formal emergency shelter, in improvised shelter, or on the streets (Robertson 1989). Nevertheless, when referring to results from specific reports or studies, the language used by the original authors will be used.

How Many Homeless Youth Are There?

As with population estimates for homeless adults, any estimate of population size is highly problematic. Since no comprehensive study on homeless youth has been done nationally, estimates are not precise, and they largely represent informed guesses about the scope of the problem.

Disagreement on estimates or reluctance of experts to estimate the total population of homeless youth reflects the lack of information, disagreement on definitions, varied methods for generating estimates, and lack of a mechanism for centralized reporting (Brennan, Huizinga, and Elliot 1979; Bucy 1987; Rothman and David 1985). Numbers based on client counts probably underestimate the population size because they are based on reports of service providers who do not include youth who have not sought help (Yates 1988).[2]

There is evidence that suggests that the size of the homeless youth population is substantial. In a recent study by the Justice Department, telephone surveys were conducted with 10,367 households and 127 institutions in 1988 and early 1989. Preliminary findings suggest that an estimated 500,000 youth under age eighteen become runaways or throwaways each year (Barden 1990). Two more dated, empirically based national estimates of the annual incidence of runaway behavior were conducted in the mid-1970s. The Opinion Research Center (ORC) conducted a study of a national sample of households for the Department of Health, Education, and Welfare. The ORC study reported that the percentage of the youth population, aged ten to seventeen, which ran away from their parents and were missing for twenty-four hours, was 1.7 percent. A second national survey also estimated the annual incidence of runaway behavior to be 1.9 percent. Based on the ORC findings, an estimated 519,500 to 635,000 youth ran away from home in 1975 (Brennan, Huizinga, and Elliot 1979). However, these youth were runaways, and an unknown number actually entered shelters or ended up on the streets. On the other hand, this figure does not include those who ran away from institutional placements. Probabilistic sampling techniques estimate that one of eight adolescents will run from home before the eighteenth birthday (Young et al. 1983).

In 1982, the number of runaway and homeless youth nationwide was estimated between 733,000 and 1,300,000 (Chelimsky 1982). In 1987, cities surveyed by the U.S. Conference of Mayors estimated that

4 percent of all homeless persons were unaccompanied youth (Solarz 1988). Also in 1987, about 333,000 youth were served in federally supported services alone.[3]

In addition to national estimates, state[4] and local[5] reports suggest that youth homelessness is a sizable and widespread phenomenon. Although most information comes from large urban areas such as New York City, Los Angeles, Chicago, and Boston, youth homelessness appears to be manifested widely.

In sum, only a limited empirical basis for a national estimate exists. However, as many as 1.3 million youth may be in emergency shelters or on the streets in the course of a year (National Network 1985). The majority of these youth are thought to return home after just a few days; however, an unknown number do not.[6] Some service providers suggest that the number of homeless youth may be increasing; however, there is no empirical evidence of an increase.[7]

Although the number is unknown, limited information suggests that the prevalence of homeless teen-age parents is noteworthy, and that they may constitute a special population among homeless youth. In 1985, an Illinois Governor's Task Force estimated that over 21,000 youth under age twenty in Illinois were homeless; of these, 7,000 were teen mothers or pregnant (Hemmens and Luecke 1988). In Pennsylvania, an estimated 1.9 percent of all homeless households statewide were estimated to consist of young parents with at least one child (Ryan, Goldstein, and Bartelt 1989).[8] A survey of seventy-seven families in the New York City temporary shelter system for families suggested that about 11.3 percent of parents were under age twenty-one (Towber 1985). A second survey of homeless families reported the presence of young families, including 4 percent of parents at the Martinique Hotel and 12 percent of parents at a city shelter who were under age twenty-one (Towber 1986).

Who Are These Homeless Youth?

A Heterogeneous Population

Current literature suggests that homeless youth constitute a diverse population (Greater Boston 1985; National Network 1985) and that there is no typical homeless youth. However, some patterns in characteristics are apparent.

Gender. Homeless youth include both males and females in varying proportions, depending upon the source of the sample. Data from shelters suggest either even numbers of males and females (Upshur 1985, in Boston; Council of Community Services 1984, in Albany, New York; New York State Council 1984) or more females (Michigan Network 1987; Miller et al. 1980; U.S. Congress, Senate, 1980). In contrast, street samples tend to include more males (Robertson 1989; Vander Kooi 1983).

Age. Ages usually range from thirteen to seventeen, with a majority from most reports over age fifteen (Council of Community Services 1984; Robertson 1989). However, several studies identified respondents or clients under age thirteen, including some as young as age nine (Rothman and David 1985; Vander Kooi 1983).

Race/ethnicity. Ethnicity in several studies in New York City tended to reflect the area served (New York State Council 1984).[9]

Distribution. Contrary to popular perception, studies in several urban areas nationally reported that most homeless youth are in fact "local kids" (New York State Council 1984; Robertson 1989; Rothman and David 1985; van Houten and Golembiewski 1978). For example, the majority of youths served in seventeen runaway and homeless youth programs nationally (72 percent) were from the immediate geographical area in which the center was located (Chelimsky 1982).[10]

Education. Many homeless youth have had interrupted or difficult school histories. Few were currently in school (Upshur 1985). For example, in one Hollywood study (mean age sixteen), most adolescents had completed the ninth grade. However, over one-quarter of the sample (28.0 percent) had been held back at least one year in school, and one-quarter reported participation in special classes including remedial reading and math and special education programs. Most had cut classes, and over three-quarters had been suspended (Robertson 1989).[11]

History of Homelessness

A pattern of episodic homelessness commonly is reported in studies of homeless youth (Institute of Medicine 1988). For example, the majority of a Hollywood street sample[12] had extensive histories of homelessness, with multiple episodes and lengthy periods of homelessness (Robertson 1989). Most had been homeless more than once (79.3 percent), and almost one-quarter had been homeless more than ten times (22.8 percent). The total time they were homeless during their lifetimes averaged over six months and ranged from five days to seven years.[13]

Recent Changes in the Population

Recent surveys of service providers nationally suggest that their contemporary clients seem to be younger, more troubled, and more likely to have multiple problems compared to clients in previous years (Miller et al. 1980; National Network 1985; Rothman and David 1985). For example, the runaway and homeless youth population in Los Angeles County is reportedly younger, more ethnically varied, and more emotionally disturbed, many coming from dysfunctional families (Yates 1988; Rothman and David 1985).[14]

How Did These Young People Become Homeless?

Homeless youth are a complex population including many youth with multiple problems. Although an array of contributory factors has been identified, no single element can be seen as the cause of youth homelessness (Miller et al. 1980; Rothman and David 1985). The literature offers several explanations of why youth become homeless in the first place and why they may remain homeless or return to homelessness. For the purposes of this discussion, causes can be loosely clustered into three categories: family issues, residential instability, and socioeconomic pressures. Some causes clearly precipitate homelessness, whereas others are more hidden. Unfortunately, no work tests the relative contribution or interaction of various factors.

Family Issues

Family problems. Family conflict or communication problems tend to be the modal reported causes of homelessness among youth.

Unfortunately, family problems tend to be tied to an undifferentiated collection of events, including conflict over sexual orientation, sexual activity, pregnancy, school, rejection by a step-parent, and alcohol and drug use (Chicago Coalition 1985; Robertson 1989; Rothman and David 1985). Early estrangement from parents and other family members often is reported by homeless adolescents, as is family disruption of various types.[15] Family disruption, such as divorce or separation, reportedly is often related to parent alcohol and drug abuse. When pressures increase in the marital relationship, communication with children becomes secondary and strained (Rothman and David 1985).

Based on a detailed review of the literature, Rothman and David (1985) suggested that families of runaways are generally dysfunctional in that (1) youth may have a poor relationship with parents; (2) parents may be separated, divorced, in trouble with the law, or abusing alcohol; (3) runaways perceive themselves as unloved or unwanted by their families; (4) adolescents may become scapegoats and divert attention from other problems in the families; or (5) physical or sexual abuse may be present.

Neglect, physical abuse, and sexual abuse. Many homeless adolescents report histories of neglect and physical and sexual abuse, although rates vary by site and method of data collection (Greater Boston 1985; Miller et al. 1980; National Network 1985; Rothman and David 1985; U.S. Department of Health and Human Services 1986; Upshur 1985).[16] For example, in seventeen shelters nationally, staff estimates of physical abuse among their clients ranged from 20 percent to 40 percent, sexual abuse ranged downward from 5 percent, and neglect ranged from 14 percent to 100 percent (Chelimsky 1982). Service providers in Los Angeles estimated that 26 percent of their clients had been victims of sexual abuse (Rothman and David 1985). Feelings of neglect and abuse were reported by one-half of the runaways in one California study: "...one-fifth of the subjects stated that their parents had so physically abused them as to 'hurt them badly'" (Miller et al. 1980, 60). Significant physical violence by a parent during the previous year was reported by 78 percent of runaways in a Columbus, Ohio, shelter (Farber et al. 1984).

Apparently, neglect and abuse contribute significantly to separations of adolescents from their homes. In a Hollywood study, many had left home at least once because of physical abuse (37.3 percent) or sexual abuse (10.7 percent) in the home. These included one-fifth of the sample (20.2 percent) who had been removed from their homes by the authorities because of neglect or abuse (Robertson 1989). Some authors consider running away from an abusive home to be a well-developed coping mechanism (Gutierres and Reich 1981).

Formerly homeless family members. There are anecdotal reports that many teen-agers become homeless when their families become homeless (Bucy 1987); however, little empirical evidence of such was found. On the contrary, available evidence on precipitating and contributing causes of homelessness contradicts the position.[17]

Throwaways. In recent literature, homeless adolescents have been identified who have not exerted choice in leaving their previous homes. They are often referred to as "push-outs" or "throwaway kids" (Barden 1990). Almost one-third (31.9 percent) of a Hollywood sample reported that they were told to leave their last dwelling (Robertson 1989). In Boston shelters, 12 percent reported having been evicted by parents, which precipitated their current episode (Greater Boston 1985).

Options. Inability to go home is a major factor in sustained youth homelessness. For example, less than half (47 percent) of current runaway and homeless clients in Los Angeles County were considered to have a realistic prospect of returning to their homes (Rothman and David 1985). In 1987, only 19 percent of youth clients in shelters in Los Angeles County were good candidates for immediate family reunification; 25 percent were chronic runaways who were very unlikely to be returned home or to placement (Yates 1988). In contrast, however, 57 percent of youth in shelters nationally were reunited with families or placed in a safe living environment (National Network 1985).

Youth alcohol and other drug use. There is little information on the contribution of alcohol and other drug use by youth to homelessness. Alcohol or other drug use seldom has been identified as a contributing factor in youth homelessness (Council of Community Services 1984). Nevertheless, the majority of youth in a Hollywood sample used illicit drugs before they became homeless (74.7 percent), and several reported that their own drug use had contributed to their leaving home (17.7 percent). Although two-thirds used alcohol before their first episode of homelessness, few (6.5 percent) reported that their own alcohol use had ever contributed to their homelessness (Robertson 1989).

Parent alcohol and other drug use. Homeless adolescents often are reported to have parents with alcohol problems, variously defined (e.g., Miller et al. 1980; National Network 1985; New York State Council 1984; Rothman and David 1985).[18] Parent alcoholism appears to be a significant but hidden factor in homelessness for many adolescents. For example, parental alcohol abuse was correlated significantly with both runaway behavior and alcohol abuse in a survey of adolescents from seventeen shelters nationally (van Houten and Golembiewski 1978).

Parent alcohol problems apparently contributed directly to residential instability and homelessness for many adolescents in a Hollywood study (Robertson, Koegel, and Ferguson 1990). The majority of homeless adolescents had lived in households in which at least one member had an alcohol problem. About one-quarter of the sample (23.7 percent) indicated that they had run away or left home at least once because their parent or step-parent had an alcohol problem which often caused arguments and physical violence.

Residential Instability

Homelessness among youth appears to be part of a long pattern of residential instability. It more accurately is described as a process than an event (Institute of Medicine 1988; Miller et al. 1980). Consistently, homeless youth report extensive moves and separations during their lifetimes. Although literal homelessness often represents a substantial part of their residential instability, their histories also often include multiple family disruptions and institutional interventions.

Foster care and other residential programs. In particular, studies report that many respondents have extensive histories of contact with public social service systems, including placements in foster care and other residential programs, many of which occurred at very early ages (Greater Boston 1985; New York State Council 1984; Rothman and David 1985).[19] For example, clients of eleven youth shelters in Massachusetts reported extensive histories of system care, including contact with multiple state and private agencies. Those who had left home earlier (57 percent left home for the first time before age thirteen) reported greater residential instability. The Greater Boston report states, "Like all system kids their lives are spent traveling through the limbo of foster care, psychiatric hospitals, emergency shelters, residential schools and the streets" (1985).

Institutional contact. Homeless adolescents also report high rates of other early institutional contacts, including inpatient psychiatric facilities[20] (Robertson 1989; Shaffer and Caton 1984) and the criminal justice system (Rothman and David 1985).[21] For example, the majority of one Hollywood sample (55.9 percent) had spent at least one night in juvenile detention or jail, and the majority of these had been detained more than once. The majority also had experienced their first detention by age fifteen, and several adolescents had been detained by age ten.

System or institutional contact appears to contribute to youth homelessness both directly and indirectly. There is some evidence that youth in placement or in institutional settings are at risk of becoming homeless upon separation from those settings. For example, 823 minors were discharged from foster care to their own responsibility in New York City in 1982 (Citizen's Committee 1983). In Illinois in 1983, of 16,000 wards of the state under age eighteen, an unsubstantiated estimate of 15 percent (or 1,650 in the Chicago area and 2,400 throughout Illinois) had run away from institutions or foster or group homes. In another example, the majority of one Hollywood study had been in various residential placements (Robertson 1989). Many had been in foster care (40.9 percent) and group homes (38.2 percent), and more than half had been in juvenile detention or jail (55.9 percent). Upon their most recent separation, about one-third of those in each of these settings spent the first night either in a shelter or on the streets; that is, one-third became homeless upon separation from placement or detention.

Institutional contact also may contribute indirectly to vulnerability to homelessness. Youths may be returned inappropriately to their prior homes due to lack of alternative longer-term placements. The Greater Boston study reports, "The lack of available out-of-home resources (e.g., foster and group homes) is often more influential in service planning than the needs of the adolescents and their families" (1985, 7). Half of the cases of first-time, out-of-home placements in one setting were returned home despite the assessment of the emergency shelter staff that this was an inappropriate placement decision (Greater Boston 1985). Additionally, some youth "age out" of the foster-care system with limited alternatives in place.

Socioeconomic Pressures

Causes of youth homelessness include socioeconomic issues, including family economics (Gordon 1979; Janus et al. 1987). Dysfunctional families may be more vulnerable to breaking down during economic crises due to problems with the welfare system, housing aid, child welfare, or employment. Many youth reported that hard economic times led to their leaving home because they were an economic burden to their families (Chicago Coalition 1985). In Iowa and Texas, for example, the increased number of homeless and push-out youth occurred as a result of family economic difficulties (National Network 1985). The lack of affordable housing creates a major obstacle for young adults trying to exit from homelessness. Youth are less likely to find adequate, affordable housing since, in a tight housing market, with high competition for housing, landlords can pick and choose among potential tenants. Unemployed or underemployed youth are a poor risk (New York State Council 1984). Furthermore, an underage youth is unable to sign a legal contract such as a lease.

What Special Problems Do Homeless Youth Have?

Survival While Homeless

Shelter, food, and income. Shelter facilities in most communities appear to be grossly inadequate to the demand.[22] Furthermore, exclusionary criteria often bar youth in most need of intervention.[23] For example, in seventeen shelters nationally, staff members reported that the three categories of youths most commonly excluded from their shelters were those with severe emotional problems, those dangerous to themselves and others, and drug addicts (Chelimsky 1982). Many youth have difficulty meeting basic needs, and of necessity many become involved in illegal and dangerous income-generating activities such as prostitution and drug dealing.

In Hollywood, a majority of the sample (79.4 percent) identified "improvised shelter" as their usual sleeping place, including abandoned buildings, vehicles, and "the streets."[24] Relatively few in the sample used formal shelters recently (15.2 percent), likely a reflection of the scarcity of shelter beds in the area.[25] Shelters or other free meal programs were the most usual sources of food; nevertheless, the majority of the sample (57.0 percent) had spent at least one day in the past month with nothing to eat. About half reported difficulty getting adequate food (48.4 percent) and clothing (51.6 percent). Many also reported difficulty finding a place to clean up (38.0 percent) or obtain medical care (30.1 percent). The majority of the sample reported legal income, although many also reported income from illegal activities such as panhandling, prostitution, and drug dealing.[26]

Illegal activities and problem behaviors. Many homeless adolescents report illegal and other problem behaviors. However, many of these behaviors appear to be part of the youths' strategy for survival while homeless. Behaviors which appear to reflect adaptation to the homeless condition include those that provide for basic needs directly (e.g., breaking into a building or trading sex for food or shelter) or those that generate income with which to meet basic needs (e.g., selling drugs or being paid for sex). In one Hollywood study, many adolescents reporting illegal behaviors reported doing so only when homeless (Robertson 1989).[27] Some adolescents also report committing offenses that result in arrest in order to secure shelter (Kufeldt and Nimmo 1987; Robertson 1989).

Physical Health Problems

More homeless adolescents appear to have impaired health status than domiciled adolescents.[28] Major health problems include sexually transmitted diseases (Chicago Coalition 1985; Robertson 1989; Rothman and David 1985), malnutrition, alcohol and drug use, pregnancy, trauma due to victimization,[29] and unusual barriers to health care[30] (Chicago Coalition 1985; Manov and Lowther 1983).

About one-quarter of the Hollywood sample rated their health as only fair or poor (Robertson 1989). A majority of the sample (65.9 percent) reported recent health problems (i.e., within the previous six months). About one-fifth (22.2 percent) noted that their health was worse since they became homeless. About one-fifth (18.7 percent) also reported that they had a health problem which was serious enough to warrant treatment but which was not treated during the past year. Although only one-third (34.4 percent) claimed current medical coverage, and almost half stated that they had no regular source of medical care, more than half reported receiving medical treatment in the previous year, which included hospitalization for one-tenth of the sample.

Sexual history. Little empirical information about sexual history is available. Homeless adolescents apparently are sexually active, as reflected in their high rates of sexually transmitted diseases and of pregnancy among young women. Most adolescents in the Hollywood sample were considered to be sexually active (i.e., they reported having sex at least once) (Robertson 1989). Of those who had sex, two-thirds had used birth control in the past year. A majority of these reported using birth control most of the time, and most (82.1 percent) reported using some sort of birth control the last time they had sex. However, only about half of those who were sexually active (i.e., 52.4 percent of those who had ever had sex) reported condom use during the last time they had sex.

Sexual orientation was reported in two Hollywood studies. In one street sample (Robertson 1989), sexual orientation was identified as 81 percent heterosexual, 5 percent gay or lesbian, and 5 percent bisexual. In the health clinic survey (Yates et al. 1988), 83 percent were heterosexual, 7.3 percent were homosexual, and 9.1 percent were bisexual.

Pregnancy. An unknown number of homeless teen-age women are pregnant. They may have become homeless because of the pregnancy, or they may have become pregnant while homeless. Unprotected sex with prostitution clients or partners while homeless may result in pregnancy.[31] In addition, given the circumstances in which they live, homeless adolescents are more vulnerable to forced sexual contact which may result in pregnancy. Homeless pregnant teen-agers are at risk for low-birthweight babies and high infant-mortality rates because they are unlikely to get prenatal care and may not have adequate health and dietary habits (Sullivan and Damrosch 1987). Malnutrition and drug and alcohol use during pregnancy can affect the health of both the young woman and the developing fetus.

There is limited information on the prevalence of pregnant teens among homeless persons. However, in 1985, an Illinois Governor's Task Force estimated that over 21,000 youth under age twenty in Illinois were homeless; of these 7,000 were teen mothers or pregnant (Hemmens and Luecke 1988). In a health clinic sample of runaways

(Yates et al. 1988), 13 percent were pregnant. In a Hollywood street sample (Robertson 1989), almost half of the females (44.4 percent) reported one or more pregnancies, although only one-third of these (or 13.9 percent of females in the sample) had ever given birth. None, however, had children with them at the time of the interview. Age at first pregnancy ranged from eleven to seventeen years. Of all females in the sample, 16.7 percent had gotten pregnant while homeless, and 11.1 percent were pregnant at time of interview. Only two females (i.e., 5.6 percent of all females in the sample) reported that pregnancy had contributed to their homelessness. However, of those who were ever pregnant, more than one-third reported getting pregnant while homeless, and about one-quarter were pregnant at the time of interview. In other words, of all females in the sample, 16.7 percent had ever gotten pregnant while homeless, and 11.1 percent were pregnant at the time of the interview.

AIDS. There is evidence from some urban areas that homeless adolescents are at high risk for exposure to human immunodeficiency virus (HIV). Homeless youth include persons in such high-risk groups for HIV infection as homosexual or bisexual males, intravenous drug users, or female partners of intravenous (IV) drug users[32] (Robertson, Koegel, and Grella 1987; Stricof et al. 1988; Yates et al. 1988; Hersch 1989). Furthermore, these adolescents reported indirect risk indicators, including high rates of other sexually transmitted diseases, multiple sex partners, minimal contraceptive use, and hard drug use (Robertson 1989; Shaffer and Caton 1984; Stricof et al. 1988; Yates et al. 1988.) In addition, despite knowledge about transmission modes, homeless adolescents may not use protection against exposure consistently (Robertson, Koegel, and Grella 1987).[33] Furthermore, homeless adolescents are reported to have excess prevalence of alcohol and drug use (Miller et al. 1980; Robertson et al. 1990; Yates et al. 1988), which may disinhibit high-risk sexual practices (Lang 1981).

Mental Health

The contemporary population of homeless adolescents generally is believed to be a multiple-problem population (Miller et al. 1980; National Network 1985) with high rates of mental health, alcohol, and drug problems, often in combination. Assessment of mental health status among homeless adolescents is problematic, as has proven true for homeless adults (Robertson, in press). Furthermore, policy makers, researchers, and service providers must guard against the "medicalization" of homeless adolescents and the premature labeling of homelessness among homeless adolescents as a psychiatric problem.

Nevertheless, with these cautions in mind, homeless adolescents have been found to be at high risk for mental health problems. Consistently, recent studies report high rates of depression (variously defined), suicide attempts, and other mental health problems (Robertson et al. 1988; Shaffer and Caton 1984; Yates et al. 1988; Speck, Ginter, and Helton 1988; Upshur 1985). Several studies also report high rates of previous psychiatric hospitalization (Robertson 1989; Shaffer and Caton 1984).

In one Hollywood study, the sample demonstrated an elevated prevalence across all mental health indicators compared to nonhomeless adolescents. Rates of DSM-III disorders (from the Diagnostic and Statistical Manual of Mental Disorders), including major depression, conduct disorder, and post-traumatic stress, were at least three times higher than those of a nonhomeless comparison group. Co-morbidity of alcohol abuse and mental health problems was also high, and dual diagnoses of major depression and alcohol abuse applied to 10.8 percent of the sample. In a New York City sample, runaways were described to have a psychiatric profile indistinguishable from that of adolescents attending a child psychiatric clinic (Shaffer and Caton 1984).

Suicide attempts. Lifetime suicide attempts were reported by 24 percent of runaways in New York City shelters (Shaffer and Caton 1984) and 18 percent of runaways using an outpatient health clinic in Los Angeles (Yates et al. 1988). About half (48.4 percent) of another Hollywood street sample had attempted suicide sometime in their lives (Robertson 1989). Of those who had made an attempt, more than half had attempted more than once (27.5 percent of the total), and more than half (26.8 percent of the total) had attempted suicide during the previous twelve months. In both the Hollywood and New York City studies, females reported higher suicide attempt rates than males (Robertson 1989; Shaffer and Caton 1984).

Mental health treatment history. In Hollywood, almost one-quarter of a street sample (23.9 percent) had ever been hospitalized overnight for mental health or emotional problems. About two-thirds of these (17.2 percent) had been hospitalized for suicide attempts (Robertson 1989).

In a New York City study, 8.5 percent of shelter clients had been hospitalized (Shaffer and Caton 1984); the authors attributed the high rate of psychiatric hospitalization in their sample to excess suicide attempts. However, an alternative explanation is posed by recent articles suggesting that psychiatric hospitalization is used increasingly as a form of social control for adolescents with problem behaviors (Warren 1981; Van Dusen 1981; Landers 1988). Although either of these explanations is plausible and consistent with both the excess suicide attempts and excess problem behaviors apparent among homeless adolescents, evaluation of their comparative contribution to excessive rates of psychiatric hospitalization among homeless adolescents has not been empirically evaluated.

Alcohol Use and Abuse

Most reports on alcohol use or abuse among homeless adolescents are anecdotal or impressionistic, and many fail to specify how alcohol abuse was measured. Nevertheless, recent empirical literature suggests that homeless adolescents are at high risk for alcohol abuse (Upshur 1985; Miller et al. 1980; Rothman and David 1985). Clearly, homeless adolescents constitute a high-alcohol-use group, as reflected both in their historic and current alcohol use. For example, a survey of 617 adolescents in seventeen shelters nationally reported that 79 percent of the sample had used alcohol and that 60 percent reported regular alcohol use (van Houten and Golembiewski 1978).[34] In their study of 117 adolescents in New York City, Shaffer and Caton (1984) reported that, on average, about one-fifth of shelter residents used alcohol to intoxication at least once per week, and those who were most "disturbed" were significantly more likely to report getting drunk weekly. In Los Angeles, about half (54.5 percent) of the runaway clients of an outpatient medical clinic reported alcohol use, a figure similar to that for nonrunaway clients (Yates et al. 1988).

Almost half of one Hollywood street sample (48.4 percent) met DSM-III criteria for a diagnosis of alcohol abuse, a figure six to eight times higher than that for nonhomeless age peers (Robertson et al. 1990).[35] Compared to nonhomeless adolescents, homeless adolescents used alcohol at a younger age, experienced greater impaired social functioning due to alcohol use, and practiced exaggerated current consumption patterns. In general, this sample was much like homeless adults in the high prevalence of abuse, correlates of abuse, pathological drinking behaviors, and high co-morbidity of alcohol abuse with depression and drug abuse. Adolescents with a history of alcohol abuse tended to have more chronic histories of homelessness and more difficulty meeting subsistence needs while homeless. They relied more on illegal behaviors to generate income. They had more extensive periods of residential instability beyond literal homelessness, greater estrangement from family members, and more histories of neglect or abuse in the home. They also were more likely to have been removed from their homes by authorities for neglect or abuse and to have spent time in institutional settings, including group homes, juvenile detention, and psychiatric inpatient facilities. They were more likely to have abused other drugs, especially cannabis, amphetamines, cocaine, and heroin or other opiates.

Despite the high prevalence of problems related to alcohol use, however, homeless adolescents appear to be a largely untreated group. For example, few in the Hollywood study (Robertson et al. 1990) had received inpatient treatment in their lifetimes (7.5 percent), and few had received any kind of treatment in the previous year other than self-help groups such as Alcoholics Anonymous. Apparent barriers to treatment included the youths' perception that they had no alcohol problem; the lack of services specifically designed for adolescents; concurrent mental health, medical, and other drug problems which complicate delivery of services to this population; and the question of priority services for the group.

Drug Use and Abuse

Little information on current and historic drug use is available, although studies suggest high rates of use (Miller et al. 1980). For example, runaway clients in a Hollywood outpatient clinic reported rates of drug abuse which were four times higher than those for nonrunaway clients (Yates et al. 1988).

The majority of one Hollywood sample (Robertson 1989) reported current use of illicit drugs.[36] More than one-third (38.7 percent) of the sample met diagnostic DSM-III criteria for drug abuse, a rate five times higher than that for nonhomeless age peers. The modal category of drug abused was cannabis, for which almost one-third of the sample met diagnostic criteria. Amphetamines were next in frequency, followed by cocaine and opiates (usually heroin), hallucinogens, and barbiturates or sedatives. Drug abuse, especially of cocaine and opiates, was more prevalent among adolescents who also abused alcohol. About one-quarter (25.8 percent) had diagnoses of both alcohol and drug abuse. The overall prevalence of substance abuse for the sample (i.e., either alcohol or drug abuse) was 61.3 percent.

Intravenous drug use is seldom assessed in studies of homeless adolescents. Nevertheless, about one-quarter of one Hollywood sample (26 percent) reported intravenous use of opiates, amphetamines, cocaine, or other drugs at some time (Robertson 1989).[37] About 35 percent of runaway clients of an outpatient health clinic reported IV drug use, compared to 3.7 percent of nonrunaway clients (Yates et al. 1988).

Will These Young People Become Homeless Adults?

Service providers have expressed concern that homeless youth may become the next generation of homeless adults (National Network 1985). Emerging evidence suggests that runaway or homeless youth may be at risk for homelessness as adults. Recent empirical studies have identified homeless adults who were homeless when they were children.[38] Emerging evidence further suggests that disproportionate numbers of homeless adults report foster placements or other institutional placements as minors.[39] Furthermore, childhood placements have been identified as a factor associated with long-term homelessness among homeless adults.[40] These findings take on added significance when one considers the high prevalence of foster and other out-of-home placements reported for homeless youth and the increasing numbers of children in out-of-home placements in the United States (*The Nation's Health* 1990).

Policy Relevance

Groups at Risk

Groups at risk for homelessness appear to be young people in such systems of care as foster care, group homes, juvenile detention, and other institutional settings. Another group at risk may be youth with serious problems in their schooling, special education needs, or mental health problems.

Gaps in Services

The principal factor in homelessness among youth appears to be the lack of an adequate supply of service and appropriate types of services. A list of services gaps and a brief overview of possible interventions was culled from current literature and is outlined briefly below.

In the short term: Shelter beds and other emergency services. Besides providing a safe place to spend the night, shelters are convenient service sites at which special programs may be available. However, many adolescents never use shelters. Only limited shelter beds are available, and shelters often exclude youth in most need of intervention because they have inadequate staff or inappropriate facilities to deal with youth who have special problems. For example, in seventeen shelters nationally, staff members reported that the three categories of youths most commonly excluded from their shelters were those with severe emotional problems, drug use problems, and those dangerous to themselves and others (Chelimsky 1982).[41] Day centers and outreach programs are also needed to serve young people who may not come into shelter settings and to provide a gateway to subsequent services.

Tailored programs and services. Special populations require tailored service provision. Special-needs groups include older and other hard-to-place youth (i.e., those who straddle the children and adult public service systems), pregnant teens, young mothers, physically and developmentally disabled youth, non-English speakers, the sexually exploited, gays or lesbians, and youth with serious mental health, alcohol, and drug problems (New York State Council 1984; Chicago Coalition 1985; Council of Community Services 1984; Robertson,

Koegel, and Ferguson 1990). For example, young mothers with children need facilities where they will not be separated from their children. In 1985, there were no emergency placements for teen mothers with children in Chicago (Chicago Coalition 1985). In addition, gay and lesbian youth need emergency shelter beds in agencies sympathetic to their lifestyles (Chicago Coalition 1985). It should be noted that many adolescents report difficulty in meeting basic food, shelter and clothing needs. The delivery of an array of services, including alcohol, drug, and mental health treatment, may be more practical after adolescents find themselves in a safe environment (Robertson, Koegel, and Ferguson 1990).

Comprehensive service approach. Since homeless youth have diverse needs which cross agency jurisdictions, they require a comprehensive service approach (New York State Council 1984). Homeless youth need housing, education, vocational training, health care, mental health care, and substance and alcohol abuse services. Case management may be needed to link physical health, family support, and legal assistance. Trained professional and other staff are needed to deal with this multiproblem population (Rothman and David 1985; Robertson, Koegel, and Ferguson 1990).

Special public and special education systems. Programs are needed to enable homeless young people to complete high school or alternative education, specialized employment and training programs (Citizen's Committee 1983; National Network 1985). Employment, job-readiness training, and other supportive services are needed before youth can secure and maintain employment. High-risk youth are often ill-prepared for work, requiring intensive preparation, including job training and placement. While homeless, these youth have little or no access to such programs (New York State Council 1984).

Treatment services. Mental health, alcohol, and drug treatment services are needed that are tailored to this heterogeneous and special adolescent population (New York State Council 1984; Robertson, Koegel, and Ferguson 1990). A comprehensive array of mental health services is needed to serve youth with overlapping problems, including drug and alcohol abuse, suicidal behavior, juvenile court involvement, and family tensions (National Network 1988; Robertson et al. 1988). Specialized counseling and support services are needed to help special groups such as victims of sexual abuse, suicidal youth, or those from multiproblem families.

Education programs for AIDS prevention. The high levels of IV drug use, involvement in prostitution, and gay and bisexual lifestyles place homeless adolescents at high risk for exposure to and transmission of AIDS, suggesting them as a priority target population for education and prevention programs (Robertson, Koegel, and Grella 1987; Yates et al. 1988).

Intervention programs and sites. As others have suggested, any successful intervention will require provision of services creatively tailored to the needs of this heterogeneous population. Shelters may not be the most practical site for treatment interventions, since only a small proportion of homeless youth use shelters and many shelters permit only limited stays. Interventions have successfully been located within existing community services. For example, Alcoholics Anonymous meetings were regularly held at a centrally located drop-in center, while another drop-in center was linked to a new residential alcohol treatment program for teens. Interventions also may be designed to occur in institutional settings where homeless adolescents already are found in some number. For example, one-quarter of those abusing alcohol had been in juvenile detention at least once during the previous six months. This institutional setting may provide the opportunity to address homelessness by diverting youth into residential programs or to provide educational programs or treatment interventions either in the institution or through linkage to specialized services in the community such as residential alcohol treatment programs for homeless adolescents (Robertson, Koegel, and Ferguson 1990).

In the long run: Residential options. Long-term housing and independent-living services are needed (New York State Council 1984; Upshur 1985; Rothman and David 1985), such as voluntary long-term shelters with supportive group living arrangements, a comprehensive mix of services (National Network 1985), and close links to school and job opportunities (Rothman and David 1985). Such programs are already in place for foster children (Barth 1986). Transitional services also are needed. Most services for youth are emergency or short-term, with care limited to crisis periods. Youth who lack basic skills such as money management, education, and vocational training need transition support to independent living.

Adequate discharge planning and aftercare services within the residential child care system. Many adolescents apparently are discharged on their own responsibility or run away from placement and institutional settings. Those who return to their families may leave again due to unresolved problems which triggered the original placement. The "lack of effective aftercare and discharge planning (has been identified) as a causal factor for a significant percentage of the homeless youth population," states the New York State Council (1984, 16). Independent living skills programs could be upgraded for children in foster care for whom the discharge plan is independent living (Citizen's Committee 1983). The age of eligibility for foster care or other placements could be extended to age twenty-one.

Issues for Further Research

A more thorough description of the epidemiology of homelessness among young people is needed, as is a description of the course of homelessness so that points of intervention can be identified. A careful examination of risk factors such as school performance or institutional history might help identify young people at risk. Also needed is an evaluation of the overlap between psychiatric, foster care, and homeless youth populations to test the relationship between residential instability and mental health problems. In addition, an assessment of the prevalence of special-education youth among homeless and runaway youth is warranted. A study of movement into and out of various state child-care systems also would be useful, including, for example, an evaluation of foster care and juvenile justice systems. Demonstration projects examining varied approaches to treatment for homeless adolescents would be useful, especially among those who have a chronic history of homelessness. Demonstrations of interventions with groups at high risk for homelessness would be valuable as well.

Methodologically rigorous epidemiological research on homeless youth is urgently needed which incorporates the following: (1) development of a clear behavioral-based operational definition of homelessness; (2) comparisons with nonhomeless youth; (3) varied geographic areas, not limited to large urban areas; (4) representative samples of the larger homeless youth population, with special commitment to studying youth outside of shelter or other services; (5)

use of standardized instruments to assess mental health, physical health, and other characteristics of the population; (6) tests of the reliability and validity of information provided by respondents (e.g., testing reliability of standardized instruments with this nontraditional population); and (7) longitudinal designs to assess the course and impact of homelessness on young people.

Conclusion

Homelessness among young people in the United States is a serious and complex problem. Although the size of the population is unknown, it appears to be a large and heterogeneous group. There is no single cause for their homelessness, but rather a variety of factors which eventually result in young people leaving their families or institutional homes. Most have experienced multiple episodes of homelessness, and the contemporary population appears to be younger and more troubled than prior generations. Homeless youth often have difficulty meeting basic needs, due in large part to the scarcity or inadequacy of existing services. In addition, questionable legal status limits minors' access to housing, education systems, medical and mental health services, and social welfare programs (New York State Council 1984).

In the short term, emergency and transitional services are needed for those who are currently homeless, but strategies are needed to intervene early with at-risk youth to prevent homelessness or at least reduce the number of youth who become homeless or reduce the time spent homeless. Homelessness itself presents physical and mental health risks to the youth. It also represents an interruption of normative socialization and education, which will likely affect the ability to live independently in the future.[42] The high rates of mental health disabilities, substance abuse, and other special problems among homeless youth tend to focus our attention on the young people, but their homelessness also demonstrates the inadequacies of basic social support systems.

Notes

1. The available literature on homeless adolescents has major limitations due to methodological biases. Most current data are neither comprehensive nor comparable since (1) they often come from program records (New York State Council 1984), and many youth may use multiple

services, while others use no services; (2) different definitions, language, and methods prohibit meaningful comparisons; (3) cross-sectional samples of homeless adolescents overrepresent longer-term homeless adolescents in each site, thereby overreporting factors related to chronic homelessness; (4) information from large urban areas is most prevalent, which may not generalize to homeless youth in other geographic areas; (5) the lack of rigorous sampling methods prevents generalizing beyond the adolescents studied, and (6) much information on homeless adolescents is based on surveys of service providers rather than of adolescents themselves.

2. One government report estimated that only one in 12 runaway youths is served by federally funded shelters (Yates 1988).

3. Personal communication with Don Griffin, Associate Director, National Network for Runaway and Homeless Youth.

4. In 1985, an Illinois Governor's Task Force estimated that over 21,000 youth in Illinois were homeless; of these, 7,900 were throwaways, 9,000 were sexually exploited while homeless, and 7,000 were teen mothers or pregnant (Hemmens and Luecke 1988). A survey of Kentucky service providers (McClure and Dickman 1988) estimated that 10 percent of homeless persons served in agencies statewide were between ages 13 and 18; 19 percent of homeless females and 7 percent of homeless males were in this age group. (However, the low 54 percent response rate of providers makes the validity of these findings questionable.)

   Ryan, Goldstein, and Bartelt (1989) reported that 1.3 percent of persons in a census of emergency shelters throughout Pennsylvania were youth runaways. However, estimates were likely underestimated since there are few resources for sheltering this population, and some service providers declined to participate in the survey because they did not consider their residents homeless.

5. In 1983, in Albany County, New York, runaways reported to the police constituted 2 percent of the county's population between ages 10 and 15. In a survey in Los Angeles County, most service providers declined to offer an estimate of population size because there was no reliable basis on which to make an estimate. Nevertheless, other estimates for the area ranged from 10,000 to 20,000 during summer months (Rothman and David 1985). As with homeless adults, the numbers of homeless had become highly politicized. Seasonal variation in demand for services in Los Angeles County was reported to increase in late spring and peak in summer (Rothman and David 1985).

6. According to estimates by the National Network of Runaway and Youth Services, an estimated 50 percent to 60 percent of 1.3 million youth run away for only a few days and then return home. Almost half (47.5 percent) of all youth sheltered in federally funded shelters were short-term runaways (National Network 1985).

7. It is unclear if there is an increase in the homeless youth population. Despite anecdotal reports of an increase (Chicago Coalition 1985; Bucy 1987), no strong empirical foundation for the claim was found. On the contrary, the demand for services and number of homeless youth clients served over a twelve-month period in Los Angeles County did not increase in 1988 (Yates 1988).

8. About 15 percent of 3,735 homeless households were headed by single parents (i.e., 570 single parents had at least one child). About 12.5 percent of these single parents were between ages sixteen and twenty.

9. For example, 7 percent of shelter intakes were under age thirteen (Michigan Network 1987). Also, a convenience sample of 162 homeless youths in Chicago included respondents as young as age nine (Vander Kooi 1983).

10. New York City shelter clients were mostly locals, with the majority born in New York City (New York City Council 1984; Citizens' Committee 1983). In Albany, New York, the majority were from Albany or other parts of the Capital District (58 percent); only about one-quarter were from out of state (Council of Community Services 1984).

   Community wisdom among service providers in Los Angeles County suggests that the majority of their clients were from within the county (67 percent) or within the state (18 percent) (Rothman and David 1985). More than half in one Hollywood street sample (52.3 percent) had moved into Los Angeles County during the previous six months, supporting a popular notion that most homeless adolescents in Hollywood are recent arrivals. On the other hand, more than one-quarter of the sample (26.9 percent) were born in the county, and one-fifth (19.8 percent) had been lifetime residents. Despite recent moves into the area for many, the majority had a previous history of residence in the county, and three-quarters of the sample (75 percent) had spent more than one year of their lives in Los Angeles County (Robertson 1989).

11. A history of school problems is prominent in the literature; however, its role is unclear. School problems are often hypothesized to be a precipitant of family conflict, which results in a runaway response; others suggest that school difficulties are merely symptoms of family conflict (Young et al. 1983).

12. This group was termed a street sample because only 15.2 percent identified shelters as their usual sleeping place.

13. The history of homelessness for this Hollywood street sample demonstrated several distinctive patterns. Considering total time homeless, most had been homeless less than one year (61 percent), including 17 percent of the sample which had been homeless just once and 44 percent which had multiple episodes adding up to less than one year (episodic). Thirty-nine percent reported being homeless for one year or longer (long term), including many with multiple episodes and several

with a single episode which had lasted as long as several years. The mean time of homelessness was 440 days; the median was 201 days.

14. The perception that contemporary homeless youth clients seem more troubled or have more combined problems than previous generations of clients reflects several possibilities: (1) the improved ability of staff to recognize severely troubled youth, (2) the referral of more difficult cases, or (3) changing of the population.

15. In Hollywood, many homeless adolescents never knew their father (13.6 percent) or their mother (6.2 percent). Among parents who were known, almost three-quarters had been either divorced or never married. On average, respondents had last lived with one or both biological parents six months prior to their interview (Robertson 1989).

16. Neglect and abuse often are underreported because the nature of the abuse may not emerge until a trusting relationship is developed (Robertson 1989; Rothman and David 1985).

17. However, in one study, one adolescent was identified whose first experience of homelessness was with his family. He reported that his first episode of homelessness occurred at age five when his "mother was evicted and they all slept in the park" (Robertson 1989, 31).

18. Stress caused by parental alcoholism is reported to be one reason youth leave home (Shaffer and Caton 1984). Families also may be dysfunctional because of alcohol abuse by parents (Rothman and David 1985). Miller et al. (1980) found that 41 percent of runaways reported that one or both of their parents had a problem with alcohol. Furthermore, 17 percent reported that one or both parents had a serious drug problem. Ten percent of males and 13 percent of females reported an alcoholic parent as a "type of abuse."

19. In Hollywood, 40.9 percent of a street sample had been in foster care at least once; the majority had been in foster care by age eleven, and several had their first foster placement before age five. Similar numbers had been in group homes at least once (38.2 percent), the majority by age thirteen.

20. Adolescent psychiatric inpatients in Los Angeles were found to have histories of high residential instability. The sample also had an average of 3.1 runaway episodes, and the majority (70.1 percent) had been placed in foster care or with an alternative caregiver (Mundy et al. 1989).

21. In 1983, in Albany County, New York, between 33 percent and 40 percent of inmates in jails, ages sixteen to twenty, were homeless (Council of Community Services 1984). There also is limited evidence that some homeless youth use juvenile detention as a shelter resource (Council of Community Services 1984; Robertson 1989).

22. Shelter staff nationally estimate that only 20 percent to 25 percent of homeless and runaway youth receive services (National Network 1985). In 1985, only thirty beds were available in Chicago for an estimated 4,000 homeless youth under age eighteen (Chicago Coalition 1985). In

Los Angeles in 1986, only fifty beds were available throughout the county for runaway and homeless youth (Robertson 1989). In 1983, in New York City, there were 210 emergency shelter beds for an estimated 20,000 young adults under age twenty-one. A study of Los Angeles County service providers reported that over a twelve-month period ending in 1987, more than half of the 6,396 requests for shelter by homeless and runaway youth were denied because beds were not available (i.e., 3,494 of 6,396 requests for assistance were turned away). Note that figures may include duplicate requests (Yates 1988).

23. Other adolescents are reportedly excluded if they have AIDS.

24. The "streets" included outdoor areas such as parks and beaches, loading docks, and under houses, roof tops, and bushes.

25. Only fifty beds were available for all of Los Angeles County in 1986.

26. In a sample of clients in a Hollywood health clinic, 26.4 percent of runaways reported "survival sex" (i.e., street prostitution) compared with .2 percent among nonrunaway clients (Yates 1988). In a Hollywood street sample, equal numbers of males (28 percent) and females (31 percent) reported trading sex for money, although females were more likely to report trading sex for food or shelter (28 percent compared to 18 percent for males) (Robertson 1989). Sex also had been traded for drugs by 11 percent of males and 10 percent of females. In addition, about half of one sample (51.7 percent) had ever sold drugs, some of whom did so only when homeless (20.9 percent). Although generating cash income was the principal motive for drug sales, one-fifth of the sample (19.8 percent) also sold drugs to support their own drug use (Robertson 1989).

27. One example is prostitution, where 29.7 percent of the sample reported having been paid for sex, but 22.0 percent of the sample did so only when homeless (Robertson 1989).

28. A sample of medical-clinic clients in Los Angeles reported that medical diagnoses such as cardiac arrhythmia, hepatitis, pneumonia, renal failure, and generalized adenopathy occurred significantly more often among runaway and homeless clients than among those who were living at home (Yates et al. 1988; Yates 1988).

29. Several studies report high rates of victimization, including murder (Chicago Coalition 1985). Runaway clients of an outpatient clinic in Hollywood sought treatment of trauma (3.6 percent) and rape (1.8 percent) at rates which were two and one-half and three times higher than nonrunaway clients (Yates 1988). The majority of a Hollywood sample had been victimized in the past twelve months, including high rates of physical assault (42.1 percent) and sexual assault (12.5 percent) (Robertson 1989).

30. An example of the difficulties faced by homeless youth in obtaining health care comes from the Hollywood study (Robertson 1989). One seventeen-year-old male reported that he was shot in the leg when he was

fourteen because he had borrowed money and did not pay it back. He reported that he could not go to the hospital for the gunshot wound for fear of arrest because he was a runaway, and because he had open warrants for assault. A friend eventually removed the bullet with a hot knife after both of them got "high on dope."

31. For example, one seventeen-year-old used condoms with her "dates" (prostitution clients) but no birth control with her boyfriend because she was trying to get pregnant, unknown to him (Robertson 1989).

32. About 1 percent of the AIDS cases nationally through August 1987 were adolescents (Hein et al. 1988). Among nonhomeless adolescent HIV cases in New York City, homosexuality or bisexuality (44 percent) and intravenous drug abuse (23 percent) were the leading risk-behavior categories. Female partners of high-risk males represented 45 percent of all teen-age female AIDS cases.

33. One study of homeless clients of a health clinic in a New York City shelter (Stricof et al. 1988) reported high-risk groups, including gay self-identification (20 percent of males), prostitution (10 percent to 15 percent of females), and IV drug use (5 percent). HIV sero-prevalence was reported for about 6 percent of the sample (i.e., seventy-four out of 1,111 clients, aged fifteen to twenty).

   The most detailed account of specific risk behaviors was reported by Robertson, Koegel, and Grella (1987) for a sample of ninety-three sheltered and unsheltered homeless adolescents in Hollywood (aged thirteen to seventeen). About half of the sample (51 percent) reported at least one high-risk behavior for HIV exposure. High-risk behaviors included intravenous drug use (26 percent) and high-risk sexual behaviors (44 percent), which included male homosexual contact (13 percent), sex with an IV drug user (17 percent), sex with persons who worked as prostitutes (18 percent), and sex with the respondents' own prostitution clients (32 percent). Many (20 percent) reported both sex with high-risk partners and IV drug use. Furthermore, although the majority of the sample (95 percent) knew that condom use could lower risk of exposure to the HIV virus, only about half (52 percent) used a condom during their last sexual encounter. Also, although all IV drug users in the sample knew about HIV transmission with shared needles, few (12 percent) had stopped using IV drugs as a means of reducing risk of HIV infection. Although 29 percent reported taking a blood test for HIV antibodies, none reported positive tests.

   It must be stressed that studies in New York and Los Angeles are not likely to generalize to other areas (especially those of New York prevalence). However, risk of exposure poses a real threat to homeless youth since they depend on high-risk behaviors to meet basic needs.

34. Many also reported a history of arrest for drinking (10 percent), and that drinking had interfered with their schooling (2 percent) or jobs (2 percent). Five percent reported that their drinking was a problem. In

addition, one-quarter of the sample reported weekly marijuana use, and half of the alcohol users reportedly combined alcohol and drug use at least occasionally (van Houten and Golembiewski 1978).

35. Although two-thirds of the Hollywood sample (65.6 percent) had used alcohol before their first episode of homelessness, few (6.5 percent) reported that their own alcohol use had ever contributed to their homelessness. Despite the high prevalence of alcohol abuse, only about one-quarter of the sample (25.8 percent) had ever perceived themselves to be excessive drinkers.

    Most of the sample had used alcohol at least once in their lives, and almost half (46.3 percent) had used alcohol before age thirteen. Most had gotten drunk at least once in the previous year, and almost half reported using alcohol weekly, on average. Respondents most often chose alcohol over street drugs due to its greater availability and lesser long-term health risk.

36. During the thirty days previous to the interview, the majority of the Hollywood sample reported drug use, including cannabis (64.5 percent), hallucinogens (36.6 percent), cocaine (26.9 percent), stimulants (24.7 percent), inhalants (9.7 percent), heroin (2.2 percent), other opiates (6.5 percent), and sedatives (4.3 percent) (Robertson 1989).

37. This figure is high compared to 1 percent of a random sample of sixteen- to nineteen-year-olds in Massachusetts who reported ever injecting drugs (Strunin and Hingson 1987).

38. For example, Susser, Streuning, and Conover (1987), reported high rates of childhood runaways among two samples of single adults in New York City shelters; 15 percent to 16 percent of adults reported running away for one week or longer before age seventeen. Runaway behavior was more prevalent (i.e., 23 percent to 26 percent) among those with a history of psychiatric hospitalization in the samples. In a survey of adults in Los Angeles city shelters, McChesney (1987) also reported high rates of runaway experiences as children: 25.7 percent reported having run away more than seven days, and 16.5 percent reported living in the streets, in abandoned buildings, or in a car or truck before age 18. In another study of homeless mothers in Los Angeles area shelters, McChesney (1987) identified one group of mothers who had been runaway teens.

    A street sample of homeless persons included five over age 20 who had extensive experience as homeless youths and were still homeless (Vander Kooi 1983).

39. For example, Piliavin, Sosin, and Westerfelt (unpublished manuscript) reported that 38 percent of homeless adults in a Minneapolis sample reported out-of-home care compared to an estimated 3 percent of domiciled adults nationally. Sosin, Colson, and Grossman (1988) reported that homeless adults in their Chicago sample were twice as likely to have had out-of-home care as children compared to nonhomeless respondents in their service site sample (i.e., 14.5 percent compared to 7.2 percent). For

a Los Angeles sample, McChesney reported that 17 percent had been in foster care, and 17 percent had been in group homes or other institutional placements as children (1987). Crystal reported that for a New York sample, 20 percent of women and 13 percent of men had been in institutional or foster care settings as children (1984).

Susser, Streuning, and Conover (1987) found that 23 percent of a New York sample of sheltered homeless men had been in foster care, group homes, or other special residences, or more than one of these. In a second sample of sheltered men, 17 percent reported histories of childhood placements. In both samples, out-of-home placements were significantly higher for homeless men who were former psychiatric inpatients. Susser and colleagues suggested a connection between childhood experiences of institutional separation from the family and running away during childhood. They suggested that men with adverse family histories lack available and effective kin support to protect them from the hardships of the housing crisis. In particular, half of former psychiatric inpatients had been placed away from their families at some time during childhood, and the families' relatively limited capacity to protect them from homelessness contributed to their vulnerability.

40. Piliavin, Sosin, and Westerfelt (unpublished manuscript) have suggested that placement as a youth may be associated with homelessness as an adult because of three hypothesized scenarios: i.e., (1) emotional or behavioral problems of the child which led to placement may endure into adulthood; (2) such placements may be debilitating (as has been postulated also by Mundy et al. 1989); and (3) placement may reflect weak family ties generated by the conditions necessitating care, as well as by having been in placement.

41. Other categories of young people excluded from services are those who are psychotic, suicidal, intoxicated, "chemically altered" (Rothman and David 1985), gay or lesbian, or HIV infected.

42. From the perspective of service providers, "the teenager trapped in the system or forced into the transient street life has been stripped of the normal developmental growth that fosters trust in others, self-esteem, and an understanding of the consequences of one's actions" (Greater Boston 1985, 8).

References

Adams, G. R., T. Gulotta, and M. A. Clancy. 1985. "Homeless Adolescents: A Descriptive Study of Similarities and Differences Between Runaways and Throwaways." *Adolescence* 20: 715-24.

Barden, J. C. 1990, 6 Feb. "Report on Runaways and 'Throwaways.'" *San Francisco Chronicle*.

Barth, R. P. 1986. "Emancipation Services for Adolescents in Foster Care." *Social Work* 31: 165-171.

Brennan T., D. Huizinga, and D. S. Elliott. 1979. *The Social Psychology of Runaways*. Lexington, MA: Lexington Books.

Bucy, J. 1987. Prepared statement of June Bucy, Executive Director, the National Network of Runaway and Youth Services, Washington, DC. In *The Crisis in Homelessness: Effects on Children and Families*. Hearing before the Select Committee on Children, Youth, and Families, House of Representatives. Washington, DC: Government Printing Office.

Caton, C. L. M. 1986. "The Homeless Experience in Adolescent Years." In *The Mental Health Needs of Homeless Persons*, ed. E. L. Bassuk, 63-70. San Francisco: Jossey-Bass.

Chelimsky, E. 1982. "The Problem of Runaway and Homeless Youth." In *Oversight Hearing on Runaway and Homeless Youth Program*, 2-13. Hearing before the Subcommittee on Human Resources, Committee on Education and Labor, House of Representatives, May 5, 1982. Washington, DC: Government Printing Office.

Chicago Coalition for the Homeless. 1985. *Position Paper: Youth Homelessness in Chicago*. Chicago: Youth Committee of the Chicago Coalition for the Homeless.

Citizens' Committee for Children of New York. 1983. *Homeless Youth in New York City: Nowhere to Turn*. New York: Citizens' Committee for Children of New York and the Coalition for the Homeless Runaway and Homeless Youth Advocacy Project.

Council of Community Services. 1984. *Homeless Older Adolescent (16-21 year olds) Needs in Albany County*. Albany, NY: Council of Community Services of Northeastern New York, Inc.

Croft, C. J., and M. K. Jolly. 1982. "A Second Look at the National Program for Runaway and Homeless Youth." *Juvenile and Family Court Journal* 33, no. 3: 39-45.

Crystal, S. 1984. "Homeless Men and Homeless Women." *Urban and Social Change Review* 17: 2-6.

Daley, S. 1988, 14 Nov. "New York City Street Youth: Living in the Shadow of AIDS." *New York Times*, pp. A-1, A-16.

Dennis, D. L. 1987. *Research Methodologies Concerning Homeless Persons with Serious Mental Illness and/or Substance Abuse Disorders*. Albany, NY: New York State Office of Mental Health, Bureau of Survey and Evaluation Research.

Deykin, E. Y., J. C. Levy, and V. Wells. 1986. "Adolescent Depression, Alcohol and Drug Abuse." *American Journal of Public Health* 76: 178-82.

Diesenhouse, S. 1988, 22 July. "Boston Judge Fighting Homelessness from Bench. *New York Times*.

Farber, E. D., C. Kinast, W. D. McCoard, and D. Faulkner. 1984. *Child Abuse and Neglect* 8: 295-9.

Gordon, I. S. 1979. "Running Away: Reaction or Revolution." In Vol. VII, *Adolescent Psychiatry: Development and Clinical Studies,* eds. S. C. Feinstein and P. L. Giovacchini. Chicago: University of Chicago Press.

Greater Boston Emergency Network. 1985. *Ride a Painted Pony on a Spinning Wheel Ride.* Boston: Massachusetts Committee for Children and Youth.

Gutierres, S. E., and J. W. Reich. 1981. "A Developmental Perspective on Runaway Behavior: Its Relationship to Child Abuse." *Child Welfare League of America* 60, no. 2: 89-94.

Gutman, A. 1987. *"1987: Street Youths in San Francisco."* Unpublished manuscript.

Hein, K., S. Vermund, E. Drucker, and N. Reuben. 1988. *Adolescent AIDS Cases: Epidemiologic Differences Related to Geography and Age.* Paper presented at the Society for Adolescent Medicine Annual Research Meeting in New York.

Hemmens, K. C., and M. R. Luecke. 1988. *Sheltering Homeless Youth: A Guide to Illinois Laws and Programs.* Chicago: The Chicago Law Enforcement Study Group.

Hersch, P. 1989. *"Final Report Exploratory Ethnographic Study of Runaway and Homeless Adolescents in New York and San Francisco."* Unpublished manuscript.

Hevesi, D. 1988, 1 Oct. "Running Away." *New York Times Magazine.*

Institute of Medicine. 1988. *Homelessness, Health, and Human Needs.* Washington, DC: National Academy Press.

Janus, M., A. McKormack, A. W. Burgess, and C. Hartman. 1987. *Adolescent Runaways.* Lexington, MA: Lexington Books.

Kufeldt, K., and M. Nimmo. 1987. "Youth on the Street: Abuse and Neglect in the Eighties." *Child Abuse and Neglect* 11: 531-43.

Landers, S. 1988. "Is Your Teen Moody? Misleading Ads May Lead Parents to Commit Teens Unnecessarily." *APA Monitor* Feb.: 18-9.

Lang, A. R. 1981. "Drinking and Disinhibition: Contributions from Psychological Research." In *Alcohol and Disinhibition: Nature and Meaning of the Link,* eds. R. Room and G. Collins, 48-90. Rockville, MD: U.S. Dept. of Health and Human Services, Research monograph no. 12.

Lattin, D. 1988, 10 April. "Cleaning Up." *San Francisco Examiner,* IMAGE section, 26-8, 37-8.

Manov, A., and L. Lowther. 1983. "A Health Care Approach for Hard-to-reach Adolescent Runaways." *Nursing Clinics of North America* 18: 333-42.

McChesney, K. Y. 1987. *Characteristics of the Residents of Two Inner-City Emergency Shelters for the Homeless*. Los Angeles: City of Los Angeles, Office of the City Attorney.

McClure, D., and J. Dickman. 1988. *Homelessness in Kentucky. 1986 House Concurrent Resolution 147*. Frankfort, KY: Legislative Research Commission Research, Report no. 237.

Michigan Network of Runaway and Youth Services. 1987. *Michigan Network of Runaway and Youth Services Annual Report FY 1986-87*. Lansing, MI: Michigan Network of Runaway and Youth Services.

Miller, D., D. Miller, F. Hoffman, and R. Duggan. 1980. *Runaways - Illegal Aliens in Their Own Land*. Brooklyn: Praeger.

Mundy, P., J. M. Robertson, M. Greenblatt, and M. J. Robertson. 1989. "Residential Instability in Adolescent Inpatients." *American Academy of Child and Adolescent Psychiatry* 28: in press.

Mundy, P., M. J. Robertson, J. M. Robertson, and M. Greenblatt. 1989. "The Prevalency of Psychotic Symptoms in Homeless Adolescents." *American Academy of Child and Adolescent Psychiatry*, in press.

National Network of Runaway and Youth Services, Inc. 1985. *To Whom Do They Belong?* Washington, DC: By the author.

New York State Council on Children and Families. 1984. *Meeting the Needs of Homeless Youth*. Albany, NY: By the author.

Pennbridge, J., G. L. Yates, and T. David. 1987. *High Risk Youth Program System of Care Report*. Los Angeles: Division of Adolescent Medicine, Children's Hospital of Los Angeles.

Piliavin, I., M. Sosin, and H. Westerfelt. 1989. "Conditions Contributing to Long-Term Homelessness: An Exploratory Study." Unpublished manuscript.

Robertson, M. J. 1989. *Homeless Youth: Patterns of Alcohol Use. A Report to the National Institute on Alcohol Abuse and Alcoholism*. Berkeley, CA: Alcohol Research Group.

Robertson, M. J. In press. "The Prevalence of Mental Disorder Among Homeless Persons." In *Homelessness: A Prevention-Oriented Approach*, ed. R. I. Jahiel. Baltimore: Johns Hopkins Press.

Robertson, M. J., P. Koegel, and L. Ferguson. 1990, in press. "Alcohol Use and Abuse Among Homeless Adolescents in Hollywood." *Contemporary Drug Problems*.

Robertson, M. J., P. Koegel, and C. Grella. 1987. *Street Kids and AIDS: Beliefs, Attitudes, and High Risk Behaviors for Exposure*. Paper presented at the annual meeting of the American Public Health Association, New Orleans.

Robertson, M. J., P. Koegel, P. Mundy, M. Greenblatt, and J. M. Robertson. 1988. "Mental Health Status of Homeless Adolescents in

Hollywood." Paper presented at the annual meeting of the American Public Health Association, Boston.

Rothman, J., and T. David. 1985. "Status Offenders in Los Angeles County: Focus on Runaway and Homeless Youth. Bush Program in Child and Family Policy." Los Angeles: University of California, Los Angeles.

Ruddick, S. 1988. "Debunking the Dream Machine: New Geographies of Homelessness, New Politics of Place. The Case of Street Kids in Hollywood, California." *Children's Environments Quarterly* 5: no. 1.

Ryan, P., I. Goldstein, and D. Bartelt. 1989. *Homelessness in Pennsylvania: How Can This Be?* Coalition on Homelessness in Pennsylvania and the Institute for Public Policy Studies of Temple University.

Shaffer, D., and C. L. M. Caton. 1984. *Runaway and Homeless Youth in New York City: A Report to the Ittleson Foundation*. New York: Division of Child Psychiatry, New York State Psychiatric Institute and Columbia University College of Physicians and Surgeons.

Solarz, A. L. 1988, Winter. "Children Without Homes." *Social Policy Report: Society for Research in Child Development* 3, no. 4.

Sosin, M., P. Colson, and S. Grossman. 1988. *Homelessness in Chicago: Poverty and Pathology, Social Institutions, and Social Change*. Chicago: University of Chicago, School of Social Service Administration.

Speck, N. B., D. W. Ginther, and J. R. Helton. 1988. "Runaways: Who Will Run Away Again?" *Adolescence* 23: 881-8.

Stiffman, A. R., E. Felton, J. Powell, and L. N. Robins. 1987. "Correlates of Alcohol and Illicit Drug Use in Adolescent Medical Patients." *Contemporary Drug Problems* Summer: 295-314.

Stricof, R. L., L. F. Novick, J. T. Kennedy, and I. B. Weisfuse. 1988. "Seroprevalence of Antibodies to Human Immunodeficiency Virus-I in a Facility for Runaway or Homeless Adolescents in New York City." Paper presented at the annual meeting of the American Public Health Association, Boston.

Strunan, L., and M. J. Hingson. 1987. "Acquired Immunodeficiency Syndrome and Adolescents: Knowledge, Beliefs, Attitudes, and Behaviors." *Pediatrics* 79: 825-8.

Sullivan, C. 1988, 30 Sept. "America's Troubled Children. Wards of the State. Part 5. Abandoned to the Streets." *The Christian Science Monitor*.

Sullivan, P. A., and S. P. Damrosch. 1987. "Homeless Women and Children." In *The Homeless in Contemporary Society*, eds. R. D. Bingham, R. E. Green, and S. B. White. Newbury Park, CA: Sage.

Susser, E., E. Streuning, and S. Conover. 1987. "Childhood Experiences of Homeless Men." *American Journal of Psychiatry* 144: 1599-1601.

Towber, R. I. 1985. "Characteristics of Homeless Families: December, 1985." New York: Human Resources Administration, Office of Program Evaluation. Unpublished manuscript.

Towber, R. I. 1986. "Summary Findings of a One-Day Survey of Homeless Families Housed at the Martinique Hotel and Forbell Street Shelter." New York: Human Resources Administration, Office of Program Evaluation.

U.S. Department of Health and Human Services. 1986. *Runaway and Homeless Youth: FY 1986 Annual Report to the Congress.* Washington, DC: Office of Human Development Services, Administration for Children, Youth and Families, Family and Youth Services Bureau.

U. S. Congress. Senate. 1980. Committee on the Judiciary, Subcommittee on the Constitution. *Homeless Youth: The Saga of "Pushouts" and "Throwaways" in America.* Washington, DC: Government Printing Office.

U. S. Congress. House. 1982, 5 May. Subcommittee on Human Resources, Committee on Education and Labor. Department of Health and Human Services. *FY 1980 Annual Report to the Congress on the Status and Accomplishments of the Centers Funded Under the Runaway Youth Act.* In *Oversight Hearing on Runaway and Homeless Youth Program,* 54-114. Washington, DC: Government Printing Office.

Upshur, C. C. 1985. "Research Report: The Bridge, Inc., Independent Living Demonstration." In *Amendments to the Foster Care and Adoption Assistance Program.* Hearing before the Subcommittee on Public Assistance and Unemployment Compensation, Committee on Ways and Means, House of Representatives, 99th Congress, Sept. 19, 1985, Serial 99-54. Washington, DC: Government Printing Office.

Vander Kooi, R. C. 1983. *Youths Without Homes: A Survey of Chicago Street Youths and Their Agencies.* Chicago: Chicago Community Trust.

Van Dusen, K. T. 1981. "New Widening and Relabeling: Some Consequences of Deinstitutionalization." *American Behavioral Scientist* 24: 801-10.

van Houten, T., and G. Golembiewski. 1978. *Life Stress as a Predictor of Alcohol Abuse and/or Runaway Behavior.* Washington, DC: American Youth Work Center.

Warren, C. A. B. 1981. "New Forms of Social Control: The Myth of Deinstitutionalization." *American Behavioral Scientist* 24: 724-40.

Yates, G. L. 1988, 2 Dec. "The Service Delivery System for Runaway/Homeless Youth in Los Angeles County." Paper presented at the Olive View Medical Center Research Conference on: "Homeless Adolescents: A Population in Crisis." Sylmar, CA.

Yates, G. L., R. MacKenzie, J. Pennbridge, and E. Cohen. 1988. "A Risk Profile Comparison of Runaway and Non-runaway Youth." *American Journal of Public Health* 78: 820-1.

Young, R. L., W. Godfrey, B. Matthews, and G. R. Adams. 1983. "Runaways: A Review of Negative Consequences." *Family Relations* 32: 275-81.

PART II

The Impact of Child and Youth Homelessness

4

Poverty, Homelessness, Health, Nutrition, and Children

James D. Wright

This chapter reviews research studies of the effects of poverty (and the most extreme contemporary manifestation of poverty, homelessness) on the nutritional and health status of children, and presents an analysis of health data on homeless children obtained in the national evaluation of the Johnson-Pew Health Care for the Homeless (HCH) program.

The rate of poverty among U.S. children has been increasing and is now the highest rate for any age group. Children comprise some 40 percent of the American poverty population. Many studies from a variety of disciplines confirm that poverty erodes the nutritional and health status of children. Children are also amply represented among the nation's homeless; indeed, in the data presented here, children under age sixteen comprise about one-tenth of the total homeless population. If poverty is bad for children's health, homelessness is little short of disastrous. Whatever health indicator is chosen, homeless children prove to be worse off – usually much worse off – than children in general and even poverty children in particular.

The review of previous studies examines the well-known link between poverty and infant mortality and the effects of child poverty on

The research reported in this chapter was supported by a grant from the Robert Wood Johnson Foundation (Princeton, NJ). Analysis, interpretations, and conclusions are the author's sole responsibility. The author thanks Ms. Zina McGee for her assistance in preparing this paper.

morbidity and nutrition. Previous research dealing with the effects of homelessness on child health is relatively thin but is also covered. All essential conclusions emerging from this literature are supported by the analysis of the HCH data which follows.

Background

The last decade has witnessed a dramatic transformation in the character of homelessness in the United States. Whereas in previous decades the homeless were predominantly older, largely white, broken-down, alcohol-abusive men (or at least were stereotypified as such), today a sizable fraction are women and children.[1] Indeed, women, children, and youth comprise perhaps three-eighths of the total homeless population (Wright 1988b). What are the effects of homelessness on the health and nutritional status of children and youth? How do these effects compare to those of simply being poor? What are the likely long-term consequences of these effects on the ability of homeless children to mature normally and subsequently to lead productive, independent, adult lives? The large numbers of debilitated homeless persons wandering aimlessly over the landscapes of our major cities are shocking and offensive to the standards of decency that prevail in any civilized nation. That many of these people are now women, children, and youth, groups that society has traditionally obliged itself to protect, should further offend our collective sensibilities. Skid Row drunks can be dismissed (correctly or otherwise) as largely beyond hope or in some sense personally responsible for their miseries. Homeless women fleeing an abusive family life, women who have lost their housing through abandonment by their male partners, children living in station wagons because of the loss of parental employment, or children who are themselves fleeing abusive family situations cannot be so lightly dismissed. Indifference to the plight of homeless adult men comes all too easily in an illiberal era; indifference to the plight of homeless women, and especially to homeless children, comes only to the cold of heart.

Conventional notions of childhood, youth, and adulthood tend to break down in the context of homelessness in that many children and youth are forced to do very adult things. Imagine a fourteen-year-old girl who has survived on the streets for two or three years, who hooks and hustles to support herself, who has had two or three venereal infections, perhaps a pregnancy and an abortion, who is beaten and sexually assaulted more or less routinely by her pimp and others. While only a child in chronological age, this pathetic young woman will have had more "adult" experiences than most middle-class adults. Thus, much more so than in a "normal" population, the division of young homeless people into groups of children, youth, and young adults is very arbitrary.

For purposes of this discussion, some rule-of-thumb age cut-offs have been adopted to differentiate four groups of interest: preschoolers (ages birth to five), children (ages six to twelve), early teens (ages thirteen to fifteen), and older teens (ages sixteen to nineteen).

While no one still would dispute the importance of research on the problems of homelessness, the focus here on health issues perhaps requires some explanation. It must be admitted that health problems are by no means the most serious problems homeless people face, ranking at least behind adequate shelter and nutrition on the agenda of human concerns. This is true of homeless children no less than of homeless adults. At the same time, attention to physical health can and often does play an important role in addressing many other problems. Homeless people are often simply too ill to place in employment or other counseling programs, too ill to stand in line while their applications for benefits are being processed, and too ill to search for housing within their means. Extreme poverty and general estrangement from society and its institutions further limit access to conventional health care.

Among children and youth in particular, poor physical health and especially chronic physical illness may well be found to contribute to the cycle of poverty, whereby the homeless children of today become the destitute and homeless adults of tomorrow. Recurring health problems of even minimal severity disrupt school attendance and interfere with studying and homework. Chronically poor health or physical disabilities interfere with, if not preclude, normal labor force participation, and, with it, the ability to lead an independent adult existence. Thus, poor health may be one mechanism by which homelessness reproduces itself in subsequent generations.

In general, there is scarcely any aspect of a homeless existence that does not compromise physical health or at least greatly complicate the delivery of adequate health services; this is true of both children and adults. Life without adequate shelter is extremely corrosive of physical well-being. Minor health problems that most people would relieve with something from the home medicine cabinet become much more serious for people with no access to a medicine cabinet and no money to purchase palliatives. Ailments that are routinely cured with a day or two at home in bed can become major health problems if one has neither home nor bed. Much that ails children requires little more than tender, loving care, but tenderness, love, and care are often in short supply within the context of homelessness.

The major features of a homeless existence that impact directly on physical well-being are an uncertain and often inadequate diet and sleeping location, limited or nonexistent facilities for daily hygiene, exposure to the elements, direct and constant exposure to the social environment of the streets, communal sleeping and bathing facilities (for those fortunate enough to avail themselves of shelter), unwillingness or inability to follow medical regimens or to seek health care, extended periods spent on one's feet, an absence of family ties or other social support networks to draw upon in times of illness, extreme poverty (and the consequent absence of health insurance), and a host of related factors (Brickner et al. 1985; Institute of Medicine 1988; Wright and Brickner 1985; Wright and Weber 1987).

Among homeless children and youth, there are additional complications. The shelters for women and children may well present optimal conditions for the transmission of infectious and communicable diseases, to which children are especially prone (Gross and Rosenberg 1987). Incomplete or nonexistent immunization protocols are yet another problem (Alperstein, Rappaport, and Flanigan 1988). Still a third problem is at least the possibility of widespread physical and sexual abuse. Among homeless teens, many of them runaways or "throwaways," rates of pregnancy, sexually transmitted diseases (STDS), and alcohol and drug abuse are inordinately high; so too are all the associated health problems (Wright 1989b; Yates et al. 1988).

Poverty, Homelessness, and the Health of Children

There is little doubt that many of the health and nutritional problems of homeless children and youth result from the extreme poverty characteristic of the homeless population. Although it has been asserted that many homeless people are "well, we might say, homeless by choice,"[2] this view has been rendered untenable by the research of the past decade. Most homeless people are homeless largely because they cannot afford to live in any other way (Wright 1989a).

Indeed, the abject poverty of homeless people may well be their distinguishing characteristic. The average income of the homeless (in Chicago and presumably in other cities) amounts to about one-quarter of the poverty-level income for a single individual; a large fraction of the homeless survive on no income at all (Rossi 1989; Rossi et al. 1987). Comparisons with Bogue's survey of the homeless in the late 1950s suggest that today's homeless are even poorer than the homeless of three decades past (Rossi 1989, 20); in fact, converted to constant dollars, the average income of today's homeless person is only about one-third of the average income reported by Bogue (1958).

The role of poverty in creating homelessness also implies that the recent increase in the number of homeless women (and, therefore, homeless children) is a consequence of the so-called feminization of poverty about which much recently has been written (Sidel 1986; Ehrenreich and Piven 1984; Duncan 1984). In 1984, approximately two-thirds of the nation's poor adults were women (Sidel 1986, 3); this proportion is apparently increasing. As a consequence, the poverty rate among children in the United States is about twice that of adults. In 1987, 20.6 percent of those under age eighteen were officially classified as poor. Among those aged eighteen to sixty-four, the corresponding figure was 10.8 percent. Four out of ten poor people in the United States today are children (U.S. Department of Commerce 1987, 8).

Poverty is a well-known risk factor for poor health among children. Summarizing a large body of literature succinctly, poverty is not healthy for children and other living things.

Infant Mortality

One of the most firmly established correlates in the epidemiological literature is that between poverty and infant mortality; indeed, "the correlation between poverty and high infant mortality rates is undisputed" (Miller 1985, 35). Particulars vary from study to study, but poor infants appear to be between 60 percent and 300 percent less likely to survive the first year of life than are children born to more affluent mothers (Schlesinger, Christenson, and Cautley 1986; Spurlock et al. 1987; Nersesian et al. 1985). The black-white difference in infant mortality is on the order of two to one; in fact, infant mortality among United States black babies exceeds the rate in Jamaica (Farley and Allen 1987, 47).

Exactly what factors are implicated in the correlation between poverty and premature infant death is less certain: inadequate prenatal care; low birthweights; excessive smoking, drinking, and drug use among poor pregnant mothers; and earlier-than-average first births among poor mothers are among the most commonly cited factors (Dott and Fort 1975a, 1975b; Hardoy 1986).

Infant mortality in the United States has been declining among all socioeconomic groups for decades, but the rate of decline slowed abruptly in the 1980s, especially among poor mothers (Miller 1985; Sogunro 1987). It is now more or less universally conceded that the long-standing national goal of no more than nine infant deaths per 1,000 live births by the year 1990 (set in 1979 by the U. S. Public Health Service) will go unattained. Least of all will this laudable goal be attained among blacks, the poor, or the homeless, despite its already having been attained (or exceeded) in many nations around the world.

The effects of poverty and race on infant mortality are well-documented and undisputed. One recent study (Chavkin et al. 1987) has shown a dramatically elevated rate of mortality among children born to homeless mothers; the infant mortality rate for babies born to homeless mothers in New York City between 1982 and 1984 was estimated to be 24.9 per hundred thousand, compared to a rate of 16.6 for children of mothers living in the housing projects and 12.0 for all other babies born in New York during the study period. Mortality among homeless adults is inordinately high (Alstrom, Lindelius, and Salum 1985; Wright and Weber 1987, Chap. 8); it is nearly inconceivable that the same would not be true of homeless infants and children. It is of some interest that the pregnancy rate for homeless women appears to be nearly twice that of U. S. women in general (Wright and Weber 1987, 112-113; Westoff 1986).[3]

Morbidity

Poverty negatively affects morbidity as well as mortality among children, although evidence on the point is not entirely conclusive. An early review of the appropriate studies suggested that "in addition to higher infant mortality and child mortality, poor children have more disabilities, handicaps, dental caries, visual and hearing impairments, lead poisoning, and incomplete immunizations than nonpoor children" (Egbuonu and Starfield 1982; Newburger, Newburger, and Richmond 1976). Other researchers have added anemia, chronic ear infections, learning disabilities, scabies and lice infestations, and increased suicide rates to this list (Shah, Kahan, and Krauser 1987).

Data from the National Health Survey, reported by Egbuono and Starfield, show approximately equal prevalences of most acute disorders among poor and nonpoor children, more severe *sequelae* of those acute disorders among the poor than the nonpoor, higher (but only slightly higher) rates of chronic disorders among the poor, and higher hospitalization rates for poor children (1982, 551). Analysis of the Child Health Supplement to the 1981 National Health Interview Survey (Newacheck and Starfield 1988) revealed similar results: while the reported prevalence of most disorders among children was approximately similar across income levels, poor children were affected more severely by their illnesses (as measured by bed days), were more likely to have multiple illnesses in the one-year span covered by the study, and used fewer physician services.

Gortmaker reports that "children living in poor households in the United States have traditionally received inadequate health services" despite the widespread availability of Medicaid to poor children since 1967 (1981). The same can be said of other advanced industrial nations such as Canada (Shah, Kahan, and Krauser 1987) or Great Britain (Wadsworth 1988). Access to adequate health care routinely is reported to be problematic for the poor in general (Aday, Fleming, and Anderson 1984; Davis, Gold, and Makuc 1981; Freeman et al. 1987), for poor children in particular (Levey, MacDowell, and Levey 1986; Newacheck and Halfon 1986), and also for the homeless (Elvy 1985; Health Care for the Homeless Coalition of Greater St. Louis 1986). Thus, inadequate access to appropriate care is perhaps the primary mechanism that links poverty to ill health, among both children and adults.

Nutrition

A second mechanism of some possible importance is inadequate nutrition. Unfortunately, the entire topic of hunger, malnutrition, and poverty has become politicized so intensely that the calm voice of science can barely be heard in the din. Some have claimed that an epidemic of hunger is sweeping across the poverty population of this country, a point of view that is not sustained by serious scientific research (Graham 1985). Such evidence as there is suggests modest dietary deficiencies in some nutrients among poor as opposed to nonpoor persons, not wholesale hunger or malnutrition among the nation's poor.

Much of the research on poverty, children, and malnutrition is based on inferences from anthropomorphic data (specifically, age-by-weight-by-height measurements grouped by quintiles or percentiles), not from direct nutritional intake surveys or observations. Most studies based on such approaches (e.g., Scholl et al. 1987; Shah, Kahan, and Krauser 1987) report weight-for-height abnormalities among poor children, but inherent genetic differences in biological growth potential are known to be a possible confounding factor. That the decreased growth observed among poor children results from nutritional deficiencies is, therefore, typically an inference from anthropomorphic differences; other environmental or genetic factors that might explain these differences rarely are examined in any depth.

There is a small literature focused on nutritional deficiency disorders among poor and nonpoor children. Iron-deficiency anemias, for example, are more widespread among poor children than nonpoor children, both in Canada (Shah, Kahan, and Krauser 1987) and the United States (Singer 1982). Rickets (resulting from vitamin D deficiency) is also more common in poor than nonpoor children.

Direct studies of nutritional intakes and ensuing deficiencies are relatively rare. Shah, Kahan, and Krauser (1987) report data from the Nutrition Canada Survey showing that mean intakes of all nutrients among children varied directly with family income level, with particularly pronounced differences in the intakes of vitamins A and C, folic acid (folate), and calcium. The authors suggest that "children of low-income families are usually fed lower-quality diets, which consist of more refined carbohydrates and fewer meats, fruits, and vegetables" (p. 486). Similar results are reported by Zee and associates (1985). Among 1,219 preschoolers from a poverty area of Memphis, Tennessee, between 9 percent and 18 percent were observed to have low or deficient levels of vitamins A, C, B1, and B2, and hemoglobin and serum iron. Wilton and Irvine (1983) report relatively small but consistent differences in nearly all nutrients between the daily dietary intakes of low-income and average-income children; as with other studies, the differences in intake of calcium and vitamin C were notably large.

A large national food-consumption survey conducted in the United States in 1977 and 1978 compared average dietary intakes of low-income households receiving food stamps with those of low-income households eligible for but not receiving food stamps (Human Nutrition Information Service 1982). No specific data on children are presented. The average diet of poor households was deemed "sufficient" in total calories and in eleven specific nutrients; however, fewer than 40 percent of the low-income households studied consumed diets meeting the recommended daily allowances (RDA) for all eleven nutrients. RDA-intake deficiencies were particularly widespread for total calories, calcium, magnesium, and vitamin B6.

Specific studies of dietary-intake or nutritional deficiency disorders among homeless persons, whether children or adults, are exceedingly rare. Winick (1985) has noted that the menu used by the city of New York in its shelters for homeless persons supplies at least one-third of the daily requirements for all known nutrients and is to that extent "sufficient." The shelter and soup-kitchen diets, however, are typically quite high in cholesterol, saturated fats, sugar, salt, and starch. While they may well offer adequate caloric intake, these diets are far short of optimal for the maintenance of good health. To the author's knowledge, no study has yet been published discussing dietary intakes or adequacy for homeless persons who do not avail themselves of shelters and soup kitchens and who eat mainly what they can scavenge from street sources, but it is unlikely in the extreme that such diets are adequate by any criterion.

A very few studies have remarked the disproportionate occurrence of nutritional deficiency disorders among homeless children. Wright (1989b) has reported that 2.2 percent of homeless children who received care during the first year of the National Health Care for the Homeless program were diagnosed with anemias, twice the rate for normal children seen in ambulatory pediatric clinics nationwide (see also Miller and Lin 1988). An additional 1.6 percent of the homeless children had nutritional deficiency disorders other than anemia (most of them vitamin deficiency disorders); among children in general, such deficiencies are practically nonexistent (1989b, Table 4.1). About 2 percent of the homeless children studied by Miller and Lin were diagnosed with growth problems, possibly secondary to dietary insufficiencies, similar to the results reported by Alperstein, Rappaport, and Flanigan (1988).

Morbidity among homeless children appears to be much more widespread than among children in general or among poor children in particular. Miller and Lin (1988) studied 158 homeless children in Seattle and reported that "although the majority of the children were considered to be in good or excellent health, the proportion whose health was described as 'fair' or 'poor' was four times higher than in the general U.S. pediatric population" (pp. 671-672). These authors also remark a high prevalence of abnormal anthropometry and immunization delays within this population. Homeless children appear to overutilize emergency room services, underutilize preventive health services, and have far fewer dental visits compared with the general pediatric population. Similar results for homeless children in Boston have been reported by Bassuk, Rubin, and Lauriat (1986) and for homeless children in New York by Alperstein, Rappaport, and Flanigan (1988).

Wright (1989b) has compared the health problems of homeless children seen during the first year of the National Health Care for the Homeless program with those of children included in the National Ambulatory Medical Care Survey (NAMCS). Nearly all disorders are more common among the homeless group. For example, about 7 percent of the homeless children were found to have scabies and lice infestations, compared with 0.2 percent of the NAMCS children. Upper respiratory infections were about twice as common, skin disorders four times as common, and poor dentition ten times as common. Homeless children were also more likely than normal children to suffer from chronic physical disorders. Similar patterns were observed among homeless teen-agers as well (see also Yates et al. 1988).

Mental health problems of homeless children have been studied in depth by Bassuk and Rubin (1987; see also Bassuk, Rubin, and Lauriat

1986). Depression, developmental delays of varying severity, anxiety, and learning difficulties are reported to be distressingly common. Psychiatric morbidity is also widespread among homeless adults (Bassuk 1984; Wright 1988a).

Homelessness and Child Health: New Evidence from The National Health Care for the Homeless Program

In December 1984, the Robert Wood Johnson Foundation (Princeton, New Jersey) and the Pew Memorial Trust (Philadelphia, Pennsylvania), in conjunction with the U.S. Conference of Mayors, announced grants totaling $25 million to establish Health Care for the Homeless Programs (HCH) in nineteen major United States cities. Details on the background of this grant program and on program philosophy and configuration are reported elsewhere (Wright 1987). Briefly, the program was conceived as seed money to get community-based health-care-for-the-homeless projects up and running, with the expectation that each project would secure continuation funding from various federal, state, and local sources once program grants expired. The health care components of the Stuart B. McKinney Homeless Assistance Act were modeled on the HCH experience and assure that all of the nineteen HCH projects will survive, in fact, beyond the Johnson-Pew grant program.

Although there was wide variation among the nineteen projects in approach, configuration, and specific program goals, all shared a common and very strong community-based health care orientation. For the most part, the HCH projects were not sited in conventional health care settings; rather, they were located out in the community, in facilities used by the homeless population. Thus, HCH facilities are found in shelters, soup kitchens, missions, drop-in centers, alcohol detoxification facilities, juvenile court, and more or less anywhere else that homeless people are known to gather. Specific HCH health facilities ran the entire gamut from fully equipped medical clinics to little more than nursing stations.

The Social and Demographic Research Institute of the University of Massachusetts was funded by the Johnson Foundation to conduct research on the national HCH program. Details of the research design and data collection protocols also are provided elsewhere (Wright 1985;

Wright et al. 1987). Briefly, each significant encounter between a homeless client and HCH staff generated a written medical note reported on a contact form. This form obtained limited demographic and other identifying information but was otherwise used as an open-ended progress note on which a care provider recorded his or her assessment of the client's problems and the treatment plan. Coding of the health information from these forms was done exclusively by registered nurses, using a modified version of the International Classification of Diseases (ICD) codes, ninth edition.

Data on the health of homeless children who received services through HCH during the first year of the program are reported in Wright (1989b). The remainder of this chapter updates that presentation to include all children seen in the HCH program between start up and the end of data collection in December 1987. All told, nearly 100,000 homeless and destitute persons received health and related social services through HCH during that period; about one-tenth of the clients were children and youth under the age of sixteen. For reasons discussed elsewhere (Wright et al. 1987), data from two of the nineteen project cities are excluded from this analysis.

Although the majority (62 percent) of HCH clients were adult men, a sizable minority (28 percent) were adult women, and another sizable although smaller fraction (10 percent) were homeless children. Thus, adult women and dependent children comprised about three-eighths of the total client load. In some cities that worked aggressively in shelters for women and children, these groups comprised well more than half the total.

The gender composition of HCH adults (among adults only, 27 percent are women and 73 percent are men) is very similar to that reported in other studies of the adult homeless population.[4] However, the heavy preponderance of males is true only of the adults; at all ages under twenty, boys and girls appear in the data in approximately equal numbers. Compared with adults, the children are somewhat likelier to be members of ethnic minorities, but the difference is not large. The children (ages zero to sixteen) are heavily concentrated in the one-to-five-year age category (63 percent). An additional quarter are in the six-to-twelve-year-old category (24 percent), with the remainder (13 percent) being young adolescents (ages thirteen to fifteen).

Health Problems of Homeless Children

Selected health data for HCH children (ages zero to twelve) are shown in Table 4.1. For reasons discussed elsewhere, HCH data for persons seen only one time are generally not reliable; all HCH data in this and subsequent tables are based only on clients seen at least twice.[5] For comparison, the table also shows corresponding data for children included in the National Ambulatory Medical Care Survey conducted in 1985. Data for the survey were supplied by a national probability sample of ambulatory care physicians (N=2,879); those in pediatric practice were included in the physician sampling frame. For a systematic probability sample of the ambulatory patients seen in a randomly stipulated week, the physicians filled out a short questionnaire giving limited background information and an account of principal health problems. Data for about 72,000 ambulatory care patients were generated.[6]

NAMCS data shown in Table 4.1 are restricted to patients under age ten living in the large urban areas (N=6,309). These data are roughly comparable to the HCH data in two important senses: (1) both data sets describe clinical populations, that is, persons presenting at ambulatory clinics for attention to their health conditions, and (2) the medical information contained in both data sets has been provided by health care professionals. At the same time, the two data sets are grossly noncomparable in many other respects.[7] The NAMCS data reported in this and subsequent tables may be taken as useful, heuristic reference points with which to compare the health problems confronted by homeless children, but these comparisons are not in any sense precise.

The general configuration of illness among homeless children is similar to that of children in general, although somewhat different from the configuration observed among homeless adults (acute disorders are more common, and chronic disorders less common, among the children than the adults). That is to say, the health problems faced by homeless children are not exotic or unusual disorders; they are, rather, the same health problems all children face. By far the most common disorders observed among the children are minor upper respiratory infections, followed by minor skin ailments and ear disorders (mostly otitis media), then gastrointestinal problems, trauma, eye disorders, and lice

TABLE 4.1

Health Problems of Homeless Children Compared with Children in the National Ambulatory Medical Care Survey

	HCH[a]				NAMCS[b]			
	Boys		Girls		Boys		Girls	
Years	0-5	6-12	0-5	6-12	0-5	6-10	0-5	6-10
(N=)	767	286	723	292	2,368	954	2,132	855

Chronic Physical Disorders

CA[c]	–	–	.1	–	.3	.9	.2	–
BENIGN	–	–	.6	.7	.3	.6	.6	.8
ENDOCR	.9	1.0	1.5	–	.4	.7	.4	.8
DM	.1	.3	.1	–	.2	.2	.1	–
NEUR	.5	1.0	.6	.3	.5	1.3	.5	.8
NEUROSYM	.9	3.1	.4	1.4	NA	NA	NA	NA
SEIZPROB	.7	.3	1.0	1.0	.1	.1	–	.2
EYE	10.0	5.6	6.9	8.6	5.9	10.8	5.9	12.0
EAR	38.1	15.4	33.2	11.6	20.6	10.9	19.3	12.6
CARDIAC	1.3	.7	1.0	.7	.3	.1	.2	.2
VASCULAR	.4	.3	.7	–	–	.1	–	.1
HTN	.3	.3	.1	.3	.1	–	.3	.2
COPD	3.3	6.3	1.5	2.7	4.3	4.4	3.6	4.7
GI	9.6	8.7	10.9	10.6	5.0	2.9	4.2	3.4
TEETH	4.2	13.6	4.8	14.7	.8	.3	.8	.2
LIVER	.1	.3	–	–	–	–	–	–
RENAL	.1	–	–	–	–	.1	.2	.8
LIMB	.8	.3	.4	1.0	.9	.9	.8	.2
PVD	.3	.7	.3	.3	–	–	–	–
ARTH	.5	–	.3	–	.3	.2	.6	.5
OTHMS	1.4	2.4	.3	1.7	.7	1.7	.2	1.8
ANYCHRON	12.4	14.7	10.9	9.9	11.8	11.0	9.8	9.8

Nutritional Disorders

NUTDEF	2.3	.7	2.1	.7	–	.1	.1	–
OBESE	.9	1.4	.1	1.4	–	.2	.1	.4
ANEMIA	2.5	1.4	1.9	2.4	1.2	.7	.9	.2

Acute Physical Disorders

MINURI	52.5	39.2	49.9	45.9	19.6	18.3	20.2	20.7
SERURI	3.1	2.1	3.2	1.7	1.8	1.2	1.9	2.6
GISYMP	11.6	4.9	11.5	9.6	NA	NA	NA	NA
GENITO	1.4	.7	1.7	5.1	.5	1.8	2.2	2.7
MALEGU	1.8	1.4	–	–	2.1	1.4	–	–
FEMGU	–	–	.8	2.4	–	–	.6	.6

TABLE 4.1 (Continued)

	HCH[a]				NAMCS[b]			
	Boys		Girls		Boys		Girls	
Years	0-5	6-12	0-5	6-12	0-5	6-10	0-5	6-10
(N=)	767	286	723	292	2,368	954	2,132	855

Acute Physical Disorders (continued)

SERSKIN	3.0	2.4	4.0	3.1	1.0	1.2	1.6	2.0
MINSKIN	23.6	15.4	25.7	20.2	4.5	3.8	6.0	6.4

Trauma

FX	.1	1.0	.4	.3	1.3	5.6	1.7	3.7
SPRAIN	.4	2.1	.4	2.1	.3	1.7	.1	.7
BRUISE	2.5	3.1	3.0	2.4	.6	2.4	.5	2.9
WOUND	3.0	5.6	2.1	2.1	1.8	3.4	.9	1.4
ABRASION	1.3	1.7	.8	3.1	.9	.8	.8	.2
BURN	2.0	.3	.8	1.0	.3	.3	.3	.1

Infectious and Communicable Disorder

INFECT	4.8	2.4	4.0	4.5	2.1	2.2	2.2	2.3
LICE	6.1	5.9	9.0	10.3	.1	.4	.1	.5
ANYPH	16.7	12.9	8.0	19.2	6.8	8.5	7.4	12.4

a. Data for child clients seen at least twice in seventeen of the nineteen HCH cities.

b. Data for urban children seen in the National Ambulatory Medical Care Survey. Note: The higher age group in the NAMCS data runs from six to ten, not six to twelve as in the HCH data.

c. Row entries are percentages of clients diagnosed with various disorders. Acronyms used to define the row entries have the following meanings:

Chronic Physical Disorders

CA	Cancer, any site
BENIGN	Benign tumors and cysts
ENDOCR	Endocrinological disorders (e.g., goiter, thyroid, and pancreas disease)
DM	Diabetes mellitus

TABLE 4.1 (Continued)

Chronic Physical Disorders (continued)

NEURO	Neurological disorders, not including seizures (e.g., Parkinson's disease, multiple sclerosis, neuritis, neuropathies)
NEUROSYM	Symptoms of neurological disorder without firm diagnoses
SEIZPROB	Seizure disorders (including epilepsy)
EYE	Disorders of the eyes (e.g., cataracts, glaucoma, decreased vision)
EAR	Disorders of the ears (e.g., otitis, deafness, cerumen impaction)
CARDIAC	Heart disease, all sorts
VASCULAR	Vascular disorders other than peripheral vascular disorders
HTN	Hypertension
COPD	Chronic obstructive pulmonary disease
GI	Gastrointestinal disorders (e.g., ulcers, hernias)
TEETH	Dentition problems (predominantly caries)
LIVER	Liver diseases (e.g., cirrhosis, hepatitis, ascites, enlarged liver or spleen)
RENAL	Kidney disease and disorder
LIMB	Disorders of the extremities consistent with PVD but without a firm diagnosis
PVD	Peripheral vascular disease
ARTH	Arthritis and related problems
OTHMS	All musculoskeletal disorders other than arthritis
ANYCHRO	Any chronic physical disorder

Nutritional Disorders

NUTDEF	Nutritional deficiencies (e.g., malnutrition, vitamin deficiencies)
OBESE	Obesity
ANEMIA	Iron-deficiency anemia

Acute Physical Disorders

MINURI	Minor upper respiratory infections (common colds and related symptoms)
SERURI	Serious respiratory infections (e.g., pneumonia, influenza, pleurisy)
GISYMP	Symptoms of GI disorders without firm diagnoses
GENITO	General genitourinary problems common to either sex (e.g., kidney, bladder problems, incontinence)
MALEGU	Genitourinary problems found among men (e.g., penile disorders, testicular dysfunction, male infertility)
FEMGU	Genitourinary problems found among women (e.g., ovarian dysfunction, genital prolapse, menstrual disorders)
SERSKIN	Serious skin disorders (e.g., carbuncles, cellulitis, impetigo, abscesses)
MINSKIN	Minor skin ailments (e.g., sunburn, contact dermatitis, psoriasis, corns and callouses)

TABLE 4.1 (Continued)

Trauma

FX	Fractures
SPR	Sprains and strains
BRU	Bruises, contusions
LAC	Lacerations, wounds
ABR	Superficial abrasions
BURN	Burns of all severities

Infectious and Communicable Disorders

INFECT	Infectious and parasitic diseases (e.g., septicemia, amebiasis, diptheria, tetanus)
LICE	Scabies and lice infestations
ANYPH	Either AIDS or tuberculosis or any sexually transmitted infection or INFECT or SERURI or LICE or SERSKIN or any combination of these
NA	Not available

---

infestations. In all these cases, differences in the rates of disorder between homeless boys and girls are relatively minor.

Differences between homeless children and children in general, in contrast, are often large and in some cases dramatically large. Although the general pattern of illness among homeless children is not atypical of children's illnesses in general, the comparative rates of occurrence are often inordinately elevated.

Consider first some of the acute disorders. Among all the NAMCS children shown in Table 4.1, a mere .2 percent are found to have lice infestations (this amounts to 13 cases of lice among 6,309 children), compared with more than 7 percent of the HCH children, a differential on the order of thirty-five to one. Nutritional deficiencies are found among about 2 percent of the HCH children and are virtually nonexistent among NAMCS children (there are only three cases of these disorders recorded in the NAMCS data). Upper respiratory infections are twice as common among homeless children as among ambulatory children in general, skin disorders about four times as common, gastrointestinal (GI) disorders about three or four times as common, ear infections nearly twice as common, and poor dentition more than ten times as common.

Children, clearly, are not immune to the deleterious effects of homelessness on physical health. That many of these children are over age five and, therefore, required to attend school, where their illnesses can then circulate to other children, is an additional point of concern.

Differences in the rates of chronic physical disorders are also troubling. About one in eight of the HCH children already have one or another chronic health condition:[8] cardiac disease, anemia, peripheral vascular disorders, neurological disorders, and the like. While the overall rate of chronic physical disorder among homeless children is about the same as that observed among ambulatory children in general, differences in specific categories are substantial, among them endocrine disorders, seizures, and cardiac and vascular disorders. All of the nutritional disorders shown in Table 4.1 are also discernibly higher among homeless children than in the comparison groups.

It is important to stress here that the best available studies of the effects of poverty on child health report relatively slight differences in the prevalence of most disorders between poor and nonpoor children, whether chronic or acute (Egbuono and Starfield 1982; Newacheck and Starfield 1988). The larger differences are found in the ensuing consequences of disease. Differentials on the order of those found in some of the rows of Table 4.1 are not to be found anywhere in the published literature on poverty and child health. The evidently disproportionate rate of illness observed among homeless children, in short, is not just a simple consequence of their impoverished circumstances. Homelessness is an independent and quite consequential risk factor in its own right.

The life chances of homeless children are obviously not bright to begin with. They are saddled, first, with the well-documented burdens of poverty, and beyond that with the unique burdens of not having a safe, stable place to live. The effects of homelessness on school performance and intellectual development are also now well known (Bassuk and Rubin 1987). It is now known that many already are afflicted with chronic physical disorders that may interfere later with labor force participation, prevent them from working altogether, or at least become life-long health problems. All this further reduces their potential for a productive and independent adult existence.

Health Problems of Homeless Youth

Table 4.2 presents an equivalent view of the health problems of homeless youth, ages thirteen through nineteen. The cell entries for this table are the same as in Table 4.1; they show the percentages of HCH clients of various age-by-gender groupings who are afflicted with various health disorders. Comparable data for NAMCS youth are again presented.

Acute disorders. As among the children, the predominant acute disorders suffered by HCH youth are upper respiratory infections, traumas, and minor skin disorders. Infestations (lice and scabies) are again quite common, and likewise genitourinary problems, especially among young women. In general, the boys are less healthy than the girls, although this pattern admits of several exceptions. Boys, particularly young men over age sixteen, show exceptionally high rates of injuries, especially sprains and lacerations. Except for trauma, there are no consistent effects for age. Rates of nearly all acute disorders and traumas are higher among HCH youth than among NAMCS youth, frequently by large margins.

Chronic physical disorders. The proportion of HCH youth with any chronic physical disorder varies from 10 percent to 20 percent and averages about 18 percent. This is nearly twice the rate of chronic disease observed among those of equivalent age in NAMCS (just under 10 percent). The most common chronic disorders observed among HCH youth are eye disorders, gastrointestinal disorders, ear problems, neurological impairments, and problems with dentition. Other chronic disorders definitely more prevalent among HCH than NAMCS youth include endocrine dysfunction, cardiac and vascular disease, and hypertension.

Nutritional disorders. As among the children, nutritional disorders are more common among HCH than NAMCS youth, anemia excepted.

Sexuality. The rate of pregnancy among HCH youth is astonishing. Among HCH girls aged thirteen to fifteen, 14 percent were pregnant at or since their first contact with HCH. Among those sixteen to nineteen, the figure is 31 percent, the highest rate of pregnancy within any HCH age group. Corresponding figures for NAMCS girls are 1 percent and 9 percent. Sexually transmitted diseases are accordingly also common (especially among the girls).[9]

TABLE 4.2

Health Problems of Homeless Youth Compared with Youth in the National Ambulatory Medical Care Survey

	HCH[a]				NAMCS[b]			
	Boys		Girls		Boys		Girls	
Years	13-15	16-19	13-15	16-19	13-15	16-19	13-15	16-19
(N=)	119	608	186	781	1,159	1,245	1,095	1,566

Chronic Physical Disorders

CA[c]	.8	.3	–	–	.5	.3	.1	.1
BENIGN	2.5	1.0	1.6	1.9	.9	.8	1.1	1.3
ENDOCR	–	1.6	–	1.5	.6	.2	.6	.8
DM	–	.3	.5	.8	.3	.3	–	.6
NEUR	–	1.0	1.1	.6	.5	1.4	.9	1.0
NEUROSYM	6.7	7.2	3.2	5.6	NA	NA	NA	NA
SEIZPROB	–	1.8	–	2.2	.3	.3	.1	.3
EYE	11.8	10.4	10.2	7.7	9.3	9.5	9.5	9.7
EAR	7.6	6.3	5.4	5.6	14.1	6.7	12.1	6.1
CARDIAC	.8	.7	1.6	1.3	.1	.6	.3	.1
VASCULAR	–	.8	1.1	1.3	.3	–	–	.1
HTN	.8	2.8	2.2	1.7	.1	.3	.2	.3
COPD	3.4	3.6	3.2	3.2	3.6	3.1	2.8	2.4
GI	10.1	7.9	4.8	6.1	2.9	3.1	3.2	3.1
TEETH	13.4	9.7	8.6	6.5	.7	.4	1.0	.3
LIVER	–	.7	–	.3	–	.1	.1	.1
RENAL	–	.2	.5	.5	–	–	–	1.4
LIMB	4.2	7.7	3.2	2.6	1.0	.6	1.0	.3
PVD	1.7	1.5	1.6	1.0	.1	–	–	.1
ARTH	.8	1.2	1.1	1.0	.9	2.1	1.5	1.4
OTHMS	3.4	8.6	3.8	4.6	3.3	3.5	3.0	2.6
ANYCHRON	10.1	18.3	15.1	20.0	9.7	10.3	9.6	10.0

Nutritional Disorders

NUTDEF	1.7	2.0	1.1	3.6	–	–	–	–
OBESE	1.7	1.0	3.2	3.3	.2	.2	.7	.2
ANEMIA	–	.5	1.1	4.2	.5	.9	1.3	.4

Acute Physical Disorders

MINURI	34.5	38.3	34.9	31.4	13.9	13.4	17.0	13.2
SERURI	5.0	4.9	2.2	2.3	1.7	.7	1.7	1.2

TABLE 4.2 (Continued)

	HCH[a]				NAMCS[b]			
	Boys		Girls		Boys		Girls	
Years	13-15	16-19	13-15	16-19	13-15	16-19	13-15	16-19
(N=)	119	608	186	781	1,159	1,245	1,095	1,566

Acute Physical Disorders (continued)

GISYMP	8.4	5.4	10.8	11.9	NA	NA	NA	NA
GENITO	8.4	9.7	10.2	16.6	.2	1.4	1.2	3.3
MALEGU	1.7	4.3	–	–	1.3	1.8	–	–
FEMGU	–	–	18.3	22.5	–	–	1.3	5.4
SERSKIN	4.2	5.9	1.1	3.5	.6	1.8	1.2	1.1
MINSKIN	28.6	18.1	15.6	16.3	7.2	11.8	9.2	10.5

Trauma

FX	2.5	5.3	1.1	1.3	7.4	6.7	3.8	2.7
SPRAIN	7.6	8.4	6.5	5.2	2.5	4.9	2.3	3.6
BRUISE	7.6	6.9	7.0	5.6	2.1	2.3	1.8	1.7
WOUND	3.4	11.3	4.8	4.1	1.8	3.9	1.3	1.1
ABRASION	5.0	4.3	2.7	2.2	.9	.7	.5	1.0
BURN	–	1.5	.5	.8	.4	.4	.5	.4

Infectious and Communicable Disorder

INFECT	–	.8	1.6	.6	.7	1.0	1.7	1.4
LICE	6.7	5.6	7.5	5.1	.1	.3	.4	.1
ACTTB	–	.6	–	–	–	–	–	.1
ANYTB	–	2.8	.5	.8	–	–	–	.1
VDUNS	1.7	3.1	12.9	8.1	2.3	3.5	3.3	2.5
SYPHIL	–	.2	–	.4	–	–	–	.3
GONN	.8	2.1	4.3	2.3	.1	.2	–	.1
ANYSTD	2.5	4.4	14.5	9.7	2.4	3.7	3.3	2.9
AIDS	–	.2	–	–	–	–	–	–
HIV+	–	.2	–	–	–	–	–	–
HEPA	–	.5	1.1	.8	–	–	.1	–
ANYPH	14.3	20.7	22.6	18.8	5.6	8.2	8.9	7.1

ADM Disorders

ETOH	4.2	4.8	4.3	3.2	–	.1	–	–
DRUG	3.4	7.9	9.1	6.4	–	.1	–	.1
MI	8.4	14.6	11.3	15.0	3.4	3.5	2.3	4.0

TABLE 4.2 (Continued)

	HCH[a]				NAMCS[b]			
	Boys		Girls		Boys		Girls	
Years	13-15	16-19	13-15	16-19	13-15	16-19	13-15	16-19
(N=)	119	608	186	781	1,159	1,245	1,095	1,566
Pregnancy								
PREG	–	–	14.0	31.1	–	–	1.1	8.7

a. Data for child clients seen at least twice in seventeen of the nineteen HCH cities.

b. Data for urban youth seen in the National Ambulatory Medical Care Survey.

c. Row entries are percentages of clients diagnosed with various disorders. Acronyms used to define the row entries have the following meanings:

Chronic Physical Disorders

CA	Cancer, any site
BENIGN	Benign tumors and cysts
ENDOCR	Endocrinological disorders (e.g., goiter, thyroid, and pancreas disease)
DM	Diabetes mellitus
NEURO	Neurological disorders, not including seizures (e.g., Parkinson's disease, multiple sclerosis, neuritis, neuropathies)
NEUROSYM	Symptoms of neurological disorder without firm diagnoses
SEIZPROB	Seizure disorders (including epilepsy)
EYE	Disorders of the eyes (e.g., cataracts, glaucoma, decreased vision)
EAR	Disorders of the ears (e.g., otitis, deafness, cerumen impaction)
CARDIAC	Heart disease, all sorts
VASCULAR	Vascular disorders other than peripheral vascular disorders
HTN	Hypertension
COPD	Chronic obstructive pulmonary disease
GI	Gastrointestinal disorders (e.g., ulcers, hernias)
TEETH	Dentition problems (predominantly caries)

TABLE 4.2 (Continued)

Chronic Physical Disorders (continued)

LIVER	Liver diseases (e.g., cirrhosis, hepatitis, ascites, enlarged liver or spleen)
RENAL	Kidney disease and disorder
LIMB	Disorders of the extremities consistent with PVD but without a firm diagnosis
PVD	Peripheral vascular disease
ARTH	Arthritis and related problems
OTHMS	All musculoskeletal disorders other than arthritis
ANYCHRO	Any chronic physical disorder

Nutritional Disorders

NUTDEF	Nutritional deficiencies (e.g., malnutrition, vitamin deficiencies)
OBESE	Obesity
ANEMIA	Iron-deficiency anemia

Acute Physical Disorders

MINURI	Minor upper respiratory infections (common colds and related symptoms)
SERURI	Serious respiratory infections (e.g., pneumonia, influenza, pleurisy)
GISYMP	Symptoms of GI disorders without firm diagnoses
GENITO	General genitourinary problems common to either sex (e.g., kidney, bladder problems, incontinence)
MALEGU	Genitourinary problems found among men (e.g., penile disorders, testicular dysfunction, male infertility)
FEMGU	Genitourinary problems found among women (e.g., ovarian dysfunction, genital prolapse, menstrual disorders)
SERSKIN	Serious skin disorders (e.g., carbuncles, cellulitis, impetigo, abscesses)
MINSKIN	Minor skin ailments (e.g., sunburn, contact dermatitis, psoriasis, corns and callouses)

Trauma

FX	Fractures
SPR	Sprains and strains
BRU	Bruises, contusions
LAC	Lacerations, wounds
ABR	Superficial abrasions
BURN	Burns of all severities

TABLE 4.2 (Continued)

Infectious and Communicable Disorders

INFECT	Infectious and parasitic diseases (e.g., septicemia, amebiasis, diptheria, tetanus)
LICE	Scabies and lice infestations
ACTTB	Active tuberculosis infection
ANYTB	Active tuberculosis infection or history of TB or on a prophylactic TB regimen without a TB diagnosis or unresolved positive PPD test
VDUNS	Venereal disease, unspecified
SYPHIL	Syphilis
GONN	Gonorrhea
ANYSTD	Any venereal infection
AIDS	Acquired Immune Deficiency Syndrome
HIV+	HIV positivity without an AIDS diagnosis
HEPA	Infectious hepatitis
ANYPH	Either AIDS or tuberculosis or any sexually transmitted infection or INFECT or SERURI or LICE or SERSKIN or any combination of these

ADM Disorders

ETOH	Alcohol problems, alcoholism
DRUG	Drug abuse, addiction
MI	Mental illness

Pregnancy

PREG	Client pregnant at or since initial contact with HCH
NA	Not available

Substance abuse and mental illness. Alcohol and drug abuse are for all practical purposes nonexistent among preteen-aged homeless but do begin to be observed in children as young as eleven or twelve. Among HCH clients aged thirteen to fifteen, about 4 percent already have problems with alcohol; 8 percent of the thirteen- to fifteen-year-old boys and 11 percent of the girls are reported to have drug-abuse problems. The numbers increase for those aged sixteen to nineteen. Alcohol and drug problems, in contrast, are essentially nonexistent among NAMCS youth of equivalent ages. Rates of psychiatric disorder are also sharply higher for homeless youth of all ages and genders than among comparable NAMCS youth.

Analysis of the NAMCS results for young adults aged sixteen to twenty-four suggests that here, as among the younger children, most disorders are at least twice as common among homeless youth as among ambulatory youth in general. With only a few exceptions, this is also true of homeless adults (Wright and Weber 1987). This, of course, is scarcely a surprise. There is virtually no aspect of a homeless existence that does not aid in the destruction of a person's physical well-being, whatever his age, race, or gender.

Conclusion

Homeless persons of all ages are exposed to, and therefore exhibit, a characteristic "package" of disorders that are directly and immediately referable to the conditions of a homeless existence. Among the acute disorders, this package includes upper respiratory infections, skin ailments, lice infestations, and trauma of all sorts; among the more chronic disorders, the package includes peripheral vascular disease, tuberculosis, GI disorders, poor dentition, and others. Among homeless women, problems related to pregnancy must be added to the list; among the children, one would add ear infections, anemia, and other nutritional deficiency disorders as well. The health problems of the homeless population are complicated further by the lack of access to medical care, poor compliance with treatment regimen, and generally unsanitary and unsafe living conditions, along with a host of other factors.

Part of the differentially poor health observed among homeless adults is due to the atypical demographic configuration of the group, the result of the homeless being largely male, disproportionally nonwhite, and extremely poor. Yet another part is ascribable to the high rates of substance abuse, particularly alcohol abuse. These points notwithstanding, multivariate analyses controlling for these (and other) factors show rather decisively that the key factor in the ill health of the homeless is not demographics and not substance abuse. The key factor is homelessness itself (Knight 1987). Among the many good reasons to "do something" about homelessness is the reason that homelessness makes people ill.

These days, the people being made ill by homelessness are increasingly children and youth, who comprise one-tenth or more of the total homeless population. Research reviewed here reveals that it is unlikely that the poor health of homeless children is a simple result of their impoverishment, although poverty is no doubt an important contributing factor. To be a poor child is one thing, but to be poor and homeless is a thing apart. It is hard to imagine a social environment less conducive to health or normal maturation and development.

Pediatricians affiliated with the New York City Children's Health Project have recently identified what they call a "homeless child syndrome," comprised of "poverty related health problems, immunization delays, untreated or under-treated acute and chronic illnesses, unrecognized disorders, school, behavioral, and psychological problems, child abuse and neglect" (Redlener 1988). It obviously would be wrong to suggest that all homeless children exhibit all aspects of this syndrome. At the same time, most homeless children probably do exhibit one or more of these problems and disorders; at the very least, they are observed more commonly among homeless children than among children in general or even among poverty-level children.

Knowing how and to what extent homelessness affects the health of children does not in itself tell us what needs to be done. Most of what has been done to date is along the lines of amelioration. There is an evident need to continue such programs as aggressive screening of homeless children for health disorders and proper treatment and health care once problems have been diagnosed. But here, as in many other areas of public health, the only ultimate, long-term solution is to be found in prevention. The negative consequences of homelessness on the health of children will be avoided only when a way is found to prevent children from being homeless in the first place.

Sad to say, this obvious truth is much easier to state than to act upon. Homelessness is a complex problem rooted ultimately in the political economy of the nation (Wright 1989a). A rising poverty rate, coupled with a continuous decline in available low-income housing, has served to price an increasingly large segment of the urban poverty population completely out of the private housing market. Inflation has reduced the purchasing power of the Aid to Families with Dependent Children program (AFDC) and other welfare programs to the point where the welfare dependent can no longer maintain stable residences with their monthly payments (Rossi 1989). Absent other sources of support, AFDC mothers with children find themselves virtually consigned to homelessness in all but the most generous states.

A reasonably aggressive, broad-scale federal assault on the problem of homelessness in all its various manifestations easily would add several tens of billions of dollars to the annual federal expenditure on housing, health, and human services (Wright 1989c). This is not the least bit likely in the "read my lips, no new taxes" spirit of the age. And so, for the foreseeable future, programs of amelioration, such as those embodied in the Stewart B. McKinney Homeless Assistance Act, must be accepted with the knowledge that such measures do not and cannot provide any final solutions to this problem.

The large numbers of children now being seen on the streets and in the shelters and other facilities providing services to homeless people mean that the homelessness of the 21st century already is being created, today. As this is being written, there are many tens of thousands of children around the nation whose lives and futures are being destroyed by forces over which they have no control. The Children's Defense Fund has estimated that "more children die each year from poverty-related causes than traffic fatalities and suicides combined" (Oberg 1987), and, while this is very likely an exaggeration, it is an exaggeration that makes a point. It is a useful if troubling question to ask: What does the very existence of homeless children say about us as a nation? What image does this present to the world?

In February 1987, the author was given an opportunity to testify at hearings before the House Select Committee on Children, Youth, and Families, and to speak about the effects of homelessness on the physical health of children. Among the several witnesses present at the hearings was Yvette Diaz, a lovely twelve-year-old Hispanic girl living with her mother and three siblings at one of the large welfare hotels in mid-town Manhattan. Yvette is a charming young lady with an engaging smile and coal-black, shoulder-length hair, soft-spoken but firm in her opinions and very sweet. In the course of her testimony, she remarked:

> If I could have anything that I could want, I wish that we could have our own apartment in a nice clean building and a place that I could go outside to play in that is safe. I want that most of all for me and my family.

A clean place to live and a safe place to play do not seem like too much to ask. As the hearings closed, a thought occurred: What kind of world is this, where such simple things can only be a dream to some children?

Notes

1. In point of fact, women and children have always comprised a sizable portion of the American homeless population, from colonial times to the present. Historical data on homeless women are reviewed in some detail in Lam (1987, Chap. 2). Detailed comparisons between the "old" homeless and the "new" are given in Rossi (1989).
2. The quotation is from impromptu remarks made at a televised news conference by ex-President Ronald Reagan.
3. The rate of venereal infection among homeless women is not much higher than that of U.S. women in general (Wright and Weber 1987); thus, the apparently higher rate of pregnancy probably does not result from greater sexual promiscuity or activity. A more likely explanation is that homeless women have lesser knowledge about or access to contraception; another possibility is a higher rate of pregnancy resulting from rape. On the inordinate rate of sexual assault on homeless women, see Kelly (1985).
4. See Knight and Lam 1987. Over a range of recent (post-1980) studies, the average proportion of women among homeless adults is around 20 percent to 25 percent, very close to the HCH figures.
5. See Wright et al. 1987, 22-9. The problem in essence is that many of the one-time contacts are very fleeting encounters that do not provide an opportunity to probe in detail into a client's health problems. In point of fact, the rates of virtually every disorder examined tend to increase as the number of client contacts increases, up to about four or five contacts, at which point the rates level off. Part of this effect is presumably substantive: sicker people return to clinic more often. Analysis suggests, however, that the larger share of the effect is methodological. Clients need to be seen a relatively large number of times before a complete and reliable health picture can be obtained.
6. A full account of methods and technical details for the NAMCS survey is given in Public Health Service, 1987, June, *1985 National Ambulatory Medical Care Survey: Public Use Data Tape Documentation*, Hyattsville, MD: U.S. Department of Health and Human Services.
7. Critically, the NAMCS data contain no measure of patient social status, parental education, or income; hence, poverty children cannot be isolated within the data set.

8. A client is considered to have a chronic physical disorder in this analysis if any of the following health problems are present (either by diagnosis or history): tuberculosis; prophylactic TB therapy; AIDS; cancer (any site); diabetes mellitus; anemia; seizure disorders; seriously impaired vision or hearing; cardiovascular disease, including stroke; hypertension; chronic obstructive pulmonary disease; liver disease; arterial disease; all colostomies; kidney disease; chronic peripheral vascular disease; all tracheotomies; amputations (other than fingers and toes); and paraplegia. The same definition applies to NAMCS patients as well.

9. Unfortunately, the data do not allow differentiation between youth who are homeless and on the streets with their families and those who are already out on their own. The impression is that most of the sixteen-and-over homeless youth are already independent of their families, whereas at least some of the thirteen- to fifteen-year-olds are not. Not all of the youth shown here, in short, are runaway or throwaway kids, although, without doubt, many are.

References

Aday, L., G. V. Fleming, and R. Anderson. 1984. *Access to Medical Care in the US: Who Has It, Who Doesn't.* Chicago: Pluribus Press.

Alperstein, G., C. Rappaport, and J. Flanigan. 1988. "Health Problems of Homeless Children in New York City." *American Journal of Public Health* 78, no. 9: 1232-33.

Alstrom, C. H., R. Lindelius, and I. Salum. 1975. "Mortality among Homeless Men." *British Journal of Addictions* 70: 245-52.

Bassuk, E. 1984. "The Homeless Problem." *Scientific American* 251, no. 1: 40-5.

Bassuk, E., and L. Rubin. 1987. "Homeless Children: A Neglected Population." *American Journal of Orthopsychiatry* 57, no. 2: 279-86.

Bassuk, E., L. Rubin, and A. Lauriat. 1986. "Characteristics of Sheltered Homeless Families." *American Journal of Public Health* 76, no. 9: 1097-101.

Bogue, D. 1958. *Skid Row In American Cities.* Chicago: Community and Family Study Center, University of Chicago.

Brickner, P. W., L. K. Scharer, B. Conanan, A. Elvy, and M. Savarese, eds. 1985. *Health Care of Homeless People.* New York: Springer.

Chavkin, W., A. Kristal, C. Seabron, and P. E. Guigli. 1987. "The Reproductive Experience of Women Living in Hotels for the Homeless in New York City." *New York State Journal of Medicine* 87: 10-3.

Davis, K., M. Gold, and D. Makuc. 1981. "Access to Health Care for the Poor: Does the Gap Remain?" *Annual Review of Public Health* 2: 159-82.

Dott, A. B., and A. T. Fort. 1975a. "The Effect of Maternal Demographic Factors on Infant Mortality Rates." *American Journal of Obstetrics and Gynecology* 123, no. 8: 847-53.

—1975b. "The Effect of Availability and Utilization of Prenatal Care and Hospital Services on Infant Mortality Rates." *American Journal of Obstetrics and Gynecology* 123, no. 8: 854-60.

Duncan, G. 1984. *Years of Poverty, Years of Plenty.* Ann Arbor, MI: Institute for Social Research Press.

Egbuono, L., and B. Starfield. 1982. "Child Health and Social Status." *Pediatrics* 69, no. 5: 550-7.

Ehrenreich, B., and F. Piven. 1984. "The Feminization of Poverty." *Dissent* 31, Spring: 162-70.

Elvy, A. 1985. "Access to Care." In *Health Care of Homeless People,* eds. P. W. Brickner, L. K. Scharer, B. Conanan, A. Elvy, and M. Savarese, 223-31. New York: Springer.

Farley, R., and W. Allen. 1987. *The Color Line and the Quality of Life in America.* New York: Russell Sage Foundation.

Freeman, H., R. J. Blendon, L. H. Aiken, S. Sudman, C. F. Moullinix, and C. R. Corey. 1987. "Americans Report on Their Access to Care." *Health Affairs* 6, no. 1: 6-18.

Gortmaker, S. L. 1981. "Medicaid and the Health Care of Children in Poverty and Near Poverty." *Medical Care* 19, no. 6: 567-82.

Graham, G. C. 1985. "Poverty, Hunger, Malnutrition, Prematurity, and Infant Mortality in the United States." *Pediatrics* 75, no. 1: 117-25.

Gross, T. P., and M. L. Rosenberg. 1987. "Shelters for Battered Women and Their Children: An Underrecognized Source of Communicable Disease Transmission." *American Journal of Public Health* 77, no. 9: 1198-201.

Hardoy, J. E. 1986. "Poverty Kills Children." *World Health* July: 12-5.

Healthcare for the Homeless Coalition of Greater St. Louis. 1986. "Program Description." Mimeographed.

Human Nutrition Information Service. 1982, July. *Nationwide Food Consumption Survey, Survey of Food Consumption in Low-Income Households, 1979-1980.* Preliminary Report No. 10. Washington, DC: U.S. Department of Agriculture.

Institute of Medicine. 1988. *Homelessness, Health and Human Needs.* Washington, DC: National Academy Press.

Kelly, J. T. 1985. "Trauma: With the Example of San Francisco's Shelter Programs." In *Health Care of Homeless People,* eds. P. W. Brickner, L. K. Scharer, B. Conanan, A. Elvy, and M. Savarese, 77-91. New York: Springer.

Knight, J. W. 1987. "Alcohol Abuse among the Homeless." Ph.D. dissertation, Department of Sociology, University of Massachusetts, Amherst.

Knight, J. W., and J. Lam. 1987. "Health and Homelessness: A Review of the Literature." Social and Demographic Research Institute, University of Massachusetts. Unpublished manuscript.

Lam, J. 1987. "Homeless Women in America: Their Social and Health Characteristics." Ph.D. dissertation, Department of Sociology, University of Massachusetts, Amherst.

Levey, L. A., M. MacDowell, and S. Levey. 1986. "Health Care of Poverty and Nonpoverty Children in Iowa." *American Journal of Public Health* 76, no. 8: 1000-3.

Miller, C. A. 1985. "Infant Mortality in the U.S." *Scientific American* 253, no. 1: 31-7.

Miller, D., and E. Lin. 1988. "Children in Sheltered Homeless Families: Reported Health Status and Use of Health Services." *Pediatrics* 81, no. 5: 668-73.

Nersesian, W. S., M. Petit, R. Shaper, D. Lemieux, and E. Naor. 1985. "Childhood Death and Poverty: A Study of All Childhood Deaths in Maine, 1976 to 1980." *Pediatrics* 75, no. 1: 41-50.

Newacheck, P., and N. Halfon. 1986. "Access to Ambulatory Care Services for Economically Disadvantaged Children." *Pediatrics* 78: 813-9.

Newacheck, P., and B. Starfield. 1988. "Morbidity and Use of Ambulatory Care Services Among Poor and Nonpoor Children." *American Journal of Public Health* 78, no. 8: 927-33.

Newburger, E., C. Newburger, and J. Richmond. 1976. "Child Health in America: Toward a Rational Public Policy." *Milbank Memorial Fund Quarterly* 54: 249.

Oberg, C. 1987. "Pediatrics and Poverty." *Pediatrics* 79, no. 4: 567-8.

Redlener, I. E. 1988. "Caring for Homeless Children: Special Challenges for the Pediatrician." *Today's Child* 2, no. 4, whole issue.

Rossi, P. H. 1989. *Without Shelter: Homelessness in the 1990s.* New York: Priority Press.

Rossi, P. H., J. D. Wright, G. Fisher, and G. Willis. 1987. "The Urban Homeless: Estimating Composition and Size." *Science* 235, no. 4794: 1336-41.

Scholl, T. O., R. Karp, J. Theophano, and E. Decker. 1987. "Ethnic Differences in Growth and Nutritional Status: A Study of Poor Schoolchildren in Southern New Jersey." *Public Health Reports* 102, no. 3: 278-83.

Shah, C. P., M. Kahan, and J. Krauser. 1987. "The Health of Children of Low Income Families." *Canadian Medical Association Journal* 137, Sept.: 485-90.

Sidel, R. 1986. *Women and Children Last: The Plight of Poor Women in Affluent America.* New York: Viking Penguin.

Singer, J. D. 1982. *Diet and Iron Status, A Study of Relationships, United States*. U.S. Department of Health and Human Services, National Center for Health Statistics, series 11 (publication no. PHS83-1679).

Slesinger, D. P., B. A. Christenson, and E. Cautley. 1986. "Health and Mortality of Migrant Farm Children." *Social Science and Medicine* 23, no. 1: 65-74.

Sogunro, G. O. 1987. "Urban Poor and Primary Health Care: An Analysis of Infant Mortality of an Inner City Community." *Journal of Tropical Pediatrics* 33, Aug.: 173-6.

Spurlock, C. W., M. W. Hinds, J. W. Skaggs, and C. E. Hernandez. 1987."Infant Death Rates among the Poor and Nonpoor in Kentucky, 1982 to 1983." *Pediatrics* 80, no. 2: 262-9.

U.S. Department of Commerce. 1987. "Money Income and Poverty Status in the United States, 1987." *Consumer Income,* Series P-60, no. 161. Washington, D.C.: Bureau of the Census, Current Population Reports.

Wadsworth, M. E. 1988. "Inequalities in Child Health." *Archives of Disease in Childhood* 63: 353-5.

Westoff, C. 1986. "Fertility in the United States." *Science* 234, no. 31: 554-9.

Wilton, K. M., and J. Irvine. 1983. "Nutritional Intakes of Socioculturally Mentally Retarded Children vs. Children of Low and Average Socioeconomic Status." *American Journal of Mental Deficiency* 88, no. 1: 79-85.

Winick, M. 1985. "Nutritional and Vitamin Deficiency States." In *Health Care of Homeless People,* eds. P.W. Brickner, L. K. Scharer, B. Conanan, A. Elvy, and M. Savarese, 103-9. New York: Springer.

Wright, J. D. 1985. "The Health Care for the Homeless' Program: Evaluation Design and Preliminary Results." Paper presented at the Annual Meetings of the American Public Health Association, Washington, DC, November.

—1987. "The National Health Care for the Homeless Program." In *The Homeless in Contemporary Society,* eds. R. D. Bingham, R. E. Green, and S. B. White, Chap. 9. Newbury Park, CA: Sage.

—1988a. "The Mentally Ill Homeless: What is Myth and What is Fact?" *Social Problems* 35, no. 2: 182-91.

—1988b. "The Worthy and Unworthy Homeless." *Society* 25, no. 5: 64-9.

—1989a. *Address Unknown: Homelessness in Contemporary America.* Hawthorne, NY: Aldine de Gruyter.

—1989b. "Homelessness is Not Healthy for Children and Other Living Things." *Journal of Child and Youth Services.* In press.

—1989c. "Supplementary Statement on Health Care for Homeless People: A Comment." *Society.* In press.

Wright, J. D., and P. W. Brickner. 1985. "The Health Status of the Homeless: Diverse People, Diverse Problems, Diverse Needs." Paper presented at the Annual Meetings of the American Public Health Association, Washington, DC, November.

Wright, J. D., and E. Weber. 1987. *Homelessness and Health.* New York: McGraw Hill Publishing Company.

Wright, J. D., E. Weber-Burdin, J. Knight, and J. Lam. 1987. *The National Health Care for the Homeless Program: The First Year.* Amherst, MA: Social and Demographic Research Institute.

Yates, G., R. MacKenzie, J. Pennbridge, and E. Cohen. 1988. "A Risk Profile Comparison of Runaway and Non-Runaway Youth." *American Journal of Public Health* 78, no. 37: 820-1.

Zee, P., M. DeLeon, P. Robertson, and C. H. Chen. 1985. "Nutritional Improvement of Poor Urban Preschool Children: a 1983-1977 Comparison." *Journal of the American Medical Association* 253, no. 22: 3269-72.

5

Developmental and Educational Consequences of Homelessness on Children and Youth

Yvonne Rafferty

The Effects Of Homelessness On Children

Homelessness is having a variety of negative effects on the physical and emotional well-being of homeless children (cf. U.S. Conference of Mayors 1987a). Of particular concern are hunger and poor nutrition, increased health problems and inadequate health care, developmental delays, psychological problems, and educational underachievement. This discussion deals with three of these areas: developmental delays, psychological problems, and educational problems. The first two areas are only briefly reviewed, with primary emphasis paid to existing research. In contrast, the discussion of the educational impact of homelessness is based on original research conducted by Advocates for Children in 1989 (cf. Rafferty and Rollins 1989). This research project had two major components: field-based interviews with 277 families residing in New York City's shelters and hotels and analyses of New York City Board of Education's statistical data on all 9,659 homeless school-age children identified by the Board between September of 1987 and May of 1988.

Developmental Delays

Current estimates indicate that there are approximately 6,000 children under the age of six years in temporary shelters in New York City. Despite the abundance of literature documenting the importance of quality day care services to provide both social and intellectual stimulation (cf. Consortium for Longitudinal Studies 1983; Haskins 1989), the existence of such programs for homeless children is clearly inadequate.

The conditions in emergency shelter facilities in New York City are not conducive to timely development. Berezin (1988) describes the extent to which restrictive physical environments prohibit exploration and interactive play:

> The infants and toddlers spend most of their time in cribs, strollers, or the arms of their parents. Pre-school age children spend their time in small airless rooms and dangerous hallways. There is little opportunity for the kind of exploration and interactive play that we know lay the foundation for healthy physical, emotional, and cognitive growth. (pp. 2-3)

Bassuk and her colleagues assessed the developmental ability of eighty-one children (age five or younger) living in various family shelters in Massachusetts (Bassuk, Rubin, and Lauriat 1986; Bassuk and Rubin 1987). The Denver Developmental Screening Test was used to evaluate gross and fine motor skills, language, and personal and social development (Frankenburg, Goldstein, and Camp 1971). Overall, 47 percent manifested at least one developmental lag (i.e., the inability to complete a task that 90 percent of one's peers are able to complete); 33 percent had two or more; and 14 percent failed in all four areas. Furthermore, 36 percent demonstrated language delays; 34 percent could not complete the personal and social developmental tasks; 18 percent lacked gross motor skills; and 15 percent lacked fine motor coordination.

In a follow-up study, a subgroup of this sample (those sheltered in the Boston area) was compared with housed children. The mothers of both groups of children were poor and currently single, had a similar number of children, and were receiving public assistance. Of the forty-eight homeless children evaluated, 54 percent manifested at least one developmental lag compared to 16 percent of the seventy-five housed children.

The developmental impact of homelessness on language skills and cognitive ability of eighty-eight children under the age of five living in a dormitory-type shelter in Missouri also has been examined (Whitman 1987; Whitman et al. 1989). Overall, 67 percent manifested delays in their capacity to use and produce language when screened by the Peabody Picture Vocabulary Test (PPVT-R), and 42 percent scored at or below the borderline area on cognitive ability when tested with the Slosson Intelligence Test (SIT-R).

Finally, Molnar (1988) documents teachers' observations and anecdotal accounts of frequently observed behaviors among homeless children attending fourteen early-childhood programs in New York City. Of particular concern are short attention span, withdrawal, aggression, speech delays, sleep disorders, regressive behaviors, inappropriate social interaction with adults, immature peer interaction contrasted with strong sibling relationships, and immature motor behavior.

Psychological Problems

The psychological impact of homelessness on children is manifested by a greater prevalence and intensity of anxiety, depression, and behavioral disturbances among homeless children (Bassuk and Rubin 1987; Bassuk, Rubin, and Lauriat 1986; Bassuk and Rosenberg 1988). Bassuk and her colleagues interviewed 156 children in family shelters in Massachusetts. Of the children interviewed, approximately 65 percent were five years or younger, and the number of boys and girls was approximately equal.

Depression among children older than five (N=44) was evaluated using the Children's Depression Inventory, a paper-and-pencil task which assesses the frequency of personal feelings such as sadness during the prior two-week period (Kovacs 1983). Overall, 54 percent scored higher than the cut-off point, indicating a need for psychiatric evaluation; 31 percent were clinically depressed; and the average score of 10.4 was significantly higher than a score of 8.3 from a comparison group of thirty-three poor, housed children. Furthermore, as shown in

Table 5.1, homeless children were more depressed than six of eight comparison groups.

TABLE 5.1

Comparison of Massachusetts Sheltered Children and Various Other Samples on the Children's Depression Inventory (CDI)

Factor	CDI score Characteristics		
	N	*Mean*	*S.D.*
Major depressive disorder	27	13.6	.7
Dysthymic disorder	12	12.2	7.9
Homeless children	42	10.4	6.4
Child psychiatric outpatient referrals	75	9.7	.3
Comparison group with various DSM-III diagnoses	40	9.1	6.3
Adjustment disorder with depressed mood	10	8.9	6.4
Conduct/oppositional disorder	22	7.4	5.1
Partially remitted major depressive disorder	12	6.3	5.0
Recently diagnosed juvenile diabetes	61	5.9	4.3

Source: Bassuk and Rubin 1987, 283.

Anxiety was assessed using the Children's Manifest Anxiety Scale (Reynolds and Richmond 1985), a thirty-seven item checklist requiring children over the age of five to complete statements that seem true about themselves (e.g., "I worry a lot of the time;" "I am afraid of a lot of things."). Of the twenty-nine children who completed the scale, 31 percent scored at a level indicating a need for psychiatric evaluation, compared to 9 percent of a comparison group of thirty-four housed children.

Behavioral disturbances among forty-two children were assessed using the Achenbach Behavior Problem Checklist (Achenbach and Edelbrock 1983), which is completed by parents. Among the twenty-nine children between six and eleven years, 66 percent of boys and 50 percent of girls indicated a need for psychiatric evaluation. Among the thirteen children between twelve and sixteen years, 38 percent indicated a need for psychiatric evaluation.

Similar findings have been reported by mothers of homeless children in temporary shelters in New York City. Citizens Committee for Children (1984) reports that 66 percent of their sample of eighty-three homeless families observed behavior changes in their children after they became homeless. The most frequently reported behavioral changes were increases in acting-out behaviors, fighting, restlessness, depression, and moodiness.

Preschool-age homeless children have also been found to manifest behavioral disturbances (Bassuk and Rubin 1987). Bassuk and her colleagues used the Simmons Behavior Checklist (Reinherz and Gracey 1982) to ascertain the extent of behavior disturbances in fifty-five homeless children between the ages of three and five years. This twenty-eight-item checklist yields a total behavioral score in addition to eleven subscales. As shown in Table 5.2, the homeless children's overall mean score of 5.6 was significantly higher than the means for a sample of seventeen "normal" children (mean=1.9) and "disturbed" children (mean=2.3). The homeless children scored significantly higher than housed normal children on the following problems: attention, sleep, shyness, speech, withdrawal, and aggression. Interestingly, the only area in which homeless children scored significantly better than both comparison groups was in being less afraid of new things.

Given the physical and psychological conditions under which homeless children live, it is not surprising that they appear to be at increased risk for anxiety, depression, and behavioral problems. These psychological factors are also well known to interfere with capacity to learn (Jahiel 1987). Since only one study has evaluated the psychological impact of homelessness on children, additional research is needed in this area.

Educational Problems Confronting Homeless Children

According to the U.S. Department of Education (1985), there are currently 220,000 school-aged homeless children in the United States, 67,000 of whom (30 percent) do not attend school. Although this number is indeed shocking, advocates for the homeless believe it underestimates the true scope of the problem. For example, the National

Coalition for the Homeless (1987a) estimates that there are between 500,000 and 750,000 school-age homeless children nationwide, of whom 57 percent do not attend school regularly.

Table 5.2

Comparison of Normal, Emotionally Disturbed, and Massachusetts Sheltered Children on the Simmons Behavior Checklist

	Group means		
	Normal	Disturbed	Homeless
Factor scales	(N=17)	(N=17)	(N=55)
Mean total score	1.9	2.3	5.6
Attention	6.2	9.5	7.3
Sleep problems	3.7	3.7	4.5
Shyness	8.4	7.9	9.6
Speech	2.8	5.7	3.5
Dependency	7.1	8.9	7.4
Toilet training	2.7	2.9	2.8
Withdrawal	4.9	6.0	6.1
Demanding behavior	5.5	5.8	5.7
Fear of new things	4.7	4.3	3.8
Aggression	6.2	6.7	7.4
Coordination	3.6	4.6	4.1

Source: Bassuk and Rubin 1987, 282.

Even when homeless children are enrolled in school, they often are faced with a variety of ancillary problems that can interfere with their capacity to learn. The academic performance of homeless children and youth has been addressed in only a handful of studies. The first such study focused on 118 runaway youth who were living in temporary shelters in New York City (Shaffer and Caton 1984). Their major findings included the following: (1) 55 percent of the boys and 47 percent of the girls had repeated a grade; (2) 59 percent of the boys and

54 percent of the girls were more than one standard deviation behind on their reading achievement tests; (3) 16 percent of the boys and 10 percent of the girls were functionally illiterate, reading at a fourth-grade level or less; (4) 71 percent of the boys and 44 percent of the girls had been suspended or expelled from school at some time; (5) 69 percent indicated that they would like to finish high school, and (6) 41 percent expressed the desire to graduate from college.

The second study was conducted by Ellen Bassuk and her colleagues (Bassuk, Rubin, and Lauriat 1986; Bassuk and Rubin 1987). As described previously, the sample consisted of eighty-two families, with 156 children. According to their parents' report, all fifty school-aged children were attending school; 43 percent (N=21) were failing or performing below-average work; 25 percent (N=13) were in special classes; and 43 percent (N=22) had repeated a grade.

In contrast to these findings for homeless children, a follow-up to this study indicated that 23 percent of thirty-four school-aged children in permanent housing were currently failing or doing below-average work in school (Bassuk and Rosenberg 1988).

The Child Welfare League of America and Travelers Aid Society conducted a study of 163 families, including 340 children, from thirty-three different states (Maza and Hall 1988). The families participating in this study included those who were seeking aid from Travelers Aid agencies and may or may not have been in the emergency housing system previously. Their major findings included the following: 43 percent of the school-aged children were not attending school, and 30 percent of the children who were attending school were below grade level.

Project Description

In order to determine whether or not the ability to be educated is affected by homelessness, the author designed a research study with two major components. One component involved the compilation and analysis of statistical data collected by the New York City Board of Education (BOE). This information, provided in response to a request made by Advocates for Children of New York Inc. (AFC) in September 1988, was used to compare school performance, attendance, and other indices of school success of children in temporary housing with their permanently housed peers. These analyses were based on data collected by the BOE on all 9,659 school-aged children who were in one of New York City's temporary housing facilities between September 1987 and May 1988.

The other component of the study was a field-based interview of 277 families residing in temporary shelters and hotels in New York City. A detailed survey instrument was developed, including focused and closed-ended questions about family demographics, prior living arrangements, events leading to the request for emergency shelter, experiences with the shelter system, and the educational experiences of the respondents' children who were between the ages of six and nineteen years, if they were currently living with the family.

Results

The families. Two-hundred seventy-seven parents from fifteen different New York City shelters and hotels for homeless families were interviewed in the AFC study. The interviews took place between November 1988 and February 1989. Table 5.3 contains a list of the facilities, the number of families interviewed at each site, in each borough, and at each type of shelter.

The demographic characteristics of shelter respondents are presented in Table 5.4. The parents interviewed were predominantly female (87 percent). Half were single (49 percent). Their ages ranged from twenty to sixty-three, with a median of thirty-two years. Almost half (47 percent) had at least a high school diploma or GED. The majority were either African-American (74 percent) or Latino-Hispanic (22 percent). Homelessness was not a recent occurrence for most (mean=16 months, S.D.=15): 70 percent had lost their permanent housing more than six months before; 47 percent had been homeless for more than one year, and 18 percent for more than two years.

The 277 parents who participated in the study had a total of 790 children (an average of 2.85 children per family). However, not all of these children currently were living with their parent(s) at the shelter. As shown in Table 5.4, 30 percent of the parents interviewed had one child currently living with them, while 40 percent had three or more.

The majority of the participants in the study currently were receiving income from public assistance (86 percent) and food stamps (84

TABLE 5.3

Shelter/Hotel Information of Survey Respondents

Variable	N[a]		Frequency	Percentage
Name of temporary[a] facility	277	East Third Street (TI)[b]	48	17.3
		Prince George Hotel	46	16.6
		Catherine Street (TI)	35	12.6
		Saratoga (TII)[c]	26	9.4
		Prospect (TII)	22	7.9
		Regent Hotel	23	8.3
		Allerton Hotel	20	7.2
		Hamilton Hotel	19	6.9
		Harriet Tubman (TII)	19	6.9
		Colonial Hotel	14	5.1
Location of facility	277	Manhattan	212	76.5
		Queens	40	14.4
		Bronx	22	7.9
		Brooklyn	2	.7
		Staten Island	1	.4
Type of facility	277	Hotel	125	45.1
		Tier I	84	30.3
		Tier II	68	24.5

a. Five families from five shelters not listed here were also interviewed. These families were present at other facilities where we interviewed.

b. TI = Tier I Shelter.

c. TII = Tier II Shelter.

TABLE 5.4

Demographic Characteristics of Survey Respondents

Variable	N[a]		Frequency	Percentage
Gender	277	Female	241	87.0
		Male	36	13.0
Marital status	277	Single/never married	136	49.1
		Currently married	54	19.5
		Living as married	33	11.9
		Other[b]	54	19.5
Age in years	273	20-29	103	37.7
		30-39	138	50.5
		40+	32	11.7
Education	277	Grades 3-9	40	14.4
(last grade		Grades 10-11	107	38.6
completed)		High school graduate	72	26.0
		GED	18	6.5
		Some college	40	14.4
Race/ethnicity	277	African-American	204	73.6
		Latino/Hispanic	60	21.7
		Other	13	4.7
Time elapsed	277	0-6 months	83	30.0
since loss of		7-12 months	65	23.4
permanent home		13-24 months	79	28.5
		>2 years	50	18.1
Number of children	277	1	83	30.0
currently living		2	83	30.0
with parent		3	73	26.4
		4	22	7.9
		5-8	16	5.8

a. N varies due to missing data.

b. Separated/divorced/widowed.

TABLE 5.5

Emergency Housing Experiences of Survey Respondents

Variable	N		Frequency	Percentage
Where stayed after	277	Went to EAU	123	44.4
loss of home		Doubled up	112	40.4
		Other	42	15.2
Location of	244[a]	Same borough	70	28.7
shelter/hotel vs.		Different borough	174	71.3
permanent home				
Months in current	277	0-4	136	49.1
facility		5-8	56	20.2
		9-12	33	11.9
		>12	52	18.7
Number of other	277	None	95	34.3
prior		1	71	25.6
facilities[b]		2	31	10.9
		3	27	9.7
		4	16	5.8
		5	10	3.6
		6-10	17	6.0
		>10	10	3.7

a. This question did not apply to the 33 families from outside of New York City.

b. Not including present placement.

percent). Several families had no income at all, because their aid to families with dependent children (AFDC) case was closed or they were waiting for a new one to be opened. Furthermore, while all families who were living in hotels were entitled to a restaurant allowance, only 62 percent of the survey respondents who lived in commercial hotels (N=125) were receiving one. Several respondents discussed how their public assistance delivery was often interrupted, inefficient, and unresponsive to their needs. In fact, many complained that the interruption of city assistance had resulted in their homelessness.

On average, families had been in the emergency housing system for twelve months (S.D.=13). The shelter experiences of the sample are summarized in Table 5.5. The majority of families did not enter the shelter system immediately after losing their permanent home. Instead, 154 families (56 percent) spent some time elsewhere before seeking shelter from the Emergency Assistance Unit. Of these 154 families, 112 doubled up with family or friends, and 42 stayed elsewhere (regular hotel, battered women's shelter, car, or abandoned buildings).

Only 29 percent of the 244 prior New York City residents were sheltered in the same borough as the one in which their permanent home was located. Overall, only five of the thirty-three (15 percent) families who formerly lived in Queens currently were living in emergency housing in Queens. Similarly, only twelve of the sixty-seven (18 percent) families from the Bronx currently were living in the Bronx. Ironically, eight of the sixty-seven families from the Bronx currently were living in Queens. In turn, 79 percent of the thirty-three families from Queens (N=26) were living in Manhattan.

The average amount of time that survey respondents had lived in their current shelter was 7.3 months (S.D.=8.1). Almost half (49 percent) had been in their current shelter for four months or less, while 19 percent had been there for more than one year. These figures do not include the length of time a family might have spent at a different facility. In fact, 66 percent of the sample had been in at least one other shelter before their current placement, 29 percent had been in three or more other facilities, and 10 percent had been in six or more other facilities.

There was a significant positive relationship between the length of time families had been in the emergency housing system and the number of other shelters in which they had been ($r(277)=.28$, $p<.001$). Furthermore, the proportion of families who had been in more than one other shelter rose steadily with the length of time in the emergency housing system: 26 percent (N=28) of the 107 families had been in the system for zero to six months; 37 percent (N=24) of the 64 families for seven to twelve months; 54 percent (N=38) of the 70 families for thirteen to twenty-four months; and 66 percent (N=21) of the thirty-two families more than two years.

While the above findings are intended to illustrate how "bouncing" increases with time in the system, it is nonetheless significant that twenty-eight families which had been in the system for six months or less had been in more than one other shelter. In fact, of these twenty-eight families, twelve had been in two other shelters, six had been in three other shelters, three had been in four other shelters, two had been in five other shelters, one had been in six other shelters, and four had been in seven to ten other shelters. It is also significant that in each of these twenty-eight families, there were school-aged children attempting to be educated.

The children. For all of the 427 children between the ages of six and nineteen years currently living with their parent(s) in the temporary facility, series of questions pertaining to their educational experiences were asked of their parent(s). Of the children, 390 (91 percent) currently were enrolled in and attending school. Of the remainder (N=37), fourteen had dropped out, three had graduated, and the rest were awaiting placement and/or transfer. The following discussion will focus on the 390 children in school at the time of the study.

Table 5.6 contains the frequency and percentage of the 390 children at each site, in each type of shelter, and in each borough, as well as select demographic characteristics. There were approximately equal numbers of boys and girls (51 percent versus 49 percent). Their ages ranged from six to nineteen, with a median age of nine and one-half years. A majority (76 percent) were in elementary school (kindergarten through grade 6), 17 percent were in middle or junior high school (grades 7 through 9), 5 percent were in high school (grades 10 through 12), and 1 percent (N=5) were in ungraded classes, primarily citywide special education programs.

Overall, elementary school children attended 115 schools in twenty-seven school districts. As shown in Table 5.7, the majority of children (42 percent) walked to school; 29 percent took a school bus; and 28 percent took public transportation. Most attended school in Manhattan (61 percent), followed by Queens (18 percent) and the Bronx (13 percent). The majority (84 percent) attended school in the same borough in which their temporary housing was located. A sizable minority (16 percent, N=62), however, attended school in a different borough. For

TABLE 5.6

Demographic Characteristics of the Children of Survey Respondents

Variable	N		Frequency	Percentage
Name of temporary facility	390	Prince George Hotel	76 Man	19.5
		East Third (TI)	53 Man	13.6
		Catherine Street (TI)	46 Man	11.8
		Saratoga (TII)	36 Q	9.2
		Regent Hotel	34 Man	8.7
		Hamilton Hotel	32 Man	8.2
		Prospect (TII)	31 Bx	8.0
		Harriet Tubman (TII)	30 Man	.7
		Colonial Hotel	23 Q	5.9
		Allerton Hotel	22 Man	.6
		Forbell (TI)	3 Bkln	.8
		SI Respite Center (TII)	2 S.I.	.5
		Bryant Hotel	1 Man	.3
		New Crown Hotel	1 Man	.3
Type of facility	390	Hotel	189	48.5
		Tier I Shelter	102	26.2
		Tier II Shelter	99	25.4
Location of facility	390	Manhattan	295	76.6
		Queens	59	15.1
		Bronx	31	8.0
		Brooklyn	3	.8
		Staten Island	2	.5
Gender	390	Male	200	51.3
		Female	190	48.7
Age in years	390	6-7	107	27.4
		8-9	88	22.6
		10-11	77	19.7
		12-13	70	17.9
		14-19	48	12.3

TABLE 5.6 (Continued)

Variable	N		Frequency	Percentage
Grade level	390	K-2	125	32.0
		3-4	99	25.4
		5-6	74	19.0
		7-8	54	13.8
		9-12	38	9.7

Notes: TI = Tier I Shelter
TII= Tier II Shelter

example, of the 295 children in temporary shelters in Manhattan, twenty-seven attended school in Brooklyn, eighteen attended school in Bronx, ten in Queens, and three in Staten Island. These children often traveled considerable distances to maintain the continuity of their education.

New York City regulations state that, upon entering the emergency shelter system, parents are to be given the option of keeping their children in the same school which they attended while residing in permanent housing, or of transferring them to the school in the district in which the temporary shelter is located.

The decision as to where children should attend school, however, not always was made in accordance with the Chancellor's regulation. Overall, the decision concerning 119 children was made without offering the parent a choice and thus significantly influenced which school (former versus shelter) the child attended (chi square=50, p<.001). For example, 58 percent of the parents of 244 children who had been given a choice transferred them to the school in the district where their shelter or hotel was located, compared with 94 percent of the 119 children whose parents had not been given a choice.

Of the 390 children represented, 71 percent (N=276) currently were attending school in the area in which their temporary housing was

Table 5.7

School Information

Variable	N[a]		Frequency	Percentage
Transportation	390	Walks	164	42.1
to school		School bus	114	29.2
		Subway/bus	109	27.9
		Other	3	.8
Borough of school	390	Manhattan	237	60.8
		Queens	69	17.7
		Bronx	49	12.6
		Brooklyn	30	7.7
		Staten Island	5	1.3
Location of school	390	Same borough	328	84.1
vs. temporary		Different borough	62	15.9
shelter				
Attends former	387	Former school	94	24.3
school or school		Near shelter/hotel	276	71.3
where shelter		Near former shelter	' 17	4.4
is located				
School transfers	390	None	94	24.1
since loss of		1	168	43.1
permanent home		2	86	22.1
		3	23	5.9
		4-6	19	4.8

a. N varies due to missing data.

located; 24 percent (N=94) were attending their former school; and the remaining 4 percent (N=17) were attending a school in an area in which one of their former shelters was located. In discussing the available options with parents, they frequently mentioned that keeping children in their former school was generally more desirable because it provided stability, continuity of instruction, and continuity of friendships, and they were satisfied with the school and/or teacher.

Despite these advantages, the same parents often indicated that they had, nonetheless, transferred their children to the school near their temporary shelter for practical and economic reasons, because remaining in former schools had serious implications for children. Traveling long distances, sometimes from one end of the Bronx to the other end of Brooklyn, took extensive time and could be dangerous. To ensure timely arrival in school, children often had to leave their shelter before breakfast. In addition, they were unable to participate in after-school programs because of lengthy journeys back to the shelter.

Keeping children in their former schools is often an additional burden on the family and, in many cases, is not a viable alternative. Although subway and bus passes are given to New York City students, school bus transportation is not provided to those who choose to remain in their former school. Therefore, students, particularly younger children who must ride subways and/or public buses, must be accompanied by their parents to insure their safe arrival at school. Choosing this option often results in poor attendance, especially on days when the parents must report to the income maintenance center, and interferes with time that could be spent looking for an apartment or job. Ironically, for those parents who are employed, the lack of actual school bus transportation translates into the lack of a choice because parents cannot take the time from work to escort their children to and from school without jeopardizing or losing their jobs.

Many parents were found who were unaware that their children could receive free transportation if they continued attending their former school. In fact, some of the parents who had transferred their children to the local school indicated that they had done so because they could not afford the transportation and were not aware that the Board of Education was required to pay for it. Indeed, of the 109 children who were taking public transportation back and forth to school, eighteen had not been issued transportation passes.

Nor were parents aware of the existence of income maintenance procedures concerning carfare allowance for parents to escort their children to and from school. Many parents, including some who were aware of free transportation for their children, nonetheless had elected to transfer them because they could not afford to pay the cost of escorting them back and forth to school. Other parents who specifically asked if carfare were available were told erroneously by their overworked caseworker that "We don't give carfare" or "Your case is closed; you're not eligible."

Homelessness had a dramatic impact on the number of different schools children attended. As shown in Table 5.7, ninety-four children (24 percent) had never transferred, and 11 percent had transferred three or more times. The number of different schools attended, not surprisingly, was influenced by the length of time elapsed since loss of permanent housing (r(390)=.21, p<.001). Furthermore, the percentage of children who had transferred to a new school from two to six times varied according to length of homelessness: 18 percent (N=19) of the 105 children had been homeless for zero to six months: 36 percent (N=38) of the 104 children had been homeless for seven to twelve months; 31 percent (N=38) of the 122 children had been homeless for twelve to twenty-four months; and 56 percent (N=33) of the fifty-nine children had been homeless for more than two years.

The number of different schools attended, of course, was influenced by the number of different shelters or hotels in which the child had been (r(390)=.32, p<.001). The following summary illustrates the percentage of students who had transferred two to six times according to the number of prior shelters in which they had been: 13 percent (N=18) of the 142 children had been in no other shelter; 35 percent (N=37) of the 106 children had been in one other shelter; 51 percent (N=38) of the seventy-five children had been in two to three other shelters; and 64 percent (N=9) of the fourteen children had been in four or more other shelters.

Each school transfer represents time irrevocably lost. The cumulative effect of these losses, even within a quality education program, contributes to academic underachievement, holdover rates, and a loss or break in continuity of learning. In fact, many parents indicated that transferring their children to a different school every time they moved to a new shelter had detrimental educational consequences. With each transfer, school records must be transferred, frequently resulting in a delay, and transportation issues must be resolved. Parents also noted that frequent transitions had negative impact on their children's academic performance, attendance, and attitude.

For example, "Pamela" and her family have been homeless for ten months. Since losing their home, this family of two parents and two children has been in six different shelters in three different boroughs. Pamela (age eight) has transferred to a new school six times during this ten-month period. It is not surprising, therefore, that she recently has been evaluated for special education services on the basis of a suspected learning disability. Her mother reported that Pamela had been assigned to a program for learning-disabled children and would be attending a new school the following week. This would be Pamela's seventh school in ten months. In discussing the sequence of events, Pamela's mother stated:

> I think what she really needs is to stop going to a different school every month. She didn't have this learning disability before we lost our home. I think what she really needs is a permanent home, and special help with her reading and her math.

School performance. As expected, a homeless existence compromises the education of children. This fact was examined in the AFC study via reading achievement, mathematics achievement, and holdover rates. Wherever possible, the findings for children in temporary housing were compared with citywide comparison data.

1. Reading achievement. The Degrees of Reading Power (DRP) test is given to New York City students in grades 3 through 10 during the month of May. According to the Board of Education in New York City "the percent of students scoring at or above grade level has generally been treated as the single most important indicator of our student's reading achievement" (1988, 1).

As shown in Table 5.8, 3,805 students from the Board of Education data base on homeless children took the DRP test in May 1988. A majority (57.7 percent) scored below grade level, while 43 percent scored at or above grade level. In contrast, 68.1 percent of all New York City students who took the DRP in May 1988 scored at or above grade level (Board of Education 1988a). What is not known, however, is how many students in temporary housing who were supposed to take the test did not. For example, the data base indicates that there were 4,839 students in grades 3 through 10 in the spring of 1988. It is not known why DRP scores are missing for 1,034 of these students.

The findings for Districts 1, 2, and 15 (those districts with the greatest percentage of homeless students) are consistent with those discussed above. Overall, 36 percent of students in temporary housing (for whom scores are available) who took the test in a District 1 school scored at or above grade level compared with 57.4 percent for all District 1 students. Similar findings are reported for District 2 schools (39.6 percent versus 73.9 percent) and District 15 (40.7 percent versus 67.5 percent).

TABLE 5.8

Reading Achievement of Students in Temporary Housing[a]

Variable	N	Homeless children	n	%	Citywide[b] %
Overall DRP scores on May 1988 test	3,805	Below grade level	2,195	57.7	31.9
		At or above grade level	1,610	42.3	68.1
District 1	247	Below grade level	158	64.0	42.6
		At or above grade level	89	36.0	57.4
District 2	402	Below grade level	243	60.4	26.1
		At or above grade level	159	39.6	73.9
District 15	204	Below grade level	121	59.3	32.5
		At or above grade level	83	40.7	67.5

a. Data from the New York City Board of Education data base on *Students in Temporary Housing.*
b. Citywide comparison data from the New York City Board of Education *Citywide Test Results.*

2. Mathematics achievement. The citywide mathematics testing program uses the Metropolitan Achievement Test (MAT) series to assess achievement in mathematics in grades 2 through 8. According to the Board of Education data base, there were 5,174 students from temporary housing in grades 2 through 8 in the spring of 1988. Of these 5,174 students, MAT scores are available for 4,203 students. It is not known why MAT scores are missing for the remaining 971 students.

As shown in Table 5.9, of the 4,203 students from temporary housing who took the MAT in the spring of 1988, 71.9 percent scored below grade level, while 28.1 percent scored at or above grade level. In contrast, 56.7 percent of all New York City students who took the MAT in the spring of 1988 scored at or above grade level (Board of Education 1988a).

The findings for Districts 1, 2, and 15 are consistent with those reported for reading achievement. For example, 21.6 percent of the students in temporary housing who took the test in a District 1 school scored at or above grade level compared with 48.5 percent of all District 1 students who took the test. The findings for Districts 2 and 15 are slightly more dramatic (23.9 percent versus 69.8 percent for District 2, and 23.4 percent versus 59.8 percent for District 15).

3. Holdover rates. The analysis of holdover rates is based on all students who appeared on the Board of Education students-in-temporary-housing data base between September 1987 and May 1988 (N=9,659). As shown in Table 5.10, of the 8,070 students on which this analysis is based, 54 percent were in an age-appropriate grade; 11.6 percent (N=938) were two years or more over age for their grade, and 30 percent were one year older than similarly graded peers. Special education students who were not mainstreamed (N=1,050) and those students on file who were missing a grade code (N=539) were excluded from this analysis.

The AFC findings from the field data are almost identical to those obtained from the Board of Education data base. For example, 47 percent of the AFC sample were in an age-appropriate grade, while 11.3 percent were two years or more over age for their grade.

A second indicator of holdover rates was obtained from data collected in the AFC field study by asking parents whether or not their children currently were repeating their current grade. As shown in Table 5.10, 15 percent of our sample had been in their current grade

TABLE 5.9

Mathematics Achievement of Students in Temporary Housing

Variable	N		Homeless children			Citywide[b]
				n	%	%
Overall MAT scores on May 1988 test	4,203		Below grade level	3,021	71.9	43.5
			At or above grade level	1,182	28.1	56.7
District 1	296		Below grade level	232	78.4	51.5
			At or above grade level	64	21.6	48.5
District 2	480		Below grade level	365	76.0	30.2
			At or above grade level	115	23.9	69.8
District 15	261		Below grade level	200	76.6	40.2
			At or above grade level	61	23.4	59.8

a.   Data from the New York City Board of Education database on *Students in Temporary Housing.*

b.   Citywide comparison data from the New York City Board of Education *Citywide Test Results.*

previously. This percentage varies slightly, depending on length of homelessness. Of the 180 children who had been homeless for one year or more, 17.8 percent (N=32) currently were repeating a past grade. In contrast, of the 208 children who had been homeless twelve months or less, only 12.5 percent (N=26) currently were repeating their current grade. Although there is no citywide comparison group for this analysis, findings from the New York City Promotional Analysis Report of the Board of Education Student Information Services (Board of Education 1988c) indicate that 6.8 percent of children in regular education were not promoted at the end of the 1987-1988 school year.

TABLE 5.10

Holdover Rates of Students in Temporary Housing

Variable	N		Frequency	Percentage
Grade level by	8,070[a]	2 years or more[b]	938	11.6
age (BOE data)		1 year over age	2,443	30.3
		Proper age for grade	4,327	53.6
		1 year below age	362	4.5
Grade level by	390[c]	2 years or more	44	11.3
age (AFC data)		1 year over age	143	36.7
		Proper age for grade	187	47.9
		1 year below age	16	4.1
Currently	390	Yes	59	15.2
repeating		No	331	84.9
prior grade				

a.   Data from the New York City Board of Education database on *Students in Temporary Housing.*

b.   Two years or more over age for grade.

c.   Data from families in AFC study.

4. School attendance. School attendance findings are summarized in Table 5.11. Attendance rates are based on a total of 6,433 students who showed up in the Board of Education data base for at least one day between February 1988 and May 1988. These analyses include mainstreamed special education students. Overall, the attendance rate for students in temporary housing was much worse than for New York City students in general, when compared with findings from the school

profile data for 1987-1988 (Board of Education 1988b). The average attendance rate for homeless students in elementary school was 73.6 percent compared with 88.7 percent for all New York City elementary school students. Similarly, junior high school students who are homeless were present 63.6 percent of the time, compared with an attendance rate of 85.5 percent for all New York City students. Finally, homeless high school students were present 50.9 percent of the time, compared with the average attendance rate of 83.9 percent for all New York City high school students.

The mean attendance rate for select districts also is presented in Table 5.11. Consistent with the citywide data, students in temporary housing who attend school in Districts 1, 2, and 15 appear to have a lower mean attendance rate than the overall rate for all students in each of these three districts. For example, the mean attendance rate of homeless students in District 2 was 68 percent as opposed to 90 percent for District 2 students overall (Board of Education 1988b).

Findings from AFC field-based data indicate that school attendance also is influenced by moving into a new or different shelter or hotel. On average, children missed 4.26 days in school when they moved into their current facility. As shown in Table 5.11, 36 percent missed no days, 19 percent missed one to two days, 23 percent missed three to five days, 3 percent missed six to nine days, and 19 percent missed ten days or more.

On average, the AFC sample of children missed 3.57 (S.D.=5.9) days in school during the month prior to the study. Overall, 25 percent lost zero days, 33 percent missed one to two days, 22 percent missed three to five days, and 20 percent missed more than five days. During the past full school week prior to the interview, 62 percent had perfect attendance, 19 percent missed one day, 9 percent missed two days, and 10 percent missed three or more days.

Discussion and Conclusion

The research literature indicates that the national tragedy of homelessness among families creates a constellation of risks. It also clearly demonstrates that homelessness has a deleterious impact on children's physical, psychological, and educational needs.

TABLE 5.11

School Attendance Profile of Children in Temporary Housing

Variable	N		n	Average rate	Citywide rate
Average attendance rates (BOE data)	6,142	Elementary	4,429	73.6	88.7
		Junior high	1,108	63.6	85.5
		High school	605	50.9	83.9
Average district attendance rates (BOE data)	1,851	District 1	618	69.0	85.4
		District 2	801	67.6	89.5
		District 15	432	75.5	88.4

Variable	N		Frequency	Percentage
Days missed when moved into current shelter/hotel	388	None	138	35.4
		1-2	74	18.9
		3-5	88	22.5
		6-9	10	2.6
		10-15	55	14.3
		16-25	23	6.0
Days missed in past month	388	None	99	25.5
		1-5	212	54.6
		6-10	56	14.4
		11-20	21	5.4
Days missed in past week	390	None	241	61.8
		1	74	19.0
		2	35	9.0
		3-5	40	10.3

a. Excludes 118 students missing a grade code designation and 175 children attending the citywide special education program.

When families lose their homes and enter the emergency housing system, they generally are placed into temporary housing facilities without sufficient consideration of the impact of being moved to unfamiliar and often distant areas. Homeless families currently are warehoused in dreary shelters or cramped in seedy hotels for excessive periods of time. The living conditions in many of these facilities provide families with neither a healthy nor humane environment and, in many cases, create extraordinary hazards for children.

In addition, families frequently are bounced from one temporary facility to another, compounding the disruption in their lives and hindering their ability to maintain their public assistance benefits, employment, access to health care, and formal education. This shuttling of families away from their communities, neighbors, friends, and local schools has been linked to poorer nutrition, inadequate health care, illness, developmental delays, emotional problems, poorer school attendance, and lower academic performance among school-aged children. While these short-term effects have been documented, it can only be imagined what the long-term trauma to these children will be.

The author's research, based on the compilation and analysis of statistical data collected by the New York City Board of Education and by field-based interviews of homeless families, indicates that the ability to be educated is severely affected by homelessness. Particularly noteworthy is the finding that homelessness has a dramatic impact on the number of different schools attended, and that the number of transfers to different schools is influenced significantly by the number of different shelters or hotels in which the children have been.

Disruption in the continuity of education of homeless children also is documented by their erratic attendance. While the majority of homeless students currently are enrolled in school, their attendance is, not surprisingly, quite poor. This is demonstrated by the Board of Education data which indicated an overall attendance rate of 74 percent for elementary students (versus 89 percent citywide), 64 percent for those in junior high school (versus 85 percent citywide), and 51 percent for high school students (versus 84 percent citywide). Data obtained by the AFC mirror these findings and also indicate that transferring from school to school often translates into additional days lost. On average, students missed four to five days with each move to a new shelter or hotel.

School performance also is affected by homelessness, as demonstrated by AFC findings that only 42 percent of homeless students were reading at or above grade level, compared with 68 percent citywide. Similarly, only 28 percent of homeless students scored at or above grade level on mathematics ability, compared with 57 percent citywide. Given these shocking findings, it is not surprising that 15 percent of survey respondents currently were repeating their prior grade and that 12 percent of homeless students citywide were two years or more over age for their grade.

In conclusion, the dislocation of the homeless from their communities and the subsequent events associated with the loss of their homes make continuity of education difficult. Although continuing to attend the former school is an available option for homeless New York City children, and certainly one that would minimize the disruption in the lives of the children, it is not always a realistic choice.

It can be argued that individualized transportation services for homeless students to and from their former schools would solve some of these problems. However, this is not only unrealistic, but it would also increase the potential of stigmatizing children living in temporary housing. Instead, the cessation of the practice of bouncing families and the increase of efforts to place families in their own communities – preferably in affordable housing, but, if not, in transitional apartments – are advocated.

Works Consulted

Achenbach, T., and C. Edelbrock. 1981. "Behavioral Problems and Competencies Reported by Parents of Normal and Disturbed Children Aged Four Through Sixteen." *Monograph Social Research Child Development* 46: 1-82.

Achenbach, T., and C. Edelbrock. 1983. *Manual for the Child Behavior Checklist and Revised Behavior Profile.* Burlington, VT: Department of Psychiatry, University of Vermont.

Acker, P. J., A. H. Fiermanman, and B. P. Dreyer. 1987. "An Assessment of Parameters of Health Care and Nutrition in Homeless Children." *American Journal of Disabled Children* 141: 388.

Alperstein, G., and E. Armstein. 1988. "Homeless Children – A Challenge for Pediatricians." *Pediatric Clinics of North America* 6: 1413-25.

Alperstein, G., C. Rappaport, and J. M. Flanigan. 1988. "Health Problems of Homeless Children in New York City." *American Journal of Public Health* 78, no. 9: 1232-33.

Angel, R., and J. Worobey. 1988. "Single Motherhood and Children's Health." *Journal of Health and Social Behavior* 29: 38-52.

Association of the Bar of the City of New York. 1989a. "Report of the Committee on Legal Problems of the Homeless." *The Record* 14, no. 1: 33-88.

Association of the Bar of the City of New York. 1989b. "Report of the Committee on Legal Assistance on Preventing Homelessness Through Representation of Tenants Faced with Eviction." *The Record* 44, no. 3: 234-53.

Bach, V., and R. Steinhagen. 1987. *Alternatives to the Welfare Hotel: Using Emergency Assistance to Provide Decent Transitional Shelter for Homeless Families.* New York: Community Service Society.

Barbanel, J. 1988, 26 Jan. "Number of Homeless Far Below Shelter Forecasts." *New York Times,* pp. B1, B6.

Bassuk, E. L. 1984. "The Homeless Problem." *Scientific American* 251, no. 1:40-5.

Bassuk, E. L. 1986. "Homeless Families: Single Mothers and Their Children in Boston Shelters." In *The Mental Health Needs of Homeless Persons: New Directions for Mental Health Services,* ed. E. L. Bassuk, 45-53. San Francisco: Jossey-Bass.

Bassuk, E. L., and A. Lauriat. 1984. "The Politics of Homelessness." In *The Homeless Mentally Ill,* ed. H. R. Lamb, 301-13. Washington, DC: American Psychiatric Association.

Bassuk, E. L., and A. Lauriat. 1986. "Are Emergency Shelters the Solution?" *International Journal of Mental Health* 14, no. 4: 125-36.

Bassuk, E. L., and L. Rosenberg. 1988. "Why Does Family Homelessness Occur? A Case-Control Study." *American Journal of Public Health* 78, no. 7: 783-8.

Bassuk, E. L., and L. Rubin. 1987. "Homeless Children: A Neglected Population." *American Journal of Orthopsychiatry* 57, no. 2: 279-86.

Bassuk, E. L., L. Rubin, and A. Lauriat. 1984. "Is Homelessness a Mental Health Problem?" *American Journal of Psychiatry* 141: 1546.

Bassuk, E. L., L. Rubin, and A. Lauriat. 1986. "Characteristics of Sheltered Homeless Families." *American Journal of Public Health* 76, no. 9: 1097-1101.

Baxter, E., and K. Hopper. 1982. "The New Mendicancy: Homeless in New York City." *American Journal of Orthopsychiatry* 52: 393-407.

Benker, K. 1989, 6 Jan. Testimony presented before the New York City Council Select Committee on the Homeless.

Berezin, J. 1988. *Promises to Keep: Child Care for New York City's Homeless Children.* New York: Child Care, Inc.

Bernstein, A. B., G. Alperstein, and A. H. Fierman. 1988. *Health Care of Homeless Children.* Paper presented at Lehman College, New York City.

Bingham, R. D., R. E. Green, and S. B. White. 1987. *The Homeless in Contemporary Society.* Newbury Park, CA: Sage.

Board of Education. 1987. *Regulation of the Chancellor, No. A-780: Students in Temporary Housing.* New York City.

Board of Education. 1988a. *Citywide Test Results.* New York City: Office of Educational Assessment.

Board of Education. 1988b, 28 Sept. *Memo from June Fields on Students in Temporary Housing.* New York City: Office of Educational Data Services.

Board of Education. 1988c, June. *Promotion Analysis Report – Citywide Summary.* New York City: Student Information Services.

Brickner, P. W. 1987. "Health Care for the Homeless." In *Homelessness: Critical Issues for Policy and Practice,* 48-52. Boston, MA: Boston Foundation.

Bronfenbrenner, U. 1974. *A Report on Longitudinal Evaluations of Early Childhood Programs. Vol. 2. Is Early Intervention Effective?* DHEW Publication No. OHD 74-24. Washington, DC: Office of Child Development.

Bronfenbrenner, U. 1979. *The Ecology of Human Development.* Cambridge: Harvard University Press.

Bronfenbrenner, U. 1986. "Ecology of the Family as a Context for Human Development: Research Perspectives." *Developmental Psychology* 22, no. 6: 723-42.

Caper, A. 1987, 30 Nov. "School Reforms Sought by Wagner." *New York Newsday.*

Caton, C. 1986. "The Homeless Experience in Adolescent Years." In *The Mental Health Needs of Homeless Persons: New Directions for Mental Health Services,* ed. E. L. Bassuk, 63-70. San Francisco: Jossey-Bass.

Center for Law and Education. 1987. "Homelessness: A Barrier to Education for Thousands of Children." *Newsnotes* 38. Cambridge, MA: By the author.

Chavkin, W., A. Kristal, C. Seabron, and P. E. Guigli. 1987. "Reproductive Experience of Women Living in Hotels for the Homeless in New York City." *New York State Journal of Medicine* 87: 10-3.

Children's Defense Fund. 1987. *Children's Defense Budget: FY 1988.* Washington, DC: By the author.

Citizens Committee for Children. 1984. *7,000 Homeless Children: The Crisis Continues.* New York: By the author.

Citizens Committee for Children. 1988. *Children in Storage: Families in New York City's Barracks-Style Shelters.* New York: By the author.

Cobb, S. 1976. "Social Support as a Mediator of Life Stress." *Psychosomatic Medicine* 38: 300-14.

Community Food Resource Center. 1989a. *The Impact of Increasing New York State's Public Assistance Grant on Federal Food Stamp Benefits in New York City.* New York: By the author.

Community Food Resource Center. 1989b. *Who are New York City's Hungry?* New York: By the author.

Consortium for Longitudinal Studies. 1983. *As the Twig is Bent..Lasting Effects of Preschool Programs.* Hillsdale, NJ: Lawrence Erlbaum Associates.

Council of the City of New York Select Committee on the Homeless. 1988a. *Home Again – A Plan for New York City's Homeless Women.* New York: By the author.

Council of the City of New York Select Committee on the Homeless. 1988b. *More, Please – Thoughts on Food in the City's Shelters.* New York: by the author.

Cuomo, M. M. 1987. "The State Role – New York State's Approach to Homelessness." In *The Homeless in Contemporary Society,* eds. R. D. Bingham, R. E. Green, and S. B. White, pp. 199-215. Newbury Park, CA: Sage.

Dehavenon, A. L. 1987. *Toward a Policy for the Amelioration and Prevention of Family Homelessness and Dissolution: New York City's After-Hours Emergency Assistance Units in 1986-87.* New York: The East Harlem Interfaith Welfare Committee.

Dehavenon, A. L., and K. Benker. 1989. *The Tyranny of Indifference: A Study of Hunger, Homelessness, Poor Health and Family Dismemberment in 818 New York City Households with Children in 1988-1989.* New York: The East Harlem Interfaith Welfare Committee.

Department of Health. 1986a. *Discussion Paper of Congregate Family Shelters and Public Health.* Unpublished paper. New York: By the author.

Department of Health. 1986b. *Diarrhea in the Family Congregate Shelters of New York City – Draft No. 5.* Unpublished paper. New York: By the author.

Dumpson, J. R., and D. N. Dinkins. 1987. *A Shelter is Not a Home: Report of the Manhattan Borough President's Task Force on Housing for Homeless Families.* New York: By the author.

Felner, R. D. 1984. "Vulnerability in Childhood: A Preventive Framework for Understanding Children's Efforts to Cope with Life Stress and Transitions." In *Prevention of Problems in Childhood: Psychological Research and Applications,* eds. M. C. Roberts and L. C. Peterson, 133-69. New York: Wiley.

Felner, R. D., S. S. Farber, and J. Primavera. 1983. "Transitions and Stressful Life Events: A Model for Primary Prevention." In *Preventive Psychology: Theory, Research, and Practice,* eds. R. D. Felner, L. A. Jason, J. N. Moritsugu, and S. Farber, 199-215. New York: Pergamon Press.

Frankenburg, W. K., A. Goldstein, and P. Camp. 1971. "The Revised Denver Development Screening Test: Its Accuracy as a Screening Instrument." *Journal of Pediatrics* 79: 988-95.

Gallagher, E. 1986. *No Place Like Home.* Boston, MA: Massachusetts Committee for Children and Youth.

Garmezy, N. 1983. "Stressors of Childhood." In *Stress, Coping, and Development in Children,* eds. N. Garmezy and M. Rutter, 43-84. New York: McGraw-Hill.

Gewirtzman, R., and I. Fodor. 1987. "The Homeless Child at School: From Welfare Hotel to Classroom." *Child Welfare* 66, no. 3: 237-245.

Grinker, W. 1989, 3 Mar. New York City Council. Select Committee on the Homeless. Hearing on Human Resource Administration's Five-Year Plan.

Gross, T., and M. Rosenberg. 1987. "Shelters for Battered Women and Their Children: An Under-Recognized Source of Communicable Disease Transmission." *American Journal of Public Health,* 77, no. 9: 1198-1201.

Hartman, C. 1986. "The Housing Part of Homelessness." In *The Mental Health Needs of Homeless Persons: New Directions for Mental Health Service,* ed. E. L. Bassuk, 71-85. San Francisco: Jossey-Bass.

Haskins, R. 1989. "Beyond Metaphor: The Efficiency of Early Childhood Education." *American Psychologist* 44, no. 2: 276-82.

Hoch, C. 1987. "A Brief History of the Homeless Problem in the United States." In *The Homeless in Contemporary Society,* eds. R. D. Bingham, R. E. Green, and S. B. White, 16-32. Newbury Park, CA: Sage.

Hodes, B. 1988, 16 May. *Summary Report on the Conference on Homeless Women.* New York: Women's City Club of New York, New York City Council's Select Committee on the Homeless, and IBM Corporation.

Hopper, K., E. Susser, and S. Conover. 1985. "Economies of Makeshift: Deindustrialization and Homelessness in New York City." *Urban Anthropology* 14, no. 1-3: 183-236.

Horton, G. 1987. *No One is Responsible for These Children.* Report prepared for Ruth W. Messinger, New York City Council Member, 4th District.

Human Resources Administration. 1986, Oct. *New York City Temporary Housing Program for Families with Children: Monthly Report.* New York: By the author.

Human Resources Administration. 1987. *Summary of the 1986 Public Hearing on Social Services in New York City.* New York: By the author.

Human Resources Administration. 1988a, Dec. *Homeless Family Census (HOMES Report).* New York: By the author.

Human Resources Administration. 1988b, Dec. *New York City Emergency Housing Program for Families: Monthly Report*. New York: By the author.

Jahiel, R. I. 1987. "The Situation of Homelessness." In *The Homeless in Contemporary Society,* eds. R. D. Bingham, R. E. Green, and S. E. White. Newbury Park, CA: Sage.

Jonas, S. 1986. "On Homelessness and the American Way." *American Journal of Public Health* 76, no. 9: 1084-6.

Kovacs, M. 1983. *The Children's Depression Inventory: A Self-Rated Depression Scale for School-Age Youngsters*. Pittsburgh: University of Pittsburgh, School of Medicine.

Kozol, J. 1988. *Rachel and Her Children: Homeless Families in America*. New York: Crown.

Leavitt, R., ed. 1981. *Homeless Welfare Families: A Search for Solutions*. New York: Community Council of Greater New York.

Main, T. 1986. "The Homeless Families of New York." *Public Interest* 56: 321.

Maza, P. L., and J. A. Hall. 1988. *Homeless Children and Their Families: A Preliminary Study*. Washington, DC: Child Welfare League of America.

McChesney, K. Y. 1986. "New Findings on Homeless Families." *Family Professional* 1, no. 2: 165-74.

McChesney, K. Y. In press a. "Paths to Family Homelessness." In *Homelessness: The National Perspective*, eds. M. J. Robertson and M. Greenblatt. New York: Plenum.

McChesney, K. Y. In press b. "Growth of Homelessness: An Aggregate Rather Than Individual Problem." In *Homelessness: A Prevention-Oriented Approach,* ed. R. Jahiel. New York: John Hopkins University.

Miller, D. S., and E. H. B. Lin. 1988. "Children in Sheltered Homeless Families: Reported Health Status and Use of Health Services." *Pediatrics* 81, no. 5: 668-73.

Molnar, J. 1988. *Home is Where the Heart Is: The Crisis of Homeless Children and Families in New York City*. New York: Bank Street College of Education.

Moreno, S. 1984, 25 Oct. "Plan Offers School to Hotel Kids." *New York Newsday*.

Nann, R. 1982. *Uprooting and Surviving*. Boston: Reidel Publishing.

National Coalition for the Homeless. 1984. *Perchance to Sleep: Homeless Children Without Shelter in New York City*. New York: By the author.

National Coalition for the Homeless. 1987a. *Broken Lives: Denial of Education to Homeless Children*. Washington, DC: By the author.

National Coalition for the Homeless. 1987b. *Homelessness in the United States: Background and Federal Response. A Briefing Paper for Presidential Candidates*. Washington, DC: By the author.

National Coalition for the Homeless. 1987c. *Pushed Out: America's Homeless – Thanksgiving 1987*. Washington, DC: By the author.

National Coalition for the Homeless. 1988. *Over the Edge: Homeless Families and the Welfare System*. Washington, DC: By the author.

Neeleman, H. L., C. Gunnoe, and A. Leviton. 1979. "Deficits in Psychological and Classroom Performance of Children with Elevated Dentine Lead Levels." *New England Journal of Medicine* 300: 689-95.

Newacheck, P. W., and B. Starfield. 1988. "Morbidity and Use of Ambulatory Care Services Among Poor and Non-Poor Children." *American Journal of Public Health* 78, no. 8: 927-33.

New York State Council on Children and Families. 1984. *Meeting the Needs of Homeless Youth: A Report of the Homeless Youth Steering Committee*. Albany, NY: By the author.

New York State Rules and Regulations. 8NYCRR Section 100.2 (x) Education of Homeless Children.

Nix, C. 1985, 5 Nov. "Nearly 1,000 Violations Cited at a Hotel for the Homeless." *The New York Times*, A1.

Paone, D., and K. Kay. 1988, Nov. *Immunization Status of Homeless PreSchoolers*. Paper presented at the American Public Health Association, Boston.

Partnership for the Homeless. 1987. *National Growth in Homelessness*. New York: By the author.

Phillips, M., N. DeChillo, D. Kronenfeld, and V. Middleton-Jeter. 1988. "Homeless Families: Services Make a Difference." *Social Case Work* 69, no. 11: 48-53.

Rafferty, Y., and N. Rollins. 1989. *Learning in Limbo: The Educational Deprivation of Homeless Children*. New York: Advocates for Children.

Redlener, I. 1989, 6 Jan. Testimony presented before the New York City Council Select Committee on the Homeless. Unpublished manuscript.

Reinherz, H., and C. A. Gracey. 1982. *The Simmons Behavior Checklist: Technical Information*. Boston: Simmons School of Social Work.

Reuler, J. B., M. J. Bax, and J. H. Sampson. 1986. "Physicians House Call Services for Medically Needy, Inner-City Residents." *American Public Health Journal* 76, no. 9: 1131-34.

Reynolds, C. R., and B. O. Richmond. 1985. *Revised Children's Manifest Anxiety Scale Manual*. Los Angeles: Western Psychological Services.

Robertson, J. R., P. Koegel, and L. Ferguson. 1988, Nov. *Alcohol Use and Abuse Among Homeless Adolescents in Hollywood*. Paper presented at the Annual Meeting of the American Public Health Association, Boston.

Robertson, J. R., P. Koegel, P. Mundy, M. Greenblatt, and J. M. Robertson. 1988, Nov. *Mental Health Status of Homeless Adolescents in Hollywood*. Paper presented at the Annual Meeting of the American Public Health Association, Boston.

Rossi, P. H., and J. D. Wright. 1987. "The Determinants of Homelessness." *Health Affairs* 6, no. 1: 19-32.

Rossi, P. H., J. D. Wright, G. H. Fisher, and G. Willis. 1987. "The Urban Homeless: Estimating Composition and Size." *Science* 253: 1336-41.

Roth, L., and E. R. Fox. 1988, Nov. *Children of Homeless Families: Health Status and Access to Health Care.* Paper presented at the American Public Health Association, Boston.

Ryan, W. 1976. *Blaming the Victim.* New York: Random House.

Shaffer, D., and C. L. Caton. 1984. *Runaway and Homeless Youth in New York City: A Report to the Ittleson Foundation.* New York: Division of Child Psychiatry, New York State Psychiatric Institute, and Columbia University College of Physicians and Surgeons.

Simpson, J., M. Kilduff, and C. D. Blewett. 1984. *Struggling to Survive in a Welfare Hotel.* New York: Community Service Society.

Smith, S. J. 1988. "New Thinking About the Homeless: Prevention, Not Cure." *Governing* 1: 24-9.

Stark, L. 1987. "Blame the System, Not its Victims." In *Homelessness: Critical Issues for Policy and Practice,* 7-11. Boston: Boston Foundation.

State Education Department. 1988. *Report on the Homeless in New York State.* University of the State of New York, Albany: By the author.

State Education Department. 1989. *New York State Plan for the Education of Homeless Children and Youth.* University of the State of New York, Albany: By the author.

Stewart B. McKinney Homeless Assistance Act. Public Law 100-77 (7/22/87), codified at 42 U.S.C. SS11301-11472.

Sullivan, P. A., and S. P. Damrosch. 1987. "Homeless Women and Children." In *The Homeless in Contemporary Society,* eds. R. D. Bingham, R. E. Green, and S. B. White, 82-98. Newbury Park, CA: Sage.

Taylor, M. 1988. "Homelessness: The Nature of the Crisis – The Scope of the Problem, Past and Current Policy, and Federal Options." *Youth Policy* 10, no. 5: 18-21.

U.S. Conference of Mayors. 1987a. *The Continuing Growth of Hunger, Homelessness, and Poverty in America's Cities: 1987 – A 26-City Survey.* Washington, DC: By the author.

U.S. Conference of Mayors. 1987b. *A Status Report on Homeless Families in America's Cities: A 29-State Survey.* Washington, DC: By the author.

U.S. Conference of Mayors. 1988. *A Status Report on the Stewart B. McKinney Homeless Assistance Act of 1987.* Washington, DC: By the author.

U.S. Congress. House. Select Committee on Children, Youth, and Families. 1987a. *The Crisis in Homelessness: Effects on Children and Families. Fact sheet.* Washington, DC: Government Printing Office.

U.S. Congress. House. Select Committee on Hunger. 1987b. *Hunger Among the Homeless: A Survey of 140 Shelters, Food Stamp Participants and Homelessness.* Washington, DC: Government Printing Office.

U.S. Department of Education. 1985, 15 Feb. "Report to Congress: State Interim Report on the Education of Homeless Children." Washington, DC: By the author.

Vanderbourg, K., and A. Christofides. 1986, June. *Children in Need: The Child Care Needs of Homeless Families in Temporary Shelter in New York City.* Report prepared for Ruth W. Messinger, New York City Council member, 4th District.

Whitman, B. 1987. Testimony presented before the U.S. House of Representatives Select Committee on Children, Youth, and Families. *The Crisis in Homelessness: Effect on Children and Families.* Washington, DC: Government Printing Office.

Whitman, B., P. Accardo, M. Boyert, and R. Kendagor. 1989. *Homelessness and Cognitive Performance in Children: A Possible Link.* St. Louis: Knights of Columbus Developmental Center, Cardinal Glennon Children's Hospital. Unpublished manuscript.

Winick, M. 1985. "Nutritional and Vitamin Deficiency States." In *Health Care of Homeless People,* eds. P. Brickner, L. Scharer, B. Conanan, A. Elvy, and M. Savarese, 103-8. New York: Springer.

Wright, J. D. 1987a. Testimony presented before the U.S. House of Representatives Select Committee on Children, Youth, and Families, 73-85. *The Crisis in Homelessness: Effect on Children and Families.* Washington, DC: Government Printing Office.

Wright, J. D. 1987b. "The National Health Care for the Homeless Program." In *The Homeless in Contemporary Society,* eds. R. D. Bingham, R. E. Green, and S. B. White, 150-69. Newbury Park, CA: Sage.

Wright, J. D. 1988a. "The Mentally Ill Homeless: What is Myth and What is Fact?" *Social Problems* 35, no. 2: 182-91.

Wright, J. D. 1988b. "The Worthy and Unworthy Homeless." *Society* 25, no. 5: 64-9.

Wright, J. D., and J. A. Lam. 1987. "Homelessness and the Low-Income Housing Supply." *Social Policy* 17, no. 4: 48-53.

Wright, J. D., P. H. Rossi, J. K. Knight, E. Weber-Burdin, R. C. Tessler, C. E. Stewart, M. Geronimo, and J. Lam. 1987. "Homelessness and Health: The Effects of Life Style on Physical Well-Being Among Homeless People in New York City." In *Research on Social Problems and Public Policy,* eds. M. Lewis and J. Miller IV, 41-72. Greenwood, CT: JAI Press.

PART III

The Causes of Child and Youth Homelessness

6

Macroeconomic Issues in Poverty: Implications for Child and Youth Homelessness

Kay Young McChesney

Most homeless children and youth are homeless because they are members of homeless families. (The exceptions, runaway and throwaway youth, have been covered in Chapter 3 of this volume.) Family homelessness is the result of the interaction of structural factors that determine the level of poverty and the characteristics of the housing market (McChesney, in press). Homelessness is the result of an imbalance between the number of households living in poverty and the amount of low-income housing available – the low-income housing ratio. When there are more households living under the poverty line (the numerator of the ratio) than there are housing units that they can afford (the denominator of the ratio), a shortage of low-income housing exists.

When there is a shortage of affordable low-income housing, households do two things. Those that can, pay more – more than the 30 percent of their monthly income that the federal government defines as the amount they can "afford" to pay for housing. Those that cannot pay more double up with family or friends (McChesney 1987). The remainder become homeless. In the aggregate, when the number of poor households far exceeds the number of low-income housing units, homelessness is the inevitable result (McChesney, in press).

The author gratefully acknowledges that work on this paper was fully funded by the Center for Children and Families, University of Pittsburgh School of Medicine.

Thus, the two root causes of child and youth homelessness are poverty and the shortage of affordable housing. All children whose families are living under the poverty line (and some who are not) are at risk of becoming homeless as long as there is a shortage of affordable low-income housing. The purpose of this chapter is to outline the characteristics and causes of family poverty in the United States. This chapter will first describe the demographic characteristics of families living in poverty. Second, it will present a model of the underlying causes of family poverty that incorporates both economic and sociological theories of poverty. The model includes macroeconomic factors – the business cycle, the dual labor market, deindustrialization and the global economy, demographic changes, social factors such as sex discrimination and racial discrimination in the labor market, and policy factors such as the inadequacy of safety net programs. Third, the model will be used to describe trends in family income and family poverty over time, from 1947 through 1987, and to explain the continuing stratification of family types across the income distribution regardless of the overall state of the economy. Finally, some of the model's implications for social policy will be suggested. The underlying causes of the shortage of affordable housing in the United States will not be covered here as they are covered in Chapter 7.

Family Poverty Today

The most recent data on family poverty are from the March 1988 Current Population Survey, which reports family income for 1987. Although families[1] with children under 18 make up only 35 percent of all United States households, they comprise 46 percent of households living under the poverty line. In 1987, 5.5 million families with 12.4 million children lived in poverty. While the percentage of families living in poverty, 16.2 percent, is down from the recent 1982 high, there are still 35 percent more families living under the poverty line now than there were in 1979. The last time the family poverty rate was this high, prior to the 1980s, was in 1964 (U.S. Bureau of the Census 1989b, 11).

Some kinds of families are much worse off than others. Only 7.8 percent of married-couple families are poor, but 17.6 percent of single-father families and an astounding 46.1 percent of single-mother families are living in poverty. However, these statistics mask significant racial/ethnic differences.[2] Black married-couple families are almost twice as likely to be poor as their white counterparts, and 18.1 percent of Hispanic married-couple families are poor. Minority single-father families are also more likely to live under the poverty line than white single-father families (U.S. Bureau of the Census 1989b, 11-14).

However, the differences in poverty rates show up most strikingly in single-mother families. Black families are significantly overrepresented among poor single-mother families. Black families make up only 14 percent of all families with children under eighteen, but they represent 34 percent of single-mother families and 44 percent of poor single-mother families. Comparatively, Hispanic families are more proportionately represented. They comprise 9.5 percent of all families, 12 percent of single-mother families, and 16 percent of poor single-mother families. By contrast, white families are underrepresented among single-mother families. Although 82 percent of all families are white, they represent 63 percent of single-mother families and 53 percent of poor single-mother families (U.S. Bureau of the Census 1989b, 11-14).

Poverty rates are significantly higher in minority single-mother families, and median incomes are lower. Nearly 60 percent of all black single-mother families are poor, as are 51.8 percent of Hispanic and 38.7 percent of white single-mother families. The median income of black single-mother families is $9,710 a year, an average of $5,647 less than needed to meet the poverty line. The median income and the income deficit are about the same for Hispanic single-mother families. By contrast, white single-mother families have a median income of $17,018, and married-couple families have a median income of $34,700 (U.S. Bureau of the Census 1989a, 31-3; 1989b, 12-4, 136).

Causes of Family Poverty

Clearly, married-couple families do better economically than single-mother families. The reasons are twofold. Married couples include men, and men earn more than women. Secondly, married couples can combine two incomes should a single income not be enough to sustain the family. Hence, the percentage of married-couple families who are poor is low compared to that of single-mother families. However, there are still nearly 2 million married-couple families living below the poverty line. When they are poor, why are they poor? What do the data show?

There seem to be three different kinds of problems. First 31.1 percent of "householders"[3] under age 65 in poor married-couple families worked full-time, year-round (U.S. Bureau of the Census 1989b, 90). Their poverty is due to the fact that they do not earn a living wage – a problem which will be discussed later.

The second problem is unemployment. Forty percent of married-couple householders worked full-time less than fifty weeks of the year, or worked only part-time. Among this group, a minority – 17.4 percent – reported that they were retired, attending school, or keeping house – in other words, they might be considered voluntarily unemployed.[4] Of the rest – the involuntarily unemployed – 68 percent said that they had been unemployed because they were unable to find work, and 13 percent were unemployed part of the year because they were ill or disabled (U.S. Bureau of the Census 1989b, 97).

The third problem is illness and disability. Among the 30.4 percent of poor married couples in which the householder did not work at all in 1987, 58 percent said they had been unable to work at all because of illness or disability and a third (35 percent) said that they had been unemployed for the whole year because they were unable to find work (U.S. Bureau of the Census 1989b, 97).

In other words, married-couple householders reported three main reasons for their poverty: (1) although they worked full-time all year, they did not earn enough to support their families above the poverty line; (2) they could not find full-time, year-round work; or (3) they were too ill or disabled to work full-time, year-round. Three macroeconomic factors – the business cycle, the dual labor market, and deindustrialization and the global economy – interact to structure a labor market that does not provide full-time, year-round work for all who want it. These labor market conditions, coupled with inadequate safety net programs for the unemployed and the disabled, are major influences in family poverty.

The Business Cycle

The business cycle has a major impact on employment. When the economy contracts, as it has eight times since World War II, the unemployment rate, the discouraged-worker rate, and the involuntary part-time worker rate all go up. As shown in Figures 6.1 and 6.2, the unemployment rate and the discouraged-worker rate are especially sensitive to recessionary pressures. As shown in Figure 6.1, the rise in the unemployment rate during a recession can be dramatic. A sharp rise in oil prices in late 1979 triggered an immediate slowdown in 1980, with the delayed effects of the oil shock causing the severe sixteen-month recession of 1981-1982 (Litan 1988). At the height of that recession, the unemployment rate for men reached 9.9 percent, almost double the 5.1 rate experienced in the last good year, 1979. Nearly 11 million people reported that they had been involuntarily unemployed at some point during 1982 (U.S. Department of Labor, Bureau of Labor Statistics).[5]

As shown in Figure 6.2, the discouraged-worker rate – the percentage of people reporting that they had given up looking for work because they had been unable to find it – is also very sensitive to recessions. It also doubled, for both men and women, between 1979 and 1982. During a recession, the percentage of men working part-time, presumably because they are unable to find full-time work, also rises sharply (U.S. Department of Labor, Bureau of Labor Statistics). Eckstein and Sinai (1986) argue that postwar recessions in the United States have primarily been caused by exogenous events such as the end of wars and world oil price increases (cited in Litan 1988). Thus, during a recession, millions of households are adversely affected economically by events over which they have no control.

Unemployment Insurance and Disability Insurance

Unemployment insurance, Worker's Compensation and Disability insurance – federal "safety net" programs designed to cushion the unemployed from the effects of recession, illness and disability – are helpful to those who receive them. However, they tend to cushion the middle class (Ellwood and Summers 1986) with benefits going primarily to white males (Blank and Blinder 1986) and coverage declined markedly during the Reagan years.

Unemployment insurance is typical. Blank and Blinder (1986, 192) found that the ratio of the number of people receiving unemployment insurance to the total number of unemployed fell from a peak of 78

FIGURE 6.1

Unemployment Rates for Women and Men, 1948-1988
(percentage of civilian noninstitutionalized labor force over 16
unemployed)

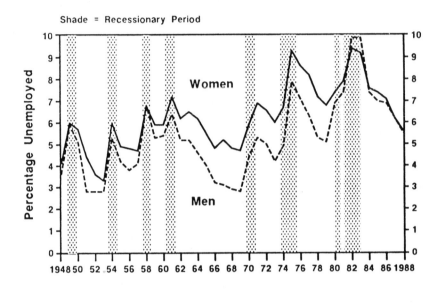

Source: U.S. Department of Labor, Bureau of Labor Statistics, Current Population
Survey, various years.

percent in 1975 to 43 percent by 1982. The maximum length of benefits
also fell, from sixty-five weeks in 1976 to thirty-four to fifty-five weeks
(depending on the state) in 1983. Even at that percentage, minority
workers are underrepresented: in Moen's (1983) sample, only 30.3
percent of the black unemployed received unemployment compensation,
compared to 49.6 percent of the white unemployed. Similarly, Blank
and Blinder (1986, 193) reported that only 14.1 percent of the nonwhite
unemployed were insured. They concluded that low-income workers
were the most likely to experience unemployment and the least likely to
receive unemployment compensation, principally because of unstable
work histories and low wages (Blank and Blinder 1986, 192).

FIGURE 6.2

Percentage of Discouraged Workers, Male and Female, in Labor Force, 1970-1988
(labor force = employed + unemployed + discouraged workers)

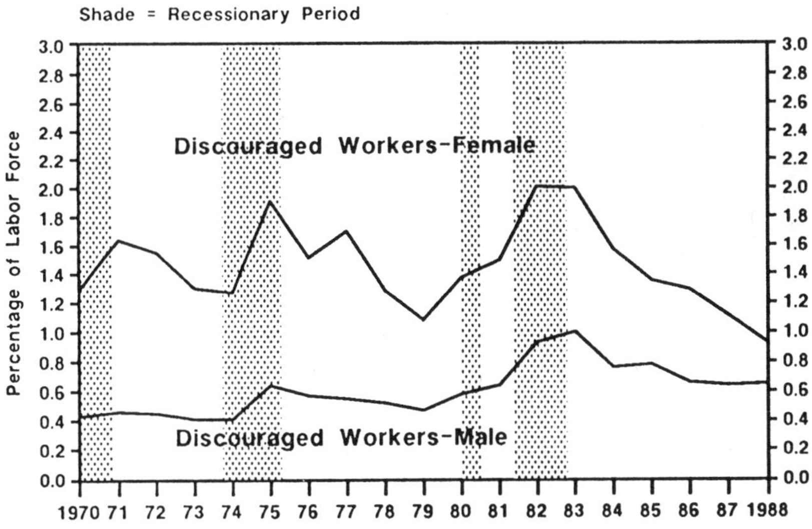

Shade = Recessionary Period

Source: U.S. Department of Labor, Bureau of Labor Statistics, Current Population Survey, various years.

Workers who are unemployed because of an injury received on the job are more fortunate. Ellwood and Summers (1986, 88) report that three-quarters of "formerly poor persons lucky enough to receive W[orker's] C[ompensation] are pushed out of poverty by this income." However, most workers who are unemployed because they are ill or disabled are not injured on the job, and there is no comparable program for them. Only persons who are totally and permanently disabled are eligible for Social Security disability, and even then only those with advocates capable enough and willing to see them through a complex and lengthy application process receive it. Two-thirds of applicants are denied; this in spite of several studies that show that between 70 and 80 percent of applicants are unable to return to work at any time within five years from the time of their application denial (Ellwood and Summers 1986, 90). Basically, there is no safety net for most of the ill or disabled, which explains why they make up a majority of the involuntarily unemployed family householders living under the poverty line.

The effects of the business cycle and the inadequacy of safety net programs for the unemployed and the ill and disabled explain the poverty of two-thirds of poor married-couple householders, but they do not explain why the third of married-couple householders who work full-time, year-round are still poor. The simple answer to this question is that the minimum wage is a poverty wage. In the mid-1960s, a person working full-time, full-year at the minimum wage could support a family of three at 115 percent of the poverty line (Children's Defense Fund 1989). The last time the minimum wage brought the income of a family of three to the poverty line was in 1978. The minimum wage was raised to $3.35 an hour in 1981. Since then, the minimum wage has been losing ground to inflation. Historically, the minimum wage was set at 40 percent to 55 percent of average hourly earnings, but by 1985 it had fallen to 38 percent of average hourly earnings (Gault and Brinner 1987).

The minimum wage rose to $3.80 an hour in April of 1990 and will rise to $4.25 in April of 1991. However, that is still well below the poverty line even for full-time workers, and many minimum wage jobs are part time. By 1988 workers needed to earn $4.86 an hour, full-time, year-round, in order to support a family of three at the poverty level. Some economists have been critical of the strategy of raising the minimum wage. They argue that this is a poorly targeted antipoverty measure, since many minimum-wage earners are teenagers from nonpoor households, and suggest that other approaches such as the negative income tax or the earned income tax credit would be preferable (Gault and Brinner 1987). However, these latter options currently have little political support. Thus, there is currently no relief in sight for the working poor.

To say that families are poor because they have inadequate earnings begs the question. The more relevant question is why some kinds of workers, especially minorities and women, are disproportionately concentrated in low-wage or minimum-wage jobs. This is the issue that is central to understanding family poverty.

Economists typically argue that workers are allocated to different jobs (some paying well, some paying poorly) solely on the basis of their productivity. Workers can be classified by the amount of "human capital" – education, training, skills, years of work experience – in which they have "invested." In this theory, the labor force is seen as "a single queue: the individuals with the highest productivity being first and those with the lowest productivity at the end. The aggregate demands of the society determine how far down the queue the market would go" (Singell 1984, 10). In other words, in good years, such as 1979 and 1987, when the economy is operating at nearly full capacity, this theory predicts that aggregate demand will structure the labor market so that people far down the end of the queue will have work. In bad years, such as 1975 and 1982, when aggregate demand falls, even people towards the middle of the queue will lose their jobs.

Employers are seen as operating on a purely rational basis. Therefore, the theory predicts that minority and women workers with equivalent qualifications will be paid the same as white men. Therefore, if women and minority workers are "last hired and first fired" as the economy moves through a business cycle, it is because they are less productive. If women and minority workers are paid lower wages, it is because they have less human capital (Lloyd and Niemi 1979).

The problem with this theory is that it does not agree with researchers' findings. It does seem to describe the labor market experience of white men fairly well, particularly the movement of white men with marginal skills in and out of the labor force through the business cycle. However, it does not seem to describe the labor market experiences of minorities and women. There are two major areas of discrepancy. First, minorities and women do not seem to be competing in the same labor market as white men. Second, women and minorities are not paid the same as white men, even when their education and experience are identical.

The Dual Labor Market

When Doeringer and Piore (1971) studied the local labor market in Boston, they decided that what they were observing was not one queue, but two – that there were two (dual) labor markets. The primary labor market had high-wage, steady jobs with full benefits and good opportunity for upward mobility. White men predominated in the primary labor market. The secondary labor market included low-wage, unstable, dead-end jobs, with few benefits. Minorities and women were concentrated in the secondary labor market. Considerable research since then has supported the finding that labor markets are segmented, rather than unitary. Although different authors find the labor market to be segmented in different ways (see Reich 1984 for a review), three markets are important: the primary (white male) market, the secondary labor market for black men, and the secondary labor market for women.

Racial Discrimination

There is considerable evidence that black men experience significant racial discrimination in the labor market in two ways: they earn significantly less than white men, and they have difficulty gaining access to the primary labor market. Black men seem to be segregated into a secondary labor market by racial discrimination. Employers perceive blacks as having fewer skills and less education than whites (Holzer 1986) and view blacks as being "suitable" for employment in manufacturing, but not in retail establishments (Culp and Dunson 1986). Consequently, the black men tend to find work in lower wage blue-collar jobs.

Black men are paid less than white men. The human capital thesis which states that differences in black-white wages are due to differences in factors such as education does not hold up under examination. As shown in Table 6.1, even when the economy is doing well, when black and white men with the same levels of education are compared, blacks consistently earn 20 percent to 25 percent less. In 1987, among full-time, year-round workers, twenty-five years and older, black men with one to three years of high school earned $5,254 less than whites – 76 percent of white men's earnings. With four years of high school, black men earned $7,126 less – 73 percent of white men's earnings. With one to three years of college, black men earned $6,007 less – 80 percent of white men's earnings. With a college degree, black men earned $9,151 less – 74 percent of white men's earnings. And even with five or more years of college – these are the doctors and lawyers and college

TABLE 6.1

Education and Median Income by Sex and Race – Full-Time, Year-Round Workers 25 Years and Over, 1987

Full-Time year-round workers, 25 years old and over	Years of school completed				
	High school		College		
	1-3	4	1-3	4	5 or more
White Men					
Median income	22,011	26,046	30,176	35,701	42,063
Percentage of white men's income	100	100	100	100	100
Black Men					
Median income	16,757	18,920	24,169	22,550	35,815
Percentage of white men's income	76	73	80	74	85
White Women					
Median income	13,367	16,674	20,084	23,749	29,793
Percentage of white men's income	61	64	67	67	71
Black Women					
Median income	11,613	15,582	18,099	21,140	26,415
Percentage of white men's income	53	60	60	59	63

Source: U.S. Bureau of the Census 1988a.

professors – black men earned $6,248 less – 85 percent of the $42,063 median salary of their white counterparts (U.S. Bureau of the Census 1989a, 140). These are aggregate data, but in individual level studies where many human capital factors, including years of work experience, age, and on-the-job training as well as education, are controlled, black men's wages are still 20 percent less than those of white men (Shapiro 1984).

Racial discrimination also appears to be the most likely explanation for the differential in unemployment rates. Even in periods of relatively full employment, the unemployment rate for black men is two to two-and-a-half times that of white workers (Hirschman 1988). However, during recessions the rise in black unemployment is much sharper and lasts longer than the rise in white unemployment. During 1975, the first OPEC oil embargo recession, the unemployment rate for black men hit 15 percent, and during 1982-1983 their unemployment rate exceeded 20 percent, more than twice the rate for white men. As Hirschman (1988, 65) emphasizes, at 20 percent, the unemployment rate for black men during recession comes very close to the unemployment levels during the Depression. Moen (1983) also found that black male householders experienced longer spells of unemployment during the 1975 recession. The combination of the effects of wage discrimination plus the effects of unemployment can be seen by comparing black-white differences in the median earnings per year for all workers (as opposed to full-time, year-round workers as discussed above). As can be seen by comparing the statistics on men in Table 6.1 (full-time, year-round workers, twenty-five years old and over) to Table 6.2 (men twenty-five years old and over), even when the economy is booming and the demand for labor is high, as it was in 1987, the costs of unemployment add an extra six to seven percent to the difference between black men's median earnings as compared to white men for levels of education from "some high school" through four or more years of college. For example, when unemployment is factored in, black male high school graduates earn only 66 percent of their white counterparts' annual salaries. At the level of five or more years of college (professional school), the added unemployment discount falls to three percent (U.S. Bureau of the Census 1989a, 140). During a recession, when demand for labor falls, the black unemployment discount rises sharply.

In a major series of studies completed for the National Bureau of Economic Research, after taking into account human capital differences, neighborhood differences, the structure of the labor market, etc., virtually all of the authors independently come to the conclusion that racial discrimination remains the most important explanation of lower wages and higher unemployment among young black men (Freeman and Holzer 1986). Ellwood (1986, 181), for example, concludes flatly, "the problem...is race." In sum, racial discrimination is a major cause of inadequate earnings for black men. By extension, since inadequate earnings of the householder are a major cause of poverty in married-couple families, racial discrimination is an important factor in married-couple family poverty.

Deindustrialization and the Global Economy

In urban areas, especially in industrially based cities like Detroit, Cleveland, Pittsburgh, and Philadelphia, black men have traditionally been employed in manufacturing and heavy industry. During the last twenty years, the United States has been in the process of deindustrialization, moving from a manufacturing-based to a services-based economy (Bluestone and Harrison 1982). Under pressure from international competition, U.S. firms moved production from U.S. plants to Third World countries where labor costs were lower (Harrison and Bluestone 1988). Harris (1984) estimates that large manufacturing firms in the U.S. eliminated more than 900,000 jobs a year in the mid-1970s. Between 1978 and 1982 alone, she estimates a total loss of 3.5 to 4 million jobs, or one out of every four jobs in large manufacturing facilities (cited in Harrison and Bluestone 1988, 37). In the process of deindustrialization, cities were transformed from centers of goods processing to centers of information processing, and the new jobs that were created were primarily white-collar jobs that required high levels of education, the sort of jobs that black men have traditionally had difficulty gaining access to, even when they had the requisite human capital (Kasarda 1988).

The result, particularly in large rust-belt cities, was a mismatch between the structure of a discriminatory labor market and the urban labor force. Kasarda (1988) shows that as the manufacturing jobs typically held by blacks were (partially) replaced by white-collar, information-processing jobs typically held by whites, the result was massive unemployment among blacks. While the unemployment rate for white men in the central cities declined, the unemployment rate for black men skyrocketed, for example, from 7.6 percent in 1969 to 30.4 percent in 1985 in the Northeast, and from 8.3 percent in 1969 to 32.8 percent in 1985 in the Midwest. Combining unemployment rates with the rates of men not in school and not in the labor force, Kasarda (1988, 187) shows that nationally, by 1985, central city black men aged twenty-five to sixty-four had a real unemployment rate of 35.0 percent, and central city black men aged sixteen to sixty-four had a real unemployment rate of 51.2 percent. In the Midwest and the Northeast, these figures were as high as 45.6 percent for mature men and 68.0 percent for young black men.

Building on Kasarda's work, Wilson and Neckerman (1986) show that the high unemployment rate, combined with high death and institutionalization rates among young black men, result in an acute shortage of "marriageable" black men – men who can support wives and children – in the central cities (see also Wilson 1987). They conclude that the "increasing delay of first marriage and the low rate of remarriage among black women seem to be directly tied to the increasing labor force problems of [black] men" (Wilson and Neckerman 1986, 256). In short, they blame the extremely high proportion of single-mother families among black families in the central cities on the combined effects of structural changes in the economy and racial discrimination. Thus, black men in the central cities[6] have become "economically redundant" to society, to the women they might have married, and to the children they might have supported, had they been employed (cf. Harris 1983).

Wilson's argument linking black male joblessness with increasing rates of black single-mother families in the central cities makes sense. However, he has been criticized for thus implying that what black women need is *men* – employed men. In his work, he does not address the question of why single mothers cannot support themselves without men.

Additional Causes of Poverty in Single-Mother Families

In our society, single mothers are poor because they are women. Being women, they are segregated into "pink collar" occupations and are paid less than men. Being single, they cannot offset this wage disadvantage by combining their income with that of a man. Being single mothers, they have sole responsibility for both the support and care of their children. In our society, unlike most other industrialized nations, single mothers must fulfill both of these responsibilities without the assistance of either the fathers of their children or the state. These disadvantages are crippling to single mothers, and, as a result, they have by far the highest rates of poverty of any demographic group.

Sex Discrimination

Women are paid less than men. Through most of the post-war period, women's wages have been fixed at roughly 60 percent of men's wages. Slowly, during the Reagan recovery, they have risen to about 65 percent of men's wages (Smith and Ward 1989, 10). In the past, economists theorized that this wage gap was due to women's lesser human capital, assuming that wage differences could be attributed to childbearing and childrearing responsibilities, which resulted in women having less education and work experience. However, as with minority men, a comparison of the median income of full-time, year-round working women with those of white men shows a wage gap – in this case of between 30 percent and 40 percent. As shown in Table 6.1, white women with one to three years of high school earned 61 percent of the wages of white men with the same education; with four years of high school, 64 percent; with one to three years of college, 67 percent; with a college degree, 67 percent of white men's wages; and with five or more years of college, 71 percent. The additional wage discount for black women ranged from 4 percent to 8 percent. Thus, black women with five or more years of college (again, these are the doctors and lawyers and college professors) earned only 63 percent of the income earned by white men with comparable education (U.S. Bureau of the Census 1989a, 140, 144).

In an extensive analysis of longitudinal (PSID) data that included differences in education, on-the-job training, work experience, career interruptions, absenteeism, and quit rates, among other things, Corcoran, Duncan, and Hill (1984) found that human capital differences accounted for only one-third of the wage gap between white women and white men and only about one-quarter of the wage gap between black women and white men. This yields an estimate of the wage discount for white women of about 23 percent, and a wage discount for black women of about 31 percent. Such a wage discount is a significant factor in the poverty experienced by single-mother families.

The evidence that women compete in a separate, occupationally segregated labor market is likewise beyond dispute. Women are concentrated in low-paying occupations like secretary, clerk, bank teller, teacher and social worker, and are underrepresented in higher-paying occupations like truck driver, plumber, accountant, and engineer. In a study of 373 U.S. firms in 1984, Bielby and Barron (cited in Bergmann 1989, 45) found that "in 60 percent of them men and women were perfectly segregated by job title – there was not a single job type in these establishments to which the employer assigned workers of both sexes. Most of the remaining establishments had substantial segregation" (Bergmann 1989, 45). Nationally, Holden and Hansen (1987, 224-5), in a typical analysis, found that in 1981 fully 63.4 percent of "women in the labor force would have to switch occupations in order to be distributed like male workers." The index of segregation for full-time women workers was 62 percent, while for part-time women workers, it was 68.7 percent.

Studies of comparable worth show that when "men's" occupations are compared to "women's" occupations with equivalent requirements of education and skill, the pink collar occupations pay significantly less (Blau and Ferber 1986). Mellor (1982), for example, found that for each increase of 10 percent in the proportion of women in an occupation median weekly wages fell by $13 (Abrahamson and Sigelman 1987). In addition, even in occupations where women are the majority, when men are employed in the same job title, the men are paid more on average. Bergmann (1989), using data on median weekly earnings for women and men in narrowly defined occupations from the U.S. Bureau of Labor Statistics, gives some illustrative examples. She found that male secretaries earned $365[7] per week, while women earned $278; male bookkeepers earned $326 per week, while women earned $263; male hotel clerks earned $279 a week, while women hotel clerks earned $191 (Bergmann 1989, 47). In short, women experience significant sex discrimination in wages and in their choice of occupations.

In addition, they are subject to the "last hired, first fired" syndrome, just as are minority men. As can be seen in Figures 6.1 and 6.2, the unemployment rate and the discouraged-worker rate for women rise sharply during times of recession, just as the rates for men do. However, women are always at a disadvantage compared to men. In good years, as shown in Figure 6.1, when the men's unemployment rate is down, the women's rate is typically a full point and a half higher. During recessions, the gap narrows, as both men and women experience sharp rises in unemployment, but the women's unemployment rate has remained consistently above the rate for men during the entire postwar period, with the exception of 1982.

Statistics on discouraged workers have only been collected since 1970, but, as shown in Figure 6.2, the differential in male and female discouraged-worker rates is even sharper. Even during a recession, women's rates are twice as high as those for men. During good years, women are three times as likely as men to report that they have given up looking for work because they have been unable to find any. It is also worth noting that women are three times as likely to work part-time as are men. Taken together, these trends support the theory that women constitute a reserve labor force, hired only after the supply of employable men[8] (especially white men) has been exhausted. And, were it possible to compute an additional women's unemployment cost to be added to the women's wage gap, it would likely be substantial, just as it is for black men.

Child Care and Child Support

Many single mothers are unable to work, because they do not have access to child care. Unlike many other western industrialized countries, the United States does not provide or assist with child care so that mothers of young children may work (Kamerman 1986). Most of the child care provided to working mothers in the United States is provided by relatives or privately and is paid for by the mother herself. When relatives are not available, or when wages are so low that a single mother cannot afford child care, she cannot enter the labor force.

In the United States, a single mother is left with two options for support: assistance from the children's father, or Aid to Families with Dependent Children (AFDC). Assistance from the father of her children – child support – is an option with a low rate of return. Ellwood (1988, 158) found that, while 82 percent of divorced U.S. mothers had been awarded child support, only 54 percent had received any. Among those that did, the average payment was only $2,538, not enough to pay for the cost of care for a single child so that the mother could work. Only 28 percent of mothers who were separated received any child support, and only 11 percent of never-married mothers received any child support, and for these mothers, the average payment received was less than half of the already inadequate amount received by divorced mothers.

Thus, many single mothers are forced to rely on AFDC. Average AFDC benefit levels have never been high enough to support single mothers and their children at or above the poverty level, so, by definition, mothers who are living on AFDC are living in poverty. However, the real value of AFDC payments has been declining. During the 1970s and early 1980s when inflation was high, AFDC benefits were not pegged to rises in the cost of living as were Social Security payments to the elderly. Consequently, real benefits fell. Ellwood (1988, 59) states that "by 1984, a family of four could get an average of only $6,955 in AFDC plus food stamps – a decrease of over 20 percent since 1972, adjusting for inflation...[a] total just three percent higher than the benefits were in 1960." When the cash value of food stamps is deducted, the real value of AFDC benefits fell between 30 percent and 50 percent (depending on the state) in the ten years between 1976 and 1986 (Ellwood 1988, 40).

In summary, single mothers are poor because they are women, which means that they experience significant sex discrimination in the labor market, because they are not economically connected to men, because they have sole responsibility for both the support and the care of their children, and because safety net benefits (AFDC) are inadequate.

Trends in Family Poverty

Short- and long-term macroeconomic conditions, the effects of sex discrimination and racial discrimination in the labor market, and the inadequacy of safety net programs combine with demographic changes to influence trends in family poverty since World War II. From 1948 to 1973, the economy grew rapidly. Median family income grew at an average annual rate of more than 6 percent (Danziger and Gottschalk 1986), from $15,448 (in 1987 dollars) to $33,319 for married-couple families, and from $9,745 to $14,826 for single-mother families (U.S. Bureau of the Census, Current Population Reports). Each year the average family could count on doing better than last year, since real income was rising faster than the cost of living. During the 1960s there was even a decline in family inequality (Danziger and Gottschalk 1986).

The abrupt four-fold increase in the price of oil in November, 1973, brought the post-war boom to a close. Between 1973 and 1979, inflation rose rapidly, and the economy stagnated. Median family incomes stayed about the same, according to Danziger and Gottschalk (1986), primarily because, in two-parent families, wives went to work in an attempt to maintain family income. Then, in 1979, oil prices rose rapidly again. The economy overheated and the Federal Reserve Board tightened the credit supply, sending the economy into a deep recession. Median family incomes declined: for married couples the 1979 peak of $33,553 fell to $30,636 in 1982; for single mothers, the 1979 peak of $15,470 fell to $13,501 in 1983. Since then, during the six-year Reagan expansion, median family incomes have risen slowly. By 1986, the median income for married-couple families had recovered its 1979 level, and in 1987 it rose to $34,700. Although the median income of single-mother families has risen since 1983, it still has not recovered its 1979 level, reaching only $14,620 by 1987.

Three demographic trends not yet discussed combined with these macroeconomic trends to influence median family incomes since World War II. The first is the 20th-century trend towards increased labor force participation for women. The percentage of women employed for pay outside the home has been rising since at least 1920. Shown in Figure 6.3, the percentage of women employed for pay has risen steadily from 31.3 percent in 1948 to a current high of 53.4 percent in 1988. Levy (1988) has shown that this rise in labor force participation has been accompanied by a gradual rise in women's earnings.

On the other hand, also shown in Figure 6.3, the percentage of men employed has fallen from a high of 84 percent in 1950 to its current rate of 72 percent. Levy (1988) suggests that this is partially an effect of the loss of manufacturing jobs to deindustrialization and shows that the modest rise in women's wages has been offset by a corresponding fall in men's wages due to a shift in the employment mix from "good" jobs (primary sector, better paying) to "bad" jobs (secondary sector, low paying), especially for younger, less-educated men.

FIGURE 6.3

**Percentage of Women and Men Employed, 1948–1988
(civilian noninstitutionalized members of labor
force over 16)**

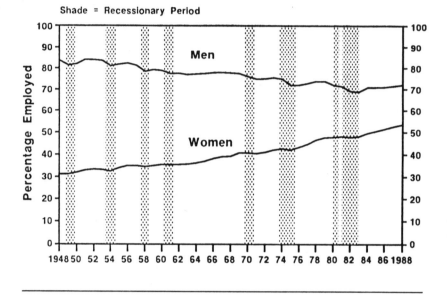

Shade = Recessionary Period

Source: U.S. Department of Labor, Bureau of Labor Statistics, Current Population Survey, various years.

The third important demographic trend is the dramatic rise in single-mother families. The proportion of all families with children under eighteen that are single-mother families has tripled, from 6.3 percent in 1950 to 19.7 percent in 1987, and there is as yet no sign that the increase is over. Given the extremely high rates of poverty in single-mother families already detailed, this change in household composition is an important factor in changes in family poverty rates.

The combined effect of macroeconomic change and demographic trends is shown in Figure 6.4. The percentage of families with children under eighteen living in poverty mirrors changes in median family income for all families. From a high of 20.3 percent in 1959, the family poverty rate fell rapidly, reaching 10.8 percent in 1969, a period when the economy was growing and antipoverty programs were in full sway. During the 1970s, the family poverty rate remained nearly level, rising only to 12.6 percent by 1979. However, with the oil-shock recessions of 1980 and 1981-1982, it rose dramatically, to 17.9 percent. Since then it has fallen only to 16.2 percent, the level of the early 1960s.

FIGURE 6.4

Percentage of Families with Children under 18 Living in Poverty, 1959-1987.

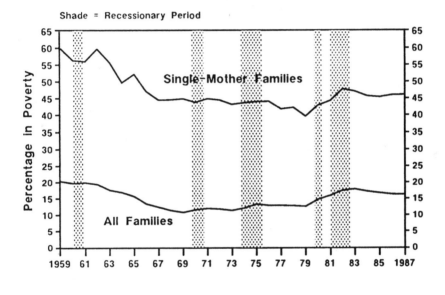

Source: U.S. Bureau of the Census, Current Population Reports, Series P-60, Nos. 160, 161.3

By 1987 the unemployment rate had fallen into the 5 percent range and the economy was at nearly full capacity (Litan 1988). Thus, the lack of response in the poverty rate for all families suggests that many families have been unable to participate in the Reagan recovery. The upper line in Figure 6.4, the percentage of single-mother families living in poverty, shows clearly that single mothers have not benefitted from the current economic expansion. Their poverty rate fell consistently from 1959 through 1979, to a record low of 39.6 percent. However, with the 1980's recessions, it rose to 47.8 percent and remains at 46.1 percent, significantly higher than in 1979.

Even these high poverty rates for single mothers mask the truly desperate plight of black single mothers. Their poverty rates have always been 20 percent to 25 percent higher than those of white single mothers. Having peaked at 63.7 percent in 1983, higher than at any time since their poverty statistics have been collected, their 1987 poverty rate was 59.5 percent, approximately the same as in 1971 (60.0 percent) when the Census Bureau switched from collecting white-nonwhite statistics to white-black statistics. Clearly, any improvement in the economy since 1982 has bypassed black single-mother families.

Policy Implications for U.S. Families

In summary, most homeless children and youth are homeless with their parents. Families are homeless because they are poor – too poor to be able to pay the market rate for housing – in the context of a shortage of affordable housing. The model presented in this discussion suggests that parents are poor because they are unable to work (sick, disabled, or without child care), because they are unable to find work (involuntarily unemployed, discouraged worker), or because they are unable to find work that pays more than a poverty wage (working poor). Thus, work is the key to ending family poverty. Providing work that pays more than a poverty wage to at least one adult in every family should be the primary goal of those who want to end child poverty in the United States. A secondary goal should be providing income support to those who are unable to work.

The availability of work is, in turn, largely determined by macroeconomic factors. Thus, the welfare of American families is inextricably bound to the health of our economy. The total number of jobs, the education and skill profiles of those jobs, and the wages they pay are primarily determined by the state of the U.S. economy. Over time, strong, sustained growth in the U.S. gross national product (GNP) yields increases in real median family income and decreases in family poverty. On the other hand, recessions or depressions (slowing of GNP growth or deflation of the GNP) spell trouble for U.S. families.

Thus, those who are concerned about U.S. families need to be concerned with social policy on a broad scale; U.S. industrial policy and economic policy are as important to the welfare of U.S. families as are more traditional areas of family policy concern. While economists differ on the details of their scenarios of the future, they seem to agree that there is reason to be concerned about a number of economic problems in the 1990s: among these, the declining position of the U.S. economy relative to the economies of the European Economic Community (EEC) (especially Germany) and Japan and the size of the federal deficit seem particularly important.

The Global Economy

During the postwar boom, the United States was the major supplier of industrial goods to the world. Europe and Japan were devastated by World War II, leaving the United States as the only major country with intact industrial capacity (Levy 1987). Now, the United States has fallen behind. In the global economy, U.S. firms must compete directly with the lower production costs of other countries. U.S. plants and equipment are old, and wages are high in comparison with production costs in Europe and Asia. As a result, U.S. wages are falling and the U.S. standard of living is stagnant in comparison to rising wages and standards of living in Europe and Asia. The policy cure is the development of a U.S. industrial strategy, including major investment in new plants and equipment, major investment in improving the quality of the U.S. labor force (education and training), and major investment in U.S. research and development (Johnston and Packer 1987; Thurow 1985). As they improve the economy, these policies will provide jobs over the long run, and that will improve the economic welfare of U.S. families.

The Federal Deficit

This type of development strategy requires capital. The United States has a low national savings rate to start with, compared with that of the EEC and Japan, but what capital there is now goes mostly to cover federal debt and consumer debt, rather than for investment (Johnston and Packer 1987). U.S. firms that want to invest in new plants and equipment or research and development must compete for capital with the federal deficit. The capital they can acquire is expensive; U.S. interest rates are higher than those in Europe and Japan (Thurow 1985). Thus, it is in the best interest of the U.S. economy and therefore of U.S. families to improve the national savings rate and to reduce the real federal deficit (over and above such fiscal sleights of hand as borrowing from Social Security trust funds).

The enormous size of the federal deficit and the shaky capitalization levels of U.S. corporations also leave the economy particularly vulnerable to new recessions. Another oil shock, or a "credit shock" – the sudden refusal of foreign creditors to lend the United States any more money to cover the federal deficit – will throw the country into a deep recession (Harrison and Bluestone 1988). Such a recession will cause family poverty to increase rapidly. Minority and single-mother families will be hardest hit. Although there is little that can be done to control exogenous shocks, their possibility emphasizes the importance of reducing deficit spending and increasing national savings.

What are the chances of avoiding a recession during the 1990s? Litan (1988) is "cautiously optimistic" that *if* the Bush administration takes realistic steps to trim the federal deficit by cutting spending and raising taxes, *and* is able to keep inflation low without tightening monetary policy, a recession may be avoided. However, he estimates that, because of current problems with the U.S. economy, even then we will be able to support only a very modest 0.7 percent to 1.5 percent annual growth rate, well below the growth rate of the last six years and not even in the same ballpark with the 6 percent annual growth rate during the 1948-1973 postwar boom. The consequences, for families, are that income inequality will continue to grow and poverty is likely to remain at its present levels, unless, of course, another recession occurs, at which point poverty levels will again rise sharply.

However, the model of the causes of family poverty presented in this chapter suggests that macroeconomic factors are not the only factors that influence the welfare of American families. Although macroeconomic factors determine the number and type of jobs available, demographic factors, interacting with sexism and racism, determine who gets the available jobs and how much they are paid. Thus, sexism and racism significantly affect the economic stratification of families – both directly, through discrimination, and indirectly, through human capital factors.

In a labor market characterized by an oversupply of workers, such as has existed in the U.S. for some 25 years, women and minorities are more likely to be unemployed or discouraged workers, and are paid less when they do find work. Thus, minority families and single-mother families are significantly more likely to be poor than white families and two-parent families.

However, the postwar baby boom of excess workers is rapidly giving way to the "baby-bust" shortage of entry-level workers expected in the 1990s. A supply-driven shortage of entry-level workers is an entirely new phenomenon for the U.S. economy in this century. The new labor shortage is already driving some firms in hi-tech suburbia to offer higher wages, education and training, and transportation to unemployed minority workers in the central cities in order to insure an adequate labor supply. If these corporate efforts catch on, they might reduce unemployment among inner-city men and decrease the number of impoverished single-mother families.

The new labor shortage will also allow policy makers to change the basic assumptions undergirding our safety net programs, from income support to employment and training. Although income support was sensible when there were not enough jobs to go around, now, with the prospect of jobs going unfilled, employment and training programs make more sense. Thus, unemployment insurance should be expanded to cover all who need it; its emphasis, however, should be changed to retraining and job placement, perhaps with relocation benefits to move job seekers to cities where they have found work (cf. President's Commission for a National Agenda for the Eighties 1981), while recipients receive temporary income support.

In addition, given the new labor market conditions, the concept of AFDC as a long-term, income-support program might well be abolished. A uniform, mandatory, payroll-deduction, child-support program, with government providing benefits up to a standard level when absent parents' wages are inadequate (similar to the Wisconsin program), should be substituted for AFDC (Ellwood 1988). In addition, for able-bodied parents who are ineligible for unemployment insurance, AFDC could become a full-fledged employment and training program, with income support, child care and health benefits for trainees, and transitional assistance for parents entering the labor force. Changes in both these directions will greatly benefit single-mother families, and there is movement toward these goals in the Moynihan Welfare Reform Act.

However, despite the labor shortage, some parents will still be too ill or disabled to work. Society has a moral obligation to provide income support, short-term or long-term, for those who cannot work – an obligation that is not now fulfilled. Just as long-term income support is now provided for the elderly, adequate long-term support must be provided for the disabled. In addition, a new short-term, income-support program should be developed for the many who are ill or unable to work for shorter periods but who are not covered by workmen's compensation. Such programs would greatly benefit eligible families.

In conclusion, however, it is essential to remember that all families living under the poverty line will be at risk of becoming homeless as long as there is a shortage of affordable low-income housing. Homelessness is the result of the low-income housing ratio – the balance between the number of households living in poverty and the amount of low-income housing available. When there are many more households living under the poverty line (the numerator of the ratio) than there are housing units that they can afford (the denominator of the ratio), homelessness is the *inevitable* result.

Thus, family homelessness has two root causes – poverty and a shortage of affordable housing. Like all ratios, the low-income housing ratio changes if either the numerator (poor households) or the denominator (affordable housing units) changes. If changes in economic policy and economic conditions or in social policy and social conditions push the family poverty rate down, all other things (the number of affordable housing units) being equal, the number of homeless families should go down. On the other hand, if the number of affordable housing units goes down, the number of homeless families will increase, even if the poverty rate stays the same. The only way the total number of families at risk of homelessness will decrease is if the total number of poor households decreases *faster* than the continuing decline in the number of affordable housing units. Thus, it is essential to remember that policy makers must work on *both* of the root causes of homelessness – poverty and a shortage of affordable housing – in order to decrease child and youth homelessness.

Notes

1. The Census Bureau defines "family" as "a group of two or more persons related by birth, marriage, or adoption who reside together" (U.S. Bureau of the Census 1988b, 156). This definition is used throughout, with the exception that only families with children under eighteen are included.

2. Since 82 percent of families with children under eighteen are white, statistics for all families are weighted toward the characteristics of white families.

3. "Householder" is the nonsexist replacement for the term "head of household." According to the Census Bureau, in a married-couple family, the householder is the person in whose name the dwelling is owned or rented, unless it is owned jointly, in which case either the husband or the wife may be listed as the householder. In practice, most families are still traditional enough to list the male spouse as the householder (U.S. Bureau of the Census 1989b, 158).

4. Data on the reasons for unemployment of married-couple householders with children under eighteen are not available for 1987. These statistics are for "all other family householders" with children under eighteen (the category left after "female family householders, no husband present" had been excluded) (U.S. Bureau of the Census 1989b, 97).

5. When a full reference is not provided for statistical data, they were provided directly by the Bureau of Labor Statistics or the Bureau of the Census.

6. Single-mother families now make up the majority – 59.9 percent – of all black families with children under eighteen in the central cities of Metropolitan Statistical Areas of 3 million or more (U.S. Bureau of the Census 1988a:76).

7. Wage estimates included have a standard error of estimate less than 10 percent.

8. Since 1970 the percentage of women in the labor force working part-time has remained steady, at just under 25 percent, with only a small rise during recessions. The part-time rate for men hovered in the eight percent range during the 1970s and has risen steadily since 1979 to a current high of 9.6 percent.

References

Abrahamson, M., and L. Sigelman. 1987. "Occupational Sex Segregation in Metropolitan Areas." *American Sociological Review* 52: 588-97.

Bergmann, B. R. 1989. "Does the Market for Women's Labor Need Fixing?" *Journal of Economic Perspectives* 3, no. 1: 43-60.

Blank, R. M., and A. S. Blinder. 1986. "Macroeconomics, Income Distribution, and Poverty." In *Fighting Poverty: What Works and What Doesn't,* eds. S. H. Danziger and D. H. Weinberg, 180-208. Cambridge: Harvard University Press.

Blau, F. D., and M. A. Ferber. 1986. *The Economics of Women, Men and Work.* Englewood Cliffs, NJ: Prentice-Hall.

Bluestone, B., and B. Harrison. 1982. *The Deindustrialization of America.* New York: Basic Books.

Children's Defense Fund. 1989. *A Vision for America's Future: An Agenda for the 1990s: A Children's Defense Budget.* Washington, DC: By the author.

Corcoran, M., G. J. Duncan, and M. S. Hill. 1984. "The Economic Fortunes of Women and Children: Lessons from the Panel Study of Income Dynamics." *Signs* 10, no. 2: 232-48.

Culp, J., and B. H. Dunson. 1986. "Brothers of a Different Color: A Preliminary Look at Employer Treatment of White and Black Youth." In *The Black Youth Employment Crisis,* R. B. Freeman and H. J. Holzer, 233-59. Chicago: University of Chicago Press.

Danziger, S., and P. Gottschalk. 1986. "How Have Families with Children Been Faring?" Madison, WI: Institute for Research on Poverty Discussion Paper No. 801-886.

Doeringer, P. B., and M. J. Piore. 1971. *Internal Labor Markets and Manpower Analysis.* Lexington, MA: D.C. Heath.

Eckstein, O., and A. Sinai. 1986. "The Mechanisms of the Business Cycle in the Postwar Era." In *The American Business Cycle: Continuity and Change,* ed. R. J. Gordon. Chicago: University of Chicago Press.

Ellwood, D. T. 1986. "The Spatial Mismatch Hypothesis: Are There Teenage Jobs Missing in the Ghetto?" In *The Black Youth Employment Crisis,* eds. R. B. Freeman and H. J. Holzer, 147-90. Chicago: University of Chicago Press.

Ellwood, D. T. 1988. *Poor Support: Poverty in the American Family.* New York: Basic Books.

Ellwood, D. T., and L. H. Summers. 1986. "Poverty in America: Is Welfare the Answer or the Problem?" In *Fighting Poverty: What Works and What Doesn't,* eds. S. H. Danziger and D. H. Weinberg, 78-105. Cambridge: Harvard University Press.

Freeman, R. B., and H. J. Holzer. 1986. *The Black Youth Employment Crisis.* Chicago: University of Chicago Press.

Gault, N., and R. Brinner. 1987, May. "Should the Minimum Wage Be Raised?" *The Review of the U.S. Economy,* p. 14-23

Granovetter, M., and C. Tilly. 1988. "Inequality and Labor Processes." In *Handbook of Sociology,* ed. N. Smelser, 175-221. Newbury Park, CA: Sage.

Harris, C. C. 1983. "Social Transitions and the Deconstruction of the Family: Reflections of Research into the Domestic Circumstances of the Victims of Economic Change." *The Tocqueville Review 5,* no. 2: 365-81.

Harris, C. S. 1984, Sept. "The Magnitude of Job Loss from Plant Closings and the Generation of Replacement Jobs: Some Recent Evidence." *Annals of the American Academy of Political and Social Science,* 475.

Harrison, B., and B. Bluestone. 1988. *The Great U-Turn: Corporate Restructuring and the Polarizing of America.* New York: Basic Books.

Hirschman, C. 1988. "Minorities in the Labor Market: Cyclical Patterns and Secular Trends in Joblessness." In *Divided Opportunities: Minorities, Poverty, and Social Policy,* eds. G. Sandefur and M. Tienda, 63-85. New York: Plenum.

Holden, K. C., and W. L. Hansen. 1987. "Part-Time Work, Full-Time Work, and Occupational Segregation." In *Gender in the Workplace,* eds. C. Brown and J. A. Pechman, 217-46. Washington, D.C.: The Brookings Institution.

Holzer, H. J. 1986. "Black Youth Nonemployment: Duration and Job Search." In *The Black Youth Employment Crisis,* eds. R. B. Freeman and H. J. Holzer, 23-70 . Chicago: University of Chicago Press.

Johnston, W. B., and A. H. Packer. 1987. *Workforce 2000.* Indianapolis: Hudson Institute.

Kamerman, S. 1986. "Women, Children and Poverty: The Policies and Female-Headed Families in Industrialized Countries." In *Women and Poverty,* eds. B. C. Gelpi, N. C. M. Hartsock, C. C. Novak and M. H. Strober, 41-63. Chicago: University of Chicago Press.

Kasarda, J. D. 1987. "Caught in the Web of Change." In *Social Problems: A Critical Thinking Approach,* eds. P. J. Baker and L. E. Anderson, 311-20. Belmont, CA: Wadsworth.

Kasarda, J. D. 1988. "Jobs, Migration, and Emerging Urban Mismatches." In *Urban Change and Poverty,* eds. M. G. H. McGeary and L. E. Lynn, Jr., 148-98. Washington, D.C.: National Academy Press.

Levy, F. 1987. *Dollars and Dreams: The Changing American Income Distribution.* New York: Russell Sage Foundation.

Levy, F. 1988. "Incomes, Families, and Living Standards." In *American Living Standards: Threats and Challenges,* eds. R. E. Litan, R. Z.

Lawrence and C. L. Schultze, 108-53. Washington, D.C.: The Brookings Institution.

Litan, R. E. 1988. "The Risks of Recession." In *American Living Standards: Threats and Challenges,* eds. R. E. Litan, R. Z. Lawrence, and C. L. Schultze, 66-107. Washington, D.C.: The Brookings Institution.

Lloyd, C. B., and B. T. Niemi. 1979. *The Economics of Sex Differentials.* New York: Columbia University Press.

McChesney, K. Y. In press. "Family Homelessness: A Systemic Problem." *Journal of Social Issues.*

McChesney, K. Y. 1987. "Women Without: Homeless Mothers and Their Children." Dissertation: University of Southern California, Los Angeles.

Mellor, E. F. 1982. "Investigating the Differences in Weekly Earnings of Women and Men." *Monthly Labor Review* 107: 17-28.

Moen, P. 1983. "Unemployment, Public Policy, and Families: Forecasts for the 1980s." *Journal of Marriage and the Family* 45, no. 4: 751-60.

Reich, M. 1984. "Segmented Labor: Time Series Hypothesis and Evidence." *Cambridge Journal of Economics* 8: 63-81.

Shapiro, D. 1984. "Wage Differentials Among Black, Hispanic and White Young Men." *Industrial and Labor Relations Review* 37: 570-81.

Singell, L. D. 1984. "Youth Employment: What Does the 1980 Census Say About its Causes and Cures?" *Journal of Urban Affairs* 6, no. 1: 5-16.

Smith, J. P., and M. Ward. 1989. "Women in the Labor Market and in the Family." *Journal of Economic Perspectives.* 3, no. 1: 9-23.

Thurow, L. C. 1985. *The Zero Sum Solution: An Economic and Political Agenda for the 80's.* New York: Simon and Schuster.

U.S. Bureau of the Census. 1988a. *Household and Family Characteristics: March 1987.* Current Population Reports, Series P-20, no. 424. Washington, DC: Government Printing Office.

U.S. Bureau of the Census. 1988b. *Poverty in the United States: 1986.* Current Population Reports, Series P-60, no. 160. Washington, DC: Government Printing Office.

U.S. Bureau of the Census. 1989a. *Money Income of Households, Families, and Persons in the United States: 1987.* Current Population Reports, Series P-60, no. 162. Washington, DC: Government Printing Office.

U.S. Bureau of the Census. 1989b. *Poverty in the United States: 1987.* Current Population Reports, Series P-60, no. 163. Washington, DC: Government Printing Office.

Wilson, W. J. 1987. *The Truly Disadvantaged: The Inner City, The Underclass, and Public Policy.* Chicago: University of Chicago Press.

Wilson, W. J., and K. M. Neckerman. 1986. "Poverty and Family Structure: The Widening Gap Between Evidence and Public Policy Issues." In *Fighting Poverty: What Works and What Doesn't,* eds. S.H. Danziger and D.H. Weinberg, 232-59. Cambridge: Harvard University Press.

7

What Is Wrong with the Housing Market

Chester Hartman and Barry Zigas

The United States housing system increasingly is failing to meet the most basic needs of its people. More and more Americans are beginning to recognize and share this perception, based on news reports, statistics on housing defects and needs, and day-to-day observations of the most extreme manifestation of our nation's housing crisis – outright homelessness.

Traditionally, Americans have expected that housing conditions in the United States would constantly improve, and, indeed, until the 1970s, this was the case. When President Roosevelt, during the Depression, spoke of "one-third of a nation ill-housed," he was referring to obscene city slums and rural shacks without running water or indoor plumbing and to levels of overcrowding associated with disease and psychosocial stress. Over the following three decades, the nation – through the workings of the economy, the housing market, and government programs – succeeded in making remarkable progress in these areas. However, it would be a serious mistake to overlook the extent to which unacceptable slum conditions and overcrowding still exist in our society.

The most dramatic evidence of housing progress, although it was not without an accompanying array of problems, was the boom in suburban single-family homeownership that followed World War II, as millions of American families found decent, new, spacious, cheap housing with lots of open space.

But was this picture of steady progress fair or complete? First, it should be recognized that not all groups participated in this roseate

© *1990 Chester Hartman*

scenario. Most obviously, very large numbers of the poor, especially racial minorities, in both urban and rural areas, continued to occupy physically substandard and overcrowded quarters. Economic and social-political factors kept them from sharing in the suburban fulfillment of the "American dream" of homeownership. The urban renewal and federal highway programs of the 1950s and 1960s ravaged their communities, displacing millions of persons, often to other substandard and, virtually always, more expensive housing, while destroying important neighborhood ties and supports. In the process the nation's low-rent housing stock was reduced drastically.

At the same time, broader changes in the economy and society were leading to a growing gap between the costs of housing and the amount which vast numbers of American households could afford to pay for their housing. As a result, the nation's housing problem now is housing affordability rather than housing quality. While outright homelessness is the most extreme and palpable manifestation of this structural gap, it is but one of the many forms the problem has taken. As shown by Hopper and Hamberg (1986), Leonard, Dolbeare, and Lazere (1989), and Dolbeare (1989), from whose work much of the following discussion is taken, the housing system and the economic system have produced homelessness.

The increase in homelessness has been fueled by the rising level of both reported and unreported unemployment, underemployment, and low-wage employment among low-income and minority households, and by the inadequacy of government income-support programs. In short, homelessness has been fueled by poverty. In 1988, 31.9 million Americans were living below the poverty line, an increase of 22 percent over the 1979 figure of 26.1 million. Unemployment is endemic among certain groups, such as young black males, and it generally is recognized that official data severely underestimate the real level of joblessness. Such data always understate, by a factor of two or three, the number of persons who have been involuntarily unemployed at some time during the year. Since rent and mortgage payments must be remitted regularly and on time, temporary unemployment among persons with little or no savings can easily lead to eviction. The minimum wage remained unchanged from 1981 through mid-1990, and the changing structure of the United States economy has meant that most new private-sector jobs are in the lower-wage service and retail sectors.

To the extent that regional shifts in employment availability induce migration, housing problems may be exacerbated, since housing stock cannot migrate along with residents.

Not only are more people living in poverty in America, but the poor are becoming poorer. The average income of families living in poverty has been declining. In 1988 the median income of families under the poverty line was $4,300 under the somewhat arbitrary poverty line figure, $700 lower in constant dollars than the comparable figure for 1979. In addition, the poverty line is far below the level of income needed to obtain decent housing. The poverty line is set at three times a recommended bare-subsistence expenditure level for food, but such a calculation totally ignores the reality of housing costs.

It is clear that the nation's income distribution is growing more polarized, augmented by changes in the tax code during the Reagan administration. Congressional Budget Office (CBO) data show that after-tax income for the top 5 percent of households by income class increased by 37 percent from 1977 to 1988, while the bottom 10 percent suffered a 10.5 percent decrease and were the only group to suffer a decrease. The top 20 percent of households now receive 52 percent of all personal income in the United States, while the bottom 20 percent receive 3 percent. Since housing costs require such a large proportion of the income of lower-income households, it is inevitable that income polarization affects how the nation is housed.

Changes in the structure of the nation's households have exacerbated these trends. Because more households are headed by a single female, for example, housing is increasingly unaffordable, given the large difference between women's and men's wages and the absence of good, inexpensive child care. In 1985, nearly half of all single-parent (mostly female-headed, largely black) households with children were living under the poverty line.

Although various government programs provide some help to some households in poverty, this aid is woefully inadequate. In 1987, 39 percent of all households living in poverty received no welfare, food stamps, Medicaid, school lunches, or public housing. (See Chapter 8 for a more detailed discussion of who does and who does not benefit from government housing programs.) Benefit levels under virtually all of these programs – Aid to Families with Dependent Children (AFDC), general assistance, disability benefits, unemployment insurance, food programs – have failed to keep up with need. In many cases, these programs were curtailed during the Reagan years, and, in all too many instances, they are made inaccessible by difficult bureaucratic hurdles.

While this brief review describes the social and economic forces leading to increased homelessness and housing-affordability problems, housing market forces are also major contributors to the problem. One, obviously, is the cutback in government housing programs, particularly those that produce housing directly for the poor through construction or rehabilitation, rather than those which rely on "gap subsidies" to house the poor in existing private-sector units (see Chapter 8).

Private housing market forces have had their own dynamic in the 1970s and 1980s, partly in response to the economic and social forces described above. The gentrification movement that began in the 1970s – a back-to-the-city movement fueled by a desire for the social and cultural amenities and the convenience of centrally located neighborhoods – initiated a more subtle but, to the poor, no less damaging form of urban renewal than the "federal bulldozer" of the 1950s and 1960s. Hundreds of thousands of persons have been uprooted by the buying, selling, speculating, and upgrading of central city housing. These forces in some ways have been more pernicious than urban renewal and highway construction programs, which provided at least some relocation and compensation services. In gentrification, whole neighborhoods, in piecemeal fashion, have been converted from lower- to higher-income occupancy. Beyond the individual and social costs of this transformation, dramatic numbers of units affordable by lower-income households have been lost. The condo conversion craze of the late 1970s and early 1980s, somewhat abated now but by no means extinct, has been one specific form of gentrification in which rental units were sold, renovated, and filtered up the economic ladder.

City governments have tended to support the gentrification process because it increases property tax revenues, the main support of local government, and reduces service needs by substituting more affluent, childless households for lower-income families.

A particularly harmful aspect of the gentrification process has been the loss of single-room-occupancy hotels (SROs) due to demolition or conversion to more lucrative uses. Few cities have intervened in this process, and those only belatedly, after most of the stock was lost. In the 1970s and early 1980s, well over 1 million such units disappeared, nearly half of the nation's total stock. These centrally located, inexpensive accommodations often provide a supportive microcommunity and some services for their residents. They are of special importance to persons with mental problems, a great many of whom have been returned to their communities as part of the deinstitutionalization movement of the early 1970s, without provision of adequate services or residential resources. Needless to say, the private sector is producing no new SROs unless the government heavily subsidizes them.

A contrary set of market phenomena – undermaintenance and abandonment – is also evident in the private housing market. Many landlords have neglected to provide adequate services and repairs and to pay their property taxes; eventually they have often walked away from their buildings. Others have "sold out to the insurance company," a euphemism for arson. In part, this neglect has been a response to the tenants' inability to pay rent. Sometimes, however, undermaintenance has been the first step in a conscious gentrification strategy to decant occupants from buildings and neighborhoods "with potential" in order to smooth the "revitalization" process. The refusal of insurance companies and lending institutions to grant insurance and mortgages in areas deemed poor financial risks has provided another support for such market forces. The unwillingness of municipal officials to use code-enforcement powers and tax-delinquency takeovers to halt these processes and to maintain the supply of affordable housing also has played an important role.

The U.S. housing industry has been reasonably productive over the past four decades. Production levels were particularly high in the 1970s. More than 20 million new units (mobile homes included) were constructed, and the 2.1 million-unit average annual rate exceeded by a considerable amount the 1.7 million average annual increase in new households, allowing for replacement of obsolete units and shifts in living patterns and household types. The 1980s, however, which began with extremely high interest rates, saw a dramatically lowered production level in the United States. Annual housing starts in the early part of the decade averaged around 1.2 million units and in more recent years generally have been only slightly higher, amounting to 1.4 million units each in 1988 and 1989. The industry is highly vulnerable to supply, the cost of credit, and a host of other macroeconomic factors.

Year-to-year fluctuations in production levels are quite wide, often in the 300,000- to 400,000-unit range. In 1983, 645,000 fewer units were started than in 1982.

The 1968 Housing Act marked the only attempt to set a national goal: 26 million units over the following ten years. In fact, housing production fell short by 8 million units, reflecting the fact that the nation has no real planning or resource-allocation system to guarantee that goals can be turned into reality. The government now has stopped setting housing-production goals and annually reviewing progress toward them, as it did for the ten years following passage of the 1968 Housing Act; such reports produced frustration and embarrassment for both Congress and the administration.

The private housing-production system generally has operated well to meet the needs of middle- and upper-income households – owners and renters alike. Only recently have younger households, even those with decent incomes, had such difficulty getting on the ownership ladder. Their inability to make down payments and monthly mortgage payments is responsible in large part for the dip in the nation's overall homeownership rate which has occurred in the last few years, reversing an upward trend dating back to World War II.

The system has not been able, however, to keep costs and rent levels low enough to meet the needs of lower-income households. The 1968 Housing Act production goal stipulated that 6 million of the 26 million units in the ten-year goal were to be subsidized for lower-income households, but the shortfall was proportionally far greater for this subset than for the larger goal. In the more than fifty years since passage of the 1937 Housing Act, the nation's first significant subsidized housing effort, a total of only 5.7 million subsidized units has been produced. The percentage of the United States housing stock that is government subsidized is far lower than in virtually any other industrialized nation. The new rental and ownership housing produced by the private market (with small notable exceptions, mainly mobile homes, which serve a limited market and are of questionable quality) simply is beyond the reach of most moderate-income consumers and virtually all low-income consumers.

As for the remaining stock of existing housing, the market reacts predictably and rationally. A shortage exists; therefore, prices rise. Neoclassic economic theory holds this to be a temporary phenomenon.

It predicts that rising prices/rents lead to new production, which in turn lowers prices/rents as supply balances demand. However, the poverty of this economic theory nowhere is more evident than in the current U.S. housing crisis. Suppliers do not rush in to fill the demand for housing for many reasons. Most obviously, very low-income people cannot afford to pay even the basic operating costs of housing in many markets, let alone the owner's costs and profit. In city after city, homeless people sleep on the streets outside dilapidated apartments abandoned by owners who cannot operate them profitably if low-income people are the tenants.

Secondly, suppliers are hindered by restrictive zoning requirements imposed by many localities. In its starkest form, restrictive or exclusionary zoning bans any construction of multifamily homes, or it requires a large lot for each home. These kinds of restrictions make it impossible to build housing that is affordable to lower-income people, even when a builder is willing to do so. Communities justify such zoning on the grounds that it helps to preserve the special character of the community, or that it maintains property values for those who have already made an investment. However, restrictive zoning often serves to exclude minorities, who also have been victims of restrictive deed covenants in the past.

Building codes also can create an obstacle to affordable housing by requiring builders to use expensive, outmoded technologies instead of newer, cheaper ones. In addition, zoning and building codes can be used to block novel and efficient uses of existing housing stock in a community, such as basement apartments or so-called "accessory units" in predominantly single-family neighborhoods.

The use of zoning to prevent development of affordable housing has become so obvious and so onerous that some states have enacted laws giving state government the power to override local ordinances where they are unduly restricting the market. Other jurisdictions have adopted inclusionary zoning ordinances, through which builders are given density bonuses (permission to build more units on a given site than the zoning normally allows) and other incentives in return for producing homes that are affordable to low- and moderate-income people. For many communities, the ability to provide affordable housing has become a major element in efforts to maintain or promote economic growth. Without affordable housing for their workers, businesses increasingly are avoiding or leaving areas with very high housing costs.

The threat to the existing stock of subsidized housing from sale; undermaintenance and abandonment of public housing; expiration of use restrictions on privately owned, subsidized projects; and termination of rental-assistance contracts severely worsens the imbalance.

Taken together, increasing poverty, the failure of safety-net programs, the loss of units available to lower-income households, the inability of the private housing market to provide for increasing numbers of Americans, rapidly rising rent levels, and the increased costs of producing housing create not only outright homelessness for hundreds of thousands and perhaps millions, but also "prehomelessness" for a far greater number of households and severe affordability problems for millions of others.

Detailed data illustrate the severity of the U.S. housing situation. The most recent comprehensive national data come from the 1985 American Housing Survey (AHS), carried out for the Department of Housing and Urban Development (HUD) by the Census Bureau. (The AHS was introduced in 1973 as a necessary supplement to the decennial Housing Census. Originally it was done yearly, with the "A" standing for "Annual." In 1981, as part of the Reagan administration budget and data cutbacks, it became biennial and the "A" became "American." The AHS data are based on a large sample rather than on a complete census enumeration. Data tabulation and publication are extremely slow; the 1985 tapes and printed tables were made available in early 1989.) A recent CBO report offers the most useful presentation of these data (Congressional Budget Office 1988). The study divides housing problems into three categories: (1) excessive costs (subdivided into costs requiring more than 30 percent or more than 50 percent of income); (2) substandard conditions requiring rehabilitation (a standard developed by CBO, defined as housing lacking either complete kitchen or plumbing facilities, or having two or more of eleven specified defects: frequent heating system or plumbing breakdowns, roof leaks, wiring defects, deficiencies in hallways of multifamily buildings, etc.); and (3) crowding (defined as units with more than two persons per bedroom). Data are also broken down by income class: very low income (50 percent or less of area median for a family of four, adjusted for family size); low income (51 percent to 80 percent of area median for a family of four, adjusted for family size); and others. The aggregate data are presented in Table 7.1.

TABLE 7.1

Housing Conditions of All Households, by Income, 1985[a]

| Housing condition[c] | Income[b] | | | |
	Very low income	Low income	Other	All
Thousands of households				
Housing costs exceed:[d]				
30 percent of income	13,900	4,370	4,040	22,300
50 percent of income	8,210	750	320	9,280
Living in housing requiring rehabilitation	2,870	1,250	2,020	6,140
Living in crowded units	1,280	760	930	2,960
Experiencing one or more of these conditions	14,890	5,660	6,520	27,070
Percentage of households in income category				
Housing costs exceed:[d]				
30 percent of income	69	31	9	28
50 percent of income	41	5	1	11
Living in housing requiring rehabilitation	13	9	4	7
Living in crowded units	6	5	2	3
Experiencing one or more of these conditions	74	41	14	33

TABLE 7.1 (Continued)

Source: Congressional Budget Office tabulations of the 1985 American Housing Survey conducted by the Bureau of the Census for the Department of Housing and Urban Development (Congressional Budget Office 1988, 9).

a. Excludes renters who paid no cash rent.
b. The income classification corresponds approximately to the definitions used in federal housing assistance programs, which target aid primarily toward very low-income households. Income categories are defined in the text.
c. Housing conditions are defined in the text.
d. Excludes households for which housing cost-to-income ratios are not computed because their housing costs are not available or because their income is zero or negative. The proportions of households with problems are calculated as a percentage of households for which these ratios are computed.

About 27 million households – one out of three in the United States – experience one or more of these problems in their housing conditions. By far the dominant problem is excessive housing costs: 22.3 million pay 30 percent or more of their income for housing; 9.3 million pay half or more. A staggering 3.6 million renter households pay more than 70 percent of their income for housing. Housing costs have become an increasing burden over recent years, especially for the poor. The proportion of poor renters (those living under the federal poverty line) paying 35 percent or more of their income for housing rose from 72 percent in 1978 to 79 percent in 1985; for poor homeowners (similarly defined), the proportion rose from 55 percent to 65 percent over the corresponding time period.

The second major problem, physically substandard housing, affects 6.1 million households. It should be noted that definitions and standards in this area always have been problematic and have changed over time. Reliability of either self-reporting or enumerator judgments is questionable. Local housing-code standards, where they exist, generally are far higher than national standards, although erratically enforced. An important background report by the National Commission on Urban Problems (the Douglas Commission), understandably long ignored because of its profoundly depressing implications, noted: "It is readily apparent that even the most conscientious user of Census data...would arrive at a total 'substandard' housing figure which grossly underestimated the number of dwelling units having serious housing code violations. To use a total thus arrived at as a figure for substandard housing is grossly inaccurate and misleading, because it flies in the face of extensive consideration given by health experts, building officials, model code drafting organizations, and the local, state, and federal court system to what have become over a period of many years, the socially, politically, and legally accepted minimum standard for housing of human beings in the United States....Even if public and private efforts eliminate all housing which is substandard under most current federal definitions, there will still be millions of dwelling units below code standard" (Sutermeister 1969). Neighborhood and environmental conditions, even more difficult to assess and quantify, are not included in the CBO standard, even though the National Housing Goal, set forth by Congress in the 1949 and 1968 Housing Acts, posits "a decent home and suitable living environment."

Slightly under 3 million households are reported to be living in overcrowded conditions, the third major housing problem. This fact is likely to represent systematic undercounting as well. Overcrowded and doubled-up households understandably are reluctant to report these conditions to a government interviewer for fear of getting into trouble with a landlord, code official, welfare agency, or immigration office.

If anything, the figure that more than 27 million experience one or more of the three major housing problems is a most conservative assessment. Because the number is several years out of date and evidence shows that these problems have been increasing, the current figure may be well into the 30 millions.

The relationship of incomes to housing problems is revealed starkly in Table 7.1: 74 percent of very low-income households experience one or more of the three problems, whereas only 14 percent of those with incomes above 80 percent of the area median do. The dominant problem, excessive cost burden, is strongly income related: 69 percent of very low-income households pay 30 percent or more of their income for housing and 41 percent pay 50 percent or more; for those with incomes over 80 percent of the area median, the corresponding figures are 9 percent and 1 percent.

Race is a variable as well. Forty-two percent of black and Hispanic households pay 30 percent or more of their income for rent, compared with 27 percent of white households; 16 percent to 17 percent of black and Hispanic households pay 60 percent or more, compared with 7.5

percent of white households. This racial disparity is partly a function of incomes, as black and Hispanic incomes are well under white incomes, but significant racial differences appear even when income is held constant. The rate of substandard housing among black households is nearly four times, and the rate among Hispanic households nearly three times, the rate among white households. Overcrowding rates show similar disparities between white and minority households, although the relationship between black and Hispanic households is reversed on this measure.

Another group with particularly severe housing problems consists of single-parent families, now showing up dramatically among the homeless. A recent study by the Harvard Joint Center for Housing Studies (Apgar and Brown 1988) estimated that in 1987 the typical single-parent family, in which the parent is less than twenty-five years old, paid 81 percent of its income for housing. For single-parent households in which the parent is twenty-five to thirty-four, the median rent-to-income ratio rose from 35 percent in 1974 to 58 percent in 1987 for a unit of similar quality.

To understand the housing cost-to-income gap, it is useful to compare the housing supply available at rents which low-income households can afford with the number of households with low incomes. For renter households earning under $10,000 a year and paying the current HUD standard of 30 percent of their income for rent ($250 per month), Figures 7.1 and 7.2 show a dramatic reversal in the supply-demand relationship. In 1970, there was a fairly large excess of supply over demand. By 1985, that relationship was totally reversed; there were nearly 4 million fewer units renting for less than $250 a month than there were renter households with incomes under $10,000 a year. The number of units renting for under $250 a month may not even be as large as appears in Figures 7.1 and 7.2, in fact, since that figure includes over 800,000 vacancies. So high a vacancy rate for low-rent units suggests poor structural or neighborhood conditions that render the units only marginally habitable. Furthermore, only 4.8 million of the 7.1 million occupied low-rent units are occupied by low-income households. For the very poorest households, the imbalance is even greater. In 1985 only 2.1 million apartments in the nation rented for $125 or less, while the number of renter households with incomes under $5,000 a year (the income level that permits a maximum of $125 rent using the 30 percent HUD standard) was 5.4 million.

FIGURE 7.1

Low-income Renters and Low-rent Units, 1970, 1978, and 1985

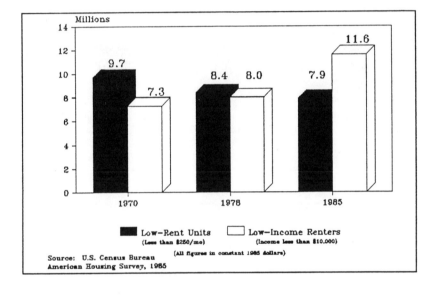

Source: Leonard, Dolbeare, and Lazare 1989, pp. 7, 9.

It is important to introduce here the limitations of the rent-to-income ratio, at least as it traditionally has been employed. The ratio is a rule of thumb, with all the imprecision that term connotes, establishing a standard for what people "should" pay for housing. For different groups and at different times, this "should" has varied. In the early days of the public housing program, it was standard that tenants should pay approximately 20 percent of income for rent; in the late 1960s, federal legislation was revised to set a 25 percent maximum under this and

FIGURE 7.2
Rental-housing Shortage for Households
Earning \$5,000 or Less, 1970 - 1985

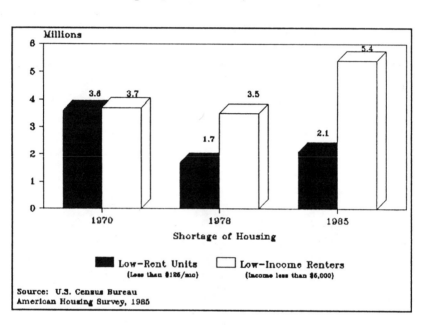

Source: U.S. Census Bureau
American Housing Survey, 1985

Source: Leonard, Dolbeare, and Lazare 1989, pp. 7, 9.

related federal subsidy programs; shortly after the Reagan administration took office, the required percentage of a tenant's income under federal programs was raised to 30 percent, not as a result of any conceptual or empirical work, but simply to lower the government's contribution by requiring tenants to devote more of their incomes to housing. Landlords often use a rough rule of thumb to decide whether an applicant for an apartment can afford it, and lending institutions use various percentage rules of thumb to decide whether to grant a mortgage. These rules, like the government's, often are bent and revised to reflect changing conditions.

The reality is that what people pay for housing is a function of ability and desire, that the distribution of actual rent-to-income ratios is enormously wide, and that some systematic variations are found, principally by income level. The lower the income, the larger the percentage of that income which is likely to be devoted to necessities, of which housing is, in most instances, the most expensive.

This reality and its implications have led to some recent and compelling work challenging the notion of a fixed rent-to-income standard.[1] This alternative view of how much a household should spend for housing is based on the fact that each household requires a basic package of necessities. If income is low, paying too much for housing can leave the household with insufficient funds for food, clothing, transportation, medical care, and other basics. Thus, what a household should spend for housing is a function of what is needed for these other necessities and what is left over for housing. Housing is a special kind of expenditure compared with expenditures for other necessities, because it is a large payment for a fixed bundle of goods and services. It is paid in advance (usually as much as a month in advance) and is contracted for an extended period of time, with severe consequences – namely, eviction – resulting from not meeting that contractual commitment. In other words, housing represents a first claim on the household budget; after paying in advance for it, remaining funds can then be used for other basics. The larger the household, the more space it needs, and, therefore, the more costly that space is, assuming a constant quality. However, at the same time, a larger household needs more for food and other basic expenses, which suggests that that household should devote a lower proportion of its income to rent if it is not to slight other necessities. Similarly, the lower the household's income, the less it has left over for the nonshelter basics after rent is paid. Thus, lower-income households, size being held constant, should pay less for housing than households with higher incomes.

This concept may be put into operation by use of budgets prepared by the Bureau of Labor Statistics (BLS) showing minimal levels of consumption needed for households of different sizes. (The BLS stopped preparing such budgets in the early 1980s, but they can be updated using consumer price index component indices.) These budgets then are applied to actual household income data in order to determine how much households of different sizes and different income levels truly can afford to spend on housing if they are not to slight other necessities. Determinations of affordability are made at the minimum level the federal government itself says is needed to maintain a "modest but adequate" standard of living. These budgets and this level are considerably higher than the federal poverty standard, but far more realistic, a fact likely not unrelated to the elimination of this data series by the BLS. The result is a sliding scale of affordability, according to which households with incomes below a certain level cannot afford to spend anything for housing if they are to have enough left for nonshelter basics (i.e., a zero percent rent-to-income standard), with the percentage standard going up with income level and down with household size. By this measure, some households can afford to pay even more than 30 percent of their income for housing without hardship.

Michael Stone has calculated the number of households paying more than they should for housing by this standard (1989, in press). Using 1985 data (available from a draft of his paper for the Economic Policy Institute; the final version will incorporate 1987 data), he calculates that nearly 27 million U.S. households, containing over 77 million people, are "shelter poor." It should be noted that this figure is based only on households living in their own homes; it does not include the homeless, those whose rent-to-income burden became so severe that they gave up, or were forced to give up, the roofs over their heads. By race, as expected, blacks suffer disproportionately: 50 percent of black and Hispanic households are shelter poor, compared with 30 percent of all households.

An astounding 14 million of these households are so poor that they could not afford their home even if it were free. Their incomes are so low that they do not have enough to meet the BLS standard for nonshelter basics. Of these 14 million households, 8 million are renters (fully 27 percent of all renter households) and 6 million are homeowners. A very large proportion of this group, probably more of the former than the latter, are at severe risk of homelessness should they be hit with even the most minor increase in housing costs.

Although, as is to be expected, the vast majority of the shelter poor have low incomes, a surprising and growing number do not. Over 10 percent have incomes over $20,000 a year, primarily households with four or more persons, illustrating the extent to which the housing affordability crisis is spreading upward. While most studies of housing affordability have focused on renters (in part because they generally have lower incomes than homeowners, in part because data on rents are somewhat better and more usable than data on homeownership payments), Stone's work reveals the extent to which homeowners also are suffering from the crisis. Nearly 25 percent of all homeowners are shelter poor (and 42 percent of renters). The shelter-poor homeowners for the most part are the low-income elderly and nonelderly, female-headed households. One out of sixteen home mortgages in this country is more than thirty days overdue, possibly in part due to the widespread replacement of fixed-payment loans by variable-rate loans, a shift motivated by lenders' desire to transfer the burden of inflation onto borrowers.

Although different from the traditional fixed rule of thumb, the shelter-poverty measure yields a total figure not too different from that derived from rule-of-thumb data. There are 27 million shelter-poor households; 26 million pay more than 30 percent of their income for housing. The shelter-poverty data, however, are far more sophisticated, analytically revealing of housing-market performance, and useful in developing policy and programs. They are especially useful in that they allow the pinpointing of kinds of groups most in danger of becoming homeless, since demographic correlations of shelter-poverty data are much more consistent and intuitively logical than correlations with data of rent-to-income ratio. For example, fully 77 percent of all renter households with six or more persons are shelter poor, indicating the vulnerability of children. Among renters with incomes under $5,000, the shelter-poverty rate is 90 percent.

The shelter-poverty approach also permits an estimate of the gross affordability gap. The per-household difference between what shelter-poor households actually pay for housing and what they can afford, using this standard, is $3,200 a year. The aggregate affordability gap, derived simply by multiplying this figure by the number of shelter-poor households, is $85 billion. Thus, it would require that amount – about six times HUD's current low-income housing budget – each year to cover the gap. It should be remembered that the homeless, those who pay no rent and have no housing, are excluded from this calculation.

Use of the more sophisticated shelter-poverty standard shows clearly that President Roosevelt's lament is no less true today, although the kind of housing problem the nation now faces is different from that of fifty years ago. Whether one regards slum conditions as a better or worse problem to endure than unaffordability, and there are good arguments to be made either way, what is remarkable is the difference in trajectory. Starting in the late 1930s, the nation saw a pronounced and rapid improvement in housing conditions. The current problem is clearly getting worse, and rapidly. In 1970, only 19 million households were shelter poor.

It is beyond question that the market has failed to meet the housing needs of the American people and that the situation is rapidly deteriorating. Part of the problem is simply the cost structure of housing. Housing in our economy is treated as a product or commodity, little or no different from any other commodity. It is produced, managed, bought, and sold largely, and for many, exclusively, with a view to profit maximization. Homeowners play a dual role, as consumers of shelter and as financial investors, and both of these motivations can play a part in their housing decisions and actions. At every phase of the housing production, management, and transaction system, the drive is to maximize profits – from land, development and construction, building materials, financing, rental, brokerage, and sales. How much housing is built, where it is built, how much it costs to build and buy, and who can afford to live in it depend on what generates the largest profits for those various actors. If it is not possible to control the market to meet social goals – and history suggests this cannot and will not be done – then it is clear that some alternative production, delivery, and operating system must be developed (Institute for Policy Studies 1989). Otherwise, an even greater deterioration in our housing standards, even more widespread homelessness, and severe affordability problems among a very large proportion – perhaps the majority – of American households surely will be seen. The nation may even arrive at the sad point where President Roosevelt's "one third of a nation" speech is no longer regarded as a lament and call to action but as a nostalgic remembrance of better times.

Notes

1. Substantial original work has been done in this area by Cushing Dolbeare, founder and chairperson of the National Low Income Housing Coalition, and by Michael Stone of the University of Massachusetts-Boston. Dolbeare terms her alternative "the market basket approach"; Stone uses the term "shelter poverty." The most recent and

comprehensive work on the subject is Stone (1990), from which information on the following pages is drawn.

References

Apgar, W. C., Jr., and H. J. Brown. 1988. *The State of the Nation's Housing, 1988.* Cambridge: Joint Center for Housing Studies of Harvard University.

Congressional Budget Office. 1988, Dec. *Current Housing Problems and Possible Federal Responses.* Washington, DC: Government Printing Office.

Dolbeare, C. N. 1989, Feb. "Low Income Housing Needs." Washington, DC: Low Income Housing Information Service.

Hopper, K., and J. Hamberg. 1986. "The Making of America's Homeless: From Skid Row to New Poor, 1954-84." In *Critical Perspectives on Housing,* eds. R. Bratt, C. Hartman, and A. Meyerson, 12-40. Philadelphia: Temple University Press.

Institute for Policy Studies Working Group on Housing. 1989. *The Right to Housing: A Blueprint for Housing the Nation.* Washington, DC: Institute for Policy Studies.

Leonard, P. A., C. N. Dolbeare, and E. Lazere. 1989. "A Place to Call Home: The Crisis in Housing for the Poor." Washington, DC: Center on Budget and Policy Priorities and the Low Income Housing Information Service.

Stone, M. 1990. "One-Third of a Nation: A New Look at Housing Affordability in America." Washington, DC: Economic Policy Institute.

Sutermeister, O. 1969. "Inadequacies and Inconsistencies in the Definition of Substandard Housing." In *Housing Code Standards: Three Critical Studies.* Research Report No. 19. Washington, DC: National Commission on Urban Problems.

PART IV

The Response to the Crisis – Housing, Welfare, and Child Welfare Policy: Part of the Solution or Part of the Problem?

8

What Is Wrong with Our Housing Programs

Chester Hartman and Barry Zigas

Housing programs in the United States have been wholly inadequate, both quantitatively and qualitatively. Government housing programs have been reasonably effective in aiding the private market to meet the needs of middle-and upper-income households, but low- and very low-income households – those which increasingly are shut out of the housing market – have received all too little government help relative to their needs. That help which has been delivered all too often has been poorly conceived and poorly administered.

Some government housing programs are successes. Clearly the most widely used forms of government housing assistance are the homeowner deductions built into the income tax. These deductions have facilitated homeownership and relatively high levels of housing consumption for millions of American families. The benefits flow largely to middle- and upper-income taxpayers. The ability to deduct mortgage-interest payments from taxable income lowers nominal interest rates through a government subsidy of those costs. This major, although indirect, subsidy, will total $46.6 billion in FY1991.

Similarly, all property taxes can be deducted by homeowners, giving them another distinct advantage over renters. Although renters also pay property taxes, albeit indirectly as part of their rents, they can take no deductions. (Some states give tenants a renter's credit on their housing payments. The credit usually amounts to only a small fraction of the homeowner's benefit and applies only to the state income tax, not to the

© *1990 Chester Hartman*

much larger federal income tax.) The property-tax deduction will save homeowners $12.4 billion in federal income taxes in FY1991.

The federal government provides still other benefits to middle- and upper-income taxpayers. For example, the government does not tax the imputed rental value of an owned home. A renter who invests $100,000 in a profit-making enterprise or interest-bearing security pays tax on the income, but the homeowner who pays $100,000 for a house is not taxed on the value of residential services he or she receives from living in that house. In addition, the increase in a home's value, when realized, is protected by the tax code. All taxes on that profit, if rolled over within a stipulated time into a home of at least equal cost, are deferred until a later date, and up to $125,000 of that capital gain may never be taxed if the homeowner cashes in after reaching the age of fifty-five and meets certain other conditions. The tax system thus gives homeownership highly preferred status and imbues it with extraordinary protection as an investment, and many state and local income-tax systems provide parallel benefits yielding deductions amounting roughly to an additional 20 percent.

As noted above, these various institutions of the internal revenue code help the well-off far more than the poorer classes. Renters are, generally speaking, less wealthy than homeowners, but they receive no benefit from these deductions. The tax system makes it so attractive to own that few who can afford homeownership choose not to do so. Ownership rates rise with income; the homeownership rate for households with incomes over $50,000 is 92 percent. Median renter income in the United States is about half that of median homeowner income. Homeowners who do not itemize their deductions get nothing from the annual deduction benefits, although they do enjoy the other features of the tax system. In fact, only about half of all homeowners find it worthwhile to itemize; for many, the newly raised standard deduction exceeds deductible expenditures. Participation rates, however, rise steeply with income. Although deductions are limited to mortgages of $1 million or less, and some minor and easily evaded restrictions were recently introduced on the deductibility of interest on home equity loans, there is otherwise no upper limit on the amount of mortgage interest that can be deducted. Since the value of the deduction is a function of the tax rate, higher- income taxpayers get greatest value from the deduction.

These features of the tax laws are extraordinarily regressive. Two-thirds of the total 1987 deduction went to taxpayers with incomes of $50,000 and more. In 1988, the average value of the deduction was $5,262 to a taxpayer with an annual income between $100,000 and $200,000; however, the average value of the deduction was only $36 to a taxpayer with an income of $10,000 a year or less – if he took it at all.

After homeowner deductions, federal support of the mortgage market is the second largest form of housing aid. It was employed most dramatically in the Depression with the creation of the Federal Housing Administration (FHA) and the resulting revolution in mortgage instruments. By providing federal mortgage insurance (later to be paralleled by the Veterans' Administration [VA] mortgage-guarantee program), the FHA created a standardized, long-term (usually thirty-year) financing system featuring low down payments (10 percent, with no down payment required under some VA programs) and fixed monthly payments. The system made homeownership possible for millions of middle- and moderate-income households. The post-World War II suburban building boom would have been impossible without FHA and VA loans and without the federal highway system that rendered suburban areas accessible. Other important creations of the federal government were (1) the central banking function of the Federal Home Loan Bank Board; (2) the special status given to savings and loan associations as the primary source of residential mortgage funds; and (3) a national secondary mortgage market, first through the Federal National Mortgage Association and later through the Government National Mortgage Association and the Federal Home Loan Mortgage Corporation – Fannie Mae, Ginnie Mae, and Freddie Mac, as they are popularly known. Some state and local housing-finance agencies have followed the federal example and provided similar types of credit assistance. It is the aim of these institutions to foster homeownership by making credit readily available on terms that permit even moderate-income families to borrow. Some rental housing also has been aided by these agencies, and some elements of their programs on occasion have reached below the standard market levels of affordability. However, by and large, this entire structure has been designed and functions to undergird and abet the existing private housing market.

At the other end of the scale has been a series of programs specifically designed to provide affordable housing for the poor and near poor. Chief among these is the low-rent public housing program, begun in the 1930s. After more than fifty years, the country has produced only 1.2 million units of public housing, subsidized by the federal government but owned and operated by local housing authorities. The program produced much satisfactory housing, certainly the best and cheapest alternative available to hundreds of thousands of poor families, as the huge waiting lists in most cities demonstrate.

Public housing programs, however, are beset with numerous problems and an exceedingly poor public image. Many of the problems of the program were built in by Congress, and some were actually inserted into the original legislation or later amendments by program opponents who hoped to weaken the program's political support. The basic financing formula obligated the federal government to pay the capital costs of constructing housing projects, while rents covered operating costs. Through annual contributions contracts the government was committed to cover the principal repayment and interest costs of bonds floated by local housing authorities. Rents originally were approximately 20 percent of tenants' income. Later, rents were capped at 25 percent; they then were raised to 30 percent of income in 1981. This system worked reasonably well during the early phases of the program. However, as operating costs rose and tenants' incomes fell relative to general income levels, insufficient funds were available for basic operating costs. Projects began to deteriorate, and housing authorities came to the verge of bankruptcy.

The changing character of the public-housing tenantry also played a major role in altering the financial picture for local housing authorities. The "submerged (white) middle class" of Depression days changed to minority households with little hope of moving ahead financially, a great many of whom were urban-renewal and highway-program displacees who had priority for public-housing vacancies. It was not until the late 1960s, when the problems of the public housing programs became too severe to ignore, that additional federal operating and modernization funds were made available. At that time, the cap on tenant rents was set at 25 percent of income. Prior to that, in an attempt to secure enough operating revenue, housing authorities were charging rents that often amounted to 50 percent, 60 percent, even 70 percent of the tenant's income. Even these additional subsidies have been insufficient to permit restoration of tens of thousands of units left vacant and uninhabitable by prior underfunding and neglect and to finance the upgrading of developments, many of which are forty and fifty years old. A recent consultant study for the Department of Housing and Urban Development (HUD) estimated that $22 billion is needed to bring existing projects up to modern standards.

Poor decisions on the location and design of public housing projects also have caused serious difficulties. In some large cities, the prototypical public housing project has been a large high-rise (sometimes with 1,500 to 2,000 or more families), of Spartan design, with few amenities, and located where land costs were low and neighborhood resistance minimal. These characteristics have ensured geographical and social isolation for the residents, as well as high levels of racial segregation. The myriad social and physical problems of the larger public housing projects often are compounded by insensitive, less-than-competent management by local housing authorities.

A more recent, highly publicized problem in public housing has been drug dealing, often from abandoned apartments. It is likely that this, as well as other social ills, is no more prevalent among the public-housing population than among persons with similar demographic characteristics living elsewhere. However, the government's role as landlord and the opportunity this role offers for an aggressive antidrug stance for national and local politicians have focused considerable attention on this issue. Public housing also has not been immune to the consequences of homelessness. In a great many instances, those who have lost their homes have turned to relatives and friends living in public housing for temporary shelter. The New York City Housing Authority estimates, based on utility usage, trash collection, observation, and other indices, that 100,000 of its 174,000 units are illegally occupied by one or more persons not on the lease.

The deteriorated state of many of the nation's public housing developments has led to efforts by the Reagan administration and the current administration to get rid of large portions of the stock through abandonment, sale (sometimes to tenants, as in Margaret Thatcher's England), and intentional undermaintenance. These efforts often have the support of local officials, particularly if the housing project is in a gentrifying area. In part, these actions are the culmination of fifty years of efforts to show that public housing "doesn't work." In part, they reflect an unwillingness to acknowledge the true costs of providing the poor with decent, affordable housing.

A great deal must be improved in the existing public housing program. The architectural, locational, and social mistakes that led to the creation of the unmanageable, Dickensian ghettos that constitute all too many projects in Chicago, St. Louis, Detroit, Oakland, Boston, Washington, and many other cities must never be repeated. But those mistakes and the vast, seemingly intractable problems they have created should not mask the importance of providing decent housing directly for low-income households through government subsidies and action. Neither should the problems mask the considerable successes of the public housing program. Prevalent public images to the contrary, only 7 percent of all family projects are both high-rise and larger than 200 units. The projects especially designed for the elderly have been particularly successful. Several studies of residents' attitudes toward public housing have found that very high degrees of overall satisfaction exist, particularly when comparisons are made with other realistic alternatives (Bratt 1986).

In the mid-1960s, Congress began to re-evaluate its reliance on public housing as the primary vehicle for providing affordable housing for low- and moderate-income people. New efforts were launched to use private-sector financing and ownership to build and manage housing that would serve this population. Instead of relying upon the direct public-housing financing programs of the 1937 U.S. Housing Act, Congress began to modify the mortgage-insurance programs that had served middle-income homeownership interests so well in the postwar years. By 1968, Congress was ready to shift the major part of its resources to such methods.

In 1968, after the urban disturbances of the previous year, the Section 236 mortgage-insurance program became the nation's primary low- and moderate-income housing-production vehicle. The program offered mortgage insurance and interest subsidies to reduce owners' actual mortgage costs. In return, owners agreed to limited cash-flow possibilities from the projects and regulated rents, which were supposed to reflect the value of the mortgage subsidies. Owners also were required to rent their units only to low- and moderate-income households. Although these income limits were purposely set higher than those for public housing, they were kept low enough to make the housing affordable to low- and moderate-income people.

At the same time it passed the Section 236 program, Congress adopted a homeownership subsidy effort (Section 235) based on the same premises – mortgage insurance and interest subsidies to facilitate homeownership among low- and moderate-income households. Again, the FHA insured mortgages made by conventional lenders and provided subsidies to reduce the eligible buyer's actual interest costs to between 1 and 3 percent. Underwriting criteria for these mortgages were more lenient than for conventional FHA homeownership, and the Nixon administration, which inherited these programs upon taking office in 1969, pursued them with zeal.

The public housing program continued in the wake of these developments, but private production programs overtook public housing as the nation's leading production and rehabilitation vehicle. In fact, in the seven years it was operating, the Section 236 program and its immediate, more limited predecessor (Section 221(d)(3)BMIR) led to the creation of nearly 600,000 units of rental housing. Section 235 accounted for well over 100,000 homeownership units.

All of these efforts were abruptly cancelled when President Nixon declared a moratorium on any further housing assistance in January 1973. All federal housing-assistance efforts were frozen by administrative order; HUD's programs were not reactivated until after the passage of the Housing and Community Development Act of 1974, over eighteen months later.

The 1974 Housing Act embodied a major shift in the federal effort, in essence abandoning the former approach of direct public development, ownership, and management, although a small number of traditional public housing projects continue to be built. It favored subsidies to permit low-income households to live in privately developed and owned units. (During the mid-1960s, leased public housing and rent-supplement programs were enacted by Congress, but these were small and ancillary to the traditional approach.) Known as the Section 8 program, the new approach embodied four separate elements: new construction, substantial rehabilitation, moderate rehabilitation, and existing housing (a portion of which is to provide additional financial assistance to moderate-income projects built under other HUD programs). Under the first three programs, private housing developers and rehabilitators (and in some instances public bodies) were promised federal subsidies to produce decent homes and rent them at regulated levels to low- and very low-income persons. Under the Section 8 existing-housing program, the consumers themselves were given certificates and permitted to locate housing in the existing supply. Owners in this program could not charge more than a so-called fair market rent established by HUD for each metropolitan area. Tenant rents under Section 8 originally were set at 25 percent of their income (the public-housing cap); then, in 1981, as part of an overall Reagan administration attempt to cut federal expenses, the required percentage was raised to 30 percent in all HUD housing-assistance programs.

Providing subsidies to bridge the gap between the costs of private-market housing and the ability of low-income households to pay, while doing nothing to control market costs except the establishment of rent ceilings beyond which Section 8 subsidies could not be used, inevitably led to high costs to the federal government. These high costs and ballooning federal deficits eventually led to the repeal of the construction and substantial rehabilitation elements of Section 8 in 1982. A small element used to further subsidize rents under HUD's Section 202 mortgage-subsidy program for the elderly and the handicapped was continued. What remains is the Section 8 certificate program for existing units and a more recent wrinkle on the idea, housing vouchers. There are some differences between the certificate and voucher programs. Housing vouchers provide a fixed monthly subsidy, set no maximum rent for units of the household's own choosing, and permit the recipients either to keep the difference if rents are below the payment standard or to pay more of their own income for the units with rent above the standard. Although proponents of housing vouchers use the term "winner take all" to characterize this program, neither program fares that well in the realities of the housing market in most parts of the country.

Enactment of the Section 8 program, particularly in its existing-housing certificate form, marked a significant new direction for national housing policy. All previous government efforts had been directed first and foremost to increasing the supply of decent, safe, and sanitary housing. Affordability was a secondary concern, often dealt with directly only as a consequence of the continuing inability to serve very low-income households even when deep subsidies had been provided for the production of new housing or for renovation. The 1974 Housing Act marked a turning point because its major goal was not the production or renovation of housing supply but an increase in the effective demand by consumers for housing that already was on the private market, or that might be produced if sufficient demand could be assured through ongoing subsidies.

The Section 8 program, as originally proposed by President Nixon, grew out of a conviction that the preceding federal efforts had focused relatively large amounts of assistance to underwrite the production of relatively few new units of affordable housing, providing large profits to owners, developers, and middlemen, while leaving the vast majority of low-income renters without any subsidies at all in a market which increasingly demanded very large percentages of low-income families' incomes for rent. Ironically, this criticism of the production programs was shared by critics on both the political left and right.

The Section 8 certificate program was based on the assumption that most, if not all, low-income renters had incomes too low to enable them to compete effectively for housing in the private market, although adequate housing might be available. Census data certainly bear out this assumption. The vast majority of low-income people today live in housing that meets federal standards for decent, safe, and sanitary conditions, but they pay unreasonably high proportions of their income in order to rent it.

It was also claimed that Section 8 would give low-income households some freedom of choice in selecting housing. Households would no longer be forced to move to publicly owned or publicly subsidized housing – "the projects" – in order to receive government assistance. With Section 8 certificates, tenants could shop freely in the marketplace, finding apartments just like "everyone else." Some advocates of the program even declared that certificates would end patterns of racial segregation in housing, as minority households moved freely throughout the metropolitan area in search of decent housing and decent neighborhoods, no longer captives of public or private enterprises set up to serve their needs.

Like most public-policy initiatives, Section 8 does not live up to the claims of either its most ardent supporters or its most dedicated detractors. A ten-year study of an earlier, experimental version of the

Section 8 program known as the experimental housing-allowance program (EHAP), highlighted some limitations in the approach:[1]

1. Only 42 percent of eligible renter households and 33 percent of eligible homeowner households participated when the allowance was made available to all who met the eligibility criteria.
2. In those subexperiments in which extraordinary outreach efforts were made to contact a limited number of eligible renter households, the participation rate was 27 percent.
3. Participation rates were lowest among minority, very poor, and large households, and those living in poor-quality dwellings.
4. In the subexperiment allowing participation in the program independent of the requirement that housing meet a minimum quality standard, participation rates more than doubled, and some two-thirds of recipients did not end up in standard housing.
5. Only one-fourth of the housing allowance, on average, was devoted to housing; the rest was used to cover other household expenses.
6. Few participants moved and thus obtained better housing, and little improvement in existing housing was triggered by the availability of this new demand-side money.

In short, the EHAP experiment showed that housing allowances are essentially an income supplement if tenants already live in good housing; if tenants do not already live in good housing, they are not likely to be able to take advantage of the program (assuming it embodies a housing-quality standard) either by moving to a better unit or by inducing the landlord to remove code violations. The housing-allowance approach assumes a supply of decent, moderately priced, vacant units appropriate to the needs of and available to people living in substandard quarters, conditions which exist in few local housing markets. The reality is that, in most areas, the vacancy rate is low for units that meet the needs of low-income households in size, rent, tenure, and location. Discrimination on the basis of race, household size or composition, source of income, or health status keeps other units out of the reach of needy households.

Results similar to those of the EHAP study have been found with respect to the Section 8 existing-housing program. In some communities, high proportions of certificate recipients cannot use them because they cannot find units meeting the program's quality and rent standards. High proportions of Section 8 existing-housing units are found to be seriously deficient when inspected. A 1979 General Accounting Office (GAO) study of five states found 42 percent of such units to be substandard. To the extent that Section 8 existing-housing certificates have been beneficial, it should be recognized that they have been serving a nonrepresentative portion of the population in need – those at the higher end of the income-eligibility scale, whites more than minorities, small more than large households, the elderly more than families. Also pertinent are the studies of housing conditions of persons receiving public assistance, which is, in effect, a housing-allowance program in which little systematic official attention is paid to how recipients fare in the housing market. The imputed housing-cost element in the general public assistance grant is insufficient to meet true housing costs in almost all states. For example, a special 1981 Census Bureau study of New York City showed that nearly half of all renter families receiving public assistance were living in units in need of rehabilitation.

On the other hand, Section 8 does serve a large clientele. More than 1 million households now participate in the certificate and voucher variants. Waiting lists for Section 8 assistance are as long or longer than for public housing. In some markets, the turn-in rate for unusable certificates is very low, and landlords have made special efforts to enroll tenants so that they can remain in their properties. Some communities have worked aggressively with certificate holders to find housing for which the certificates can be used. These efforts often have led to markedly higher success rates than when tenants are left to locate appropriate housing by themselves.

Section 8 does give tenants the financial means to pay for decent housing. Without such deep subsidies, it is difficult to imagine any housing program succeeding for very low-income people. Public housing projects, for example, do not require rents to cover any of the development costs. Yet, in 1989, public housing as a whole will require more than $1.5 billion annual operating assistance in federal funds (plus substantial local subsidies in some localities) simply to make ends meet. That amounts to, on average, more than $1,000 per year in subsidy for each public housing unit now in existence. Increasingly through the 1980s, it has become clear that the gap between the costs of decent housing and the incomes of low- and moderate-income people is widening at an accelerating rate. Even where more recent public and private subsidies have combined to provide housing for which rents need cover only routine operating, maintenance, and reserve requirements, poverty-level renters are unable in many markets to afford this housing even at 30 percent of their income. These realities demand deep subsidy programs that can cover the housing cost:income gap as a major element, if not the foundation, of ongoing federal housing efforts.

In short, there is no reason to believe that the present forms of housing allowances will, by themselves, work, if "working" implies providing people with decent housing at rents they can afford. As introduced by conservative administrations, housing allowances are intended to get the government out of the housing business gradually by substituting very flexible shorter-term commitments (vouchers are generally five-year commitments) for the permanent affordability feature of public housing and even the midterm (usually twenty-year) Section 8 commitments. In a November 6, 1981 *Washington Post* interview, Samuel Pierce, the Reagan administration's HUD secretary, stated, "We hope by 1984 or '85, that we will have interest rates down enough that it will stimulate housing so that we won't even have to use the voucher system. We hope that maybe we'll even get out of that." At the Urban League's 1985 national convention, a HUD deputy assistant secretary told the audience, "We're basically backing out of the business of housing, period."

Although there are local housing markets in which it makes sense to use existing vacancies rather than to provide new or rehabilitated housing directly for the poor, a voucher program, particularly as it has been formulated by the current and past administrations, cannot provide an answer to the nation's severe housing crisis. Vouchers can be a useful element in a comprehensive panoply of government programs, to offer choice, possibilities of racial and socioeconomic integration, and, where appropriate, efficient use of available slack in the housing stock. Vouchers must be tied to far greater controls over the private housing market, in terms of rent levels, protection of tenant rights, and assurance of long-term, if not permanent, affordability, an issue discussed in greater detail below.

The two principal federal housing programs for those not served by the private market are public housing and Section 8 (vouchers included),

but there are many others, some for rural areas and small towns under
the aegis of the Farmers Home Administration (FmHA), rather than
HUD. Table 8.1 describes the function of each of these and Table 8.2
the size of each (Congressional Budget Office 1988). Some of the more
important observations regarding the entire group of housing programs
follow (see also Leonard, Dolbeare, and Lazere 1989):

1. A total of 5.4 million households are served by all federal
    housing programs, less than one-third of those eligible to receive
    such assistance. For the most part, nonelderly, nonhandicapped,
    single individuals are ineligible to receive government housing
    assistance, regardless of how low their income is. Inclusion of
    these one-person households would produce an even lower
    proportion of those in need who actually receive program
    benefits. In 1987, only 29 percent of the 7.7 million renter
    households with incomes below the poverty line, and 18 percent
    of all poor households, lived in public housing or received
    government rental assistance. This is a considerably lower figure
    than the proportion of poverty-level households receiving school
    lunch benefits, Medicaid, or food stamps.
2. Because of the complexity of the various programs, some
    subgroups of the needy population are served better than others.
    Table 8.3 shows that, in the rental housing programs, the elderly
    have the most program benefits available to them, families with
    children the least, although little difference exists between
    availability to large and small families. In Table 8.3, the more
    relevant data on actual beneficiaries of specific major rental
    programs show that the elderly receive a disproportionate share
    of benefits under all programs, that large families (three or more
    children) do worst, and that, of all programs, public housing
    serves these large households best.
3. Only limited assistance is available to homeowners, even though
    a very large portion of those in need of assistance own their own
    homes; homeowners represent between 20 percent and 37
    percent of all households within each of the three major
    categories of housing problems – excessive housing costs,
    physically substandard units, and overcrowding (see Chapter 6).
    Virtually no assistance is available to needy homeowners who

TABLE 8.1
Overview of Major Federal Programs for Direct Housing Assistance, in Chronological Order

Program	Year authorized	Status	Type of subsidy	Description	Household Payment	Households assisted as of 9/30/87 (Thousands)	Funding for FY1989
Rental assistance programs							
Public housing	1937	Active	Project-based	Pays for developing and modernizing projects owned by local PHAs. Before 1987, funds paid off debt-service costs over 20 to 40 years. Costs are now financed with up-front grants. Since 1969, has also paid the difference between the projects operating costs and rent collections.	Generally 30% of adjusted income	1,390	$433 million for 6,243 new units; $1,647 million for modernization; and $1,618 million for operating subsidies
Section 202	1959	Active	Project-based	Provides loans for up to 40 years to nonprofit sponsors to finance construction of rental housing for the elderly and handicapped. All projects built since 1974 also receive Section 8 rental subsidies.	Generally 30% of adjusted income	153	$480 million of loan authority for 9,500 new units
Section 221 (d X 3) below-market interest rate (BMIR)	1961	No new commitments since 1968	Project-based	Provides up-front subsidies that reduced to 3% the interest rate on private 40-year mortgages for multifamily rental housing built by non profit or limited-dividend organizations. Reduces rents for income-eligible tenants.	Fixed rent sufficient to cover mortgage payments and other allowable costs	150	n.a.
Section 515 rural rental assistance	1962	Active	Project-based	FmHA provides 50-year direct loans to developers at 1% interest. Reduces rents for income-eligible tenants. Some very poor tenants receive supplementary assistance through the rural RAP and Section 8 programs.	Generally, the greater of a basic rent covering mortgage payments and allowable costs, or 30% of adjusted income	349	$555 million of loan authority for about 16,700 new units
Rent supplement	1965	No new commitments since 1973	Project-based	Reduces rents for income-eligible tenants in housing projects insured under certain FHA mortgage insurance programs. Most outstanding commitments have been converted to Section 8 assistance.	The greater of 30% of adjusted income or 30% of unit's rent	23	n.a.

TABLE 8.1 (Continued)

Program	Year authorized	Status	Type of subsidy	Description	Household Payment	Households assisted as of 9/30/87 (Thousands)	Funding for FY1989
Rental assistance programs, cont.							
Section 236	1968	No new commitments since 1973	Project-based	Provides monthly subsidies that reduce to 1% the interest rate on private 40 year mortgages for new multifamily rental projects. Reduces rents for income-eligible tenants. Since 1974, some tenants get larger subsidies through the RAP program. Many RAPs have been converted to Section 8 assistance.	Similar to Section 515	528	n.a.
Section 8 new construction and substantial rehabilitation	1974	No new commitments since 1983, except for elderly and handicapped families	Project-based	Provides rental subsidies to income-eligible households in new or substantially rehabilitated projects. Subsidy covers the difference between tenants' payments and FMR, determined by HUD and based initially on capital and operating costs. Subsidy contracts for 20 to 40 years commit owners to set aside a certain number of units for lower-income households for a period of time. Tax incentives and financing arrangements also may reduce owners' effective mortgage interest rates.	Generally 30% of adjusted income	794	$1.325 million for 9,500 new units
Section 8 loan management set-aside and property disposition	1974	Active	Project-based	Provides subsidies to units in financially troubled projects in the FHA-insured inventory and on sale of HUD-owned projects, respectively. Five to 15 year subsidy contracts with owners help ensure improved cash flows and preserve projects for lower-income tenants. Subsidies cover the difference between tenants' payments and the units' rents, which often are below-market rents because of other federal subsidies.	Generally 30% of adjusted income	414[a]	$453 million for 10,657 new units

TABLE 8.1 (Continued)

Program	Year authorized	Status	Type of subsidy	Description	Household Payment	Households assisted as of 9/30/87 (Thousands)	Funding for FY1989
Rental assistance programs, cont.							
Section 8 vouchers	1983	Active	Household-based	Similar to Section 8 certificate program in that assisted households can live in standard units of their own choosing and PHAs administer the program. Unlike certificates in that recipients may occupy units with rents above the voucher payment standard—roughly equivalent to the FMR—if they pay the difference, and may keep the difference if rents are below the payment standard. Funding committed for 5 years.	Generally 30% of adjusted income	82	$1,276 million for 47,000 new units and $79 million for 3,099 units replacing units lost because of landlords' opting out of programs or expiring contracts.
Rental housing development grant (HoDAG)	1983	Terminated 9/30/89	Project-based	Awards grants through national competitions among eligible state and local governments to help finance new construction and substantial rehabilitation of rental housing. Projects must reserve at least 20% of units for 20 years for lower-income tenants; grants cannot exceed 50% of total costs of developing the projects.	No more than 30% of adjusted income of a family whose gross income equals 50% of area median income, adjusted for family size	7[b]	No new funds appropriated
Rental rehabilitation grants	1983	Active	Project-based	Distributes grants by formula to eligible units of government to help fund moderate rehabilitation of rental housing. Also provides vouchers to current lower-income tenants who may choose to remain in the building or to relocate. Grants generally limited to between $5,000 and $8,500 per unit, depending on number of bedrooms, and cannot exceed 50% of the total rehabilitation. At least 70% of units must be occupied by lower-income households, with specified shares going to large families.	Similar to	39[c]	$150 million

TABLE 8.1 (Continued)

Program	Year authorized	Status	Type of subsidy	Description	Household Payment	Households assisted as of 9/30/87 (Thousands)	Funding for FY1989
Rental assistance programs, cont.							
Section 8 conversion assistance	1974	Active	Project-based	Provides 15-year subsidies to some dwelling units in projects formerly aided through other types of programs, primarily the rent supplement and RAP programs. Subsidy mechanisms similar to Section 8 loan management.	Generally 30% of adjusted	a	No new funds appropriated
Section 8 existing-housing certificates	1974	Active	Household-based	Aids income-eligible households, which can choose any existing unit that meets the program's property standards and whose rent does not exceed the FMR. HUD pays difference between units' actual rents and tenants' payments, with funding committed for 5 to 15 years. Administered by local PHAs, which enter contracts with landlords.	Generally 30% of adjusted income	874	$542 million for 18,000 new units with 5-year terms and $30 million for 333 new units with 15-year terms designed to replace units lost because of public housing demolition
Section 8 moderate rehabilitation	1979	Active	Project-based	Aids households in existing units brought up to standard with modest repairs. Differs from Section 8 existing-housing program only in that aid is tied to the rehabilitated unit whose rent is limited to 125% of the local FMR for existing units.	Generally 30% of adjusted	76	$323 million for 2,942 new units and $45 million for 1,270 single-room occupancy units for the homeless

TABLE 8.1 (Continued)

Program	Year authorized	Status	Type of subsidy	Description	Household Payment	Households assisted as of 9/30/87 (Thousands)	Funding for FY1989
				Homeownership assistance programs			
Section 502 rural housing loans	1949	Active	n.a.	Provides reduced-interest (as low as 1%) direct loans, generally with 33-year terms, to rural lower-income homebuyers. Households with incomes somewhat above income-eligibility cutoff (80% of area's median income adjusted for family size) may obtain direct loans roughly at the long term federal borrowing rate, which is typically below private mortgage rates.	At least 20% of adjusted income for mortgage payments, property taxes, and insurance	899	$1.267 million in loan authority for about 27,000 loans
Section 235 mortgage-interest subsidies	1968	Terminated 9/30/89	n.a.	Provides mortgage insurance and interest subsidies to private lenders on behalf of low- and moderate-income homebuyers—those with incomes below 95% of area's median income adjusted for family size. Characteristics have changed several times, with subsidies becoming more limited and their term being reduced. As authorized in 1983, interest subsidies are provided for 10 years, and the implicit interest rate cannot fall below 4%.	At least 28% of adjusted income for mortgage payments, property taxes, and insurance	159	No new funds appropriated

SOURCE: Congressional Budget Office 1988, 10-35.

NOTES: n.a. = not applicable; FHA = Federal Housing Administration; FmHA = Farmers Home Administration; FMR = fair market rent; HUD = Department of Housing and Urban Development; PHA = public housing housing agency; RAP = rental assistance payment program.

[a] No reliable data are available for separate breakouts of households assisted by Section 8 loan management, property disposition, and conversion assistance. The figure of 414,000 is the total for all three components.

[b] Number of units targeted specifically for lower-income households and for which funds had been obligated. Funds for a total of 24,000 units have been obligated through 1987.

[c] Estimated number of units occupied by lower-income households. At total of 41,638 units were completed with grants through 1987.

Table 8.2
Commitments and Outlays by Major Federal
Housing-assistance Programs 1987

Program	Households assisted end of FY1987 (Thousands)	Commitments outstanding through FY1988 (Thousands)[a]	Total outlays during FY 1987 (Millions of dollars)	Outlays per household in FY1987 (Dollars)[b]
Rental-assistance programs				
Section 8				
Existing-housing				
Vouchers	82	184	81	n.a.
Certificates	874	895	c	c
Loan management, property disposition, and conversions	414	438	3,819[c]	3,013[c]
Moderate rehabilitation	76	126	244	3,381
Subtotal, existing housing	1,446	1,643	4,144	3,033
New construction and substantial rehabilitation	794	868	3,981	5,067
Public housing	1,390	1,433	3,517[d]	2,539[d]
Other HUD programs[e]	552	551	686	1,229
Section 515 rural rental assistance	349	394	853[f]	2,525[f]
Total[g]	4,296	4,653	13,180	3,092
Homeownership-assistance programs				
Section 235 mortgage-interest subsidies	159	144	182	1,066
Section 502 rural housing loans[h]	899	876	1,900	2,062
Total[i]	1,059	1,020	2,082	1,906

Table 8.2 (Continued)

Source: Congressional Budget Office 1988, 46-7. Based on data provided by the Department of Housing and Urban Development and the Farmers Home Administration.

Note: n.a. = not available.

a. Includes commitments being processed, as well as commitments that will be funded from the 1988 appropriation. Excludes commitments expected to be lost because funds are deobligated or because landlords or homeowners drop out of the programs in 1988.

b. Estimated by dividing total outlays by the simple average of the number of households receiving assistance at the end of FY1986 and the end of FY1987. This procedure could not be used for vouchers because, between 1986 and 1987, HUD changed its methodology for counting the number of voucher recipients. Thus vouchers are excluded from the calculations of subtotal and total outlays per household.

c. Section 8 certificates are included in loan management, property disposition, and conversions.

d. Includes outlays for operating subsidies, for the up-front capital costs of new construction and modernization activities undertaken during 1987, and for debt service of construction and modernization activities taken before 1974.

e. Includes currently active Section 236 and rent-supplement programs.

f. Total outlays include household subsidies provided under the FmHA's rental-assistance payments program and mortgage-interest subsidies provided to the developers.

g. The total does not equal the sum of the number of households assisted under the various programs; rather, it has been adjusted to avoid double-counting households receiving more than one subsidy. These households include 189,000 households assisted through Section 236 as well as either rent supplement or Section 8, and about 46,000 households assisted through both Section 515 and Section 8.

h. Includes 141,000 assisted households whose loans were sold to private investors in 1987. Total outlays do not include the loss of $1 billion associated with these asset sales, however.

i. Although at the end of 1987 over 26,000 commitments for new homebuyers were still being processed, an estimated 66,000 households are expected to leave the programs in 1988. Thus, the total number of outstanding commitments is declining.

live outside the small towns and rural areas serviced by the Farmers Home Administration.

4. A very significant portion of the existing subsidized housing stock is seriously threatened. The precarious condition of a great many public housing projects has been described. More than half of all public-housing households live in projects needing moderate to substantial rehabilitation just to meet HUD standards. Nearly 1 million Section 8 existing-housing and voucher contracts will expire between FY1990 and FY1994. The cost of renewing them, under terms similar to those of the original contracts, is a staggering $73 billion. Under the reasonable assumption that market rents will rise, increasing the required per-unit subsidy, the cost is even greater. Finally, nearly 250,000 low- and moderate-rent units in privately owned developments built with federal mortgage subsidies may be lost when the use restrictions contained in the original contracts with the owners expire. If these restrictions are allowed to lapse, owners will be free to rent the units to others at higher market-level rents, convert them to condominiums, or otherwise free themselves from the original commitment to house the poor and near poor. According to the National Low Income Housing Preservation Commission, some $10 billion over the next fifteen years, in addition to legislation to require owners to extend these commitments, is required to retain these units.

During the last half of the Carter administration and during the Reagan administration, some important and superficially contradictory trends occurred in the federal low-rent housing effort. Appropriations for HUD's subsidized housing program fell from a peak of $32.2 billion in FY1978 to $9.8 billion in FY1988. In constant 1987 dollars, the drop was from $53 billion to $9.5 billion. New lending authority for FmHA's direct-loan programs dropped over this same period from $3.7 billion to $2.1 billion ($6.8 billion to $2 billion in constant 1987 dollars). On the other hand, the number of net new households receiving such assistance increased between 1977 and 1988 by 3 million (2.2 million renter households and 0.8 million homebuyers). However, the number of new rental commitments made each year has declined steadily from 1978 to 1983 (from 375,000 to 78,000) and more

TABLE 8.3

Distribution of the Eligible Population and of Rental Aid Under Various Programs, 1988
(In percentages)

	Type of household[a]				
	Elderly, no children	Nonelderly, no children	With 1 or 2 children	With 3 or more children	All
As a percentage of very low-income renters					
Eligible population in 1988	29	29	29	13	100
Percentage of total aid received by type of household					
Section 8 existing-housing vouchers[b]	32	15	38	15	100
Section 8 new construction and substantial rehabilitation	68	10	17	5	100
Public housing	38	15	29	19	100
Other HUD programs[c]	41	19	30	10	100
Section 515 rural rental assistance	51	16	25	9	100
Total	43	14	30	13	100

Source: Congressional Budget Office 1988, 56. Estimates based on data provided by the Department of Housing and Urban Development and the Farmers Home Administration.

TABLE 8.3 (Continued)

a. Income category and household types are defined in the text. Federal statistics on housing aid to the elderly commonly include commitments to households headed by handicapped individuals. In this table, however, figures for the elderly include the share of aid that goes to the handicapped elderly, while aid to other handicapped households is reflected primarily in the category of nonelderly households without children present. Overall, the handicapped occupy an estimated 8 percent of public housing units and 12 percent of Section 8 new-construction units.

b. Includes Section 8 moderate rehabilitation, loan management, property disposition, and conversion assistance.

c. Includes Section 236 and rent-supplement programs.

erratically since 1983, but still at far lower levels than in the Carter administration (see Figure 8.1, which also indicates a similar trend for homebuyer assistance [Congressional Budget Office 1988]).

The explanation of this apparent contradiction lies primarily in the changing mix of housing-subsidy programs and, to a lesser extent, in budgetary sleight-of-hand. Basically, the shift from new construction and rehabilitation (under the Section 8 program as well as the lingering public-housing commitments) to subsidies for existing housing has altered the budgetary impact markedly, apart from the changes it has wrought in the nature and effectiveness of the federal effort. Most new housing-assistance commitments are provided through annual appropriations of long-term budget authority, committing the government to expenditures of funds for the full term of the commitment. Thus, a program or an addition to a program contains, in the year in which it passes, the full funding for the duration of that contract. Programs embodying five-year commitments appear to cost far less than those which entail fifty-year or twenty-year commitments, apart from any differences in per-unit costs among the programs themselves.

The manner in which construction and modernization projects are to be financed has constituted a further change. Until 1987, the federal government made annual payments to cover the principal and interest on construction and modernization bonds floated by local housing authorities, a fairly inexpensive system in times of low interest rates (even lower for the tax-exempt local bonds). With high interest rates,

FIGURE 8.1

Net New Commitments for Renters and
New Commitments for Homebuyers, 1977-1988

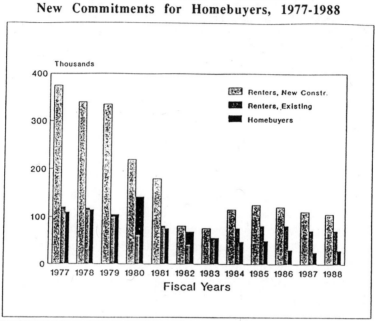

Source: Congressional Budget Office based on data provided by the Department of Housing and Urban Development and the Farmers Home Administration.

Note: Net new commitments for renters represent net additions to the available pool of rental aid and are defined as the total number of commitments for which new funds are appropriated in any year. To avoid double-counting, these numbers are adjusted for the number of commitments for which funds are deobligated or canceled that year; the number of commitments for units converted from one type of assistance to another; in the FmHA Section 515 program, the number of units that receive more than one subsidy; and, starting in 1985, the number of commitments specifically designed to replace those lost because private owners of assisted housing opt out of the programs or because public housing units are demolished.

New commitments for homebuyers are defined as the total number of new loans that the FmHA may make (or that HUD may subsidize) each year based on the maximum lending authority set by the Congress. This measure of program activity is meant to indicate how many new homebuyers can be helped each year and is therefore not adjusted to account for homeowners who leave the programs in any year because of mortgage repayments, prepayments, or foreclosures. Thus, it does not represent net additions to the total number of assisted homeowners and therefore cannot be added to net new commitments for renters.

however, these forty-year new-construction bonds and twenty-year modernization bonds show up as extraordinarily large budget outlays. In an effort to save money and eliminate these huge outlays, HUD, starting in 1987, began to finance all such projects with up-front capital grants, which reduce budget authority requirements by one-half to two-thirds.

Thus, the sharp reduction in federal budgetary outlays over the past ten years reflects the reduced number of new households being assisted each year; the change in program mix (far shorter time commitments, the average term of new commitments falling from twenty-four years in 1977 to twelve years in 1988, and lower per-unit costs to subsidize existing as opposed to new housing); and the change in the manner of financing public housing.

In summary, at a time when the housing market increasingly is unable to meet the needs of lower-income Americans, federal housing programs, while providing help for an increasing number of needy households, are falling well behind the need. The percentage of poor being helped by government housing programs is up, but the number of households *not* served has gone up to a much greater degree. Federal aid has shifted to reliance on assistance that reduces tenant costs in existing homes. This massive shift away from programs that add to the supply of housing for the poor to "tenant-based" subsidies does not increase the housing supply. In 1980, 86 percent of incremental HUD-subsidized units were new or rehabilitated Section 8 or public-housing units; by 1988 that figure had fallen to 33 percent.

What then should be the directions and directives for federal housing programs if the nation is to move closer to the National Housing Goal of "a decent home and suitable living environment for every American family," established by Congress in 1949 and reiterated in the 1968 Housing Act? Although this discussion concerns federal policy, similar conclusions apply to state and local efforts, which have in many cases increased admirably in response to federal cutbacks, but which by and large share the inadequacies of the federal effort.

First, there is clear need to devote far greater amounts of the federal budget to housing. Recent proposals by the National Low Income Housing Coalition and the Leadership Conference on Civil Rights have placed the minimal need at close to $40 billion a year. Expressed differently, an additional two cents of every federal-budget dollar, beyond the roughly one cent now spent on direct housing subsidies are needed. Covering the growing gap between what people can afford and what housing costs will require much more money than now is spent.

At a minimum, parity should be demanded between federal government spending on indirect subsidies to aid the well-off who own homes and government spending to aid those most in need. The total amount spent on HUD-subsidized housing from the 1930s, when public housing was introduced, through FY1988 ($111 billion) is just slightly more than the indirect homeowners' tax subsidy in 1987 and 1988 alone, a vast proportion of which is the homeowners' mortgage-interest and property-tax deductions (Dolbeare 1989).

Secondly, in designing the kinds of housing programs needed, permanent affordability and low basic and initial costs must be guiding principles. Both of these goals can best be met by increasing reliance on nonprofit, nonspeculative housing producers, owners, and managers. Private-market actors understandably seek to maximize their profits from all phases of the housing operation, keeping housing costs high and out of the reach of lower-income consumers. If the subsidy system is tied to owners who are constantly seeking profit maximization, without adequate controls on their activities, such problems as excessive costs, political opposition, and the lapse of use restrictions now faced in privately owned developments that for years have benefited from very large mortgage-interest subsidies will continue.

On the other hand, if housing programs are placed under the control of private nonprofit and public entities whose aim is to provide the best housing at the lowest cost for the most people – entities such as churches and synagogues, labor unions, neighborhood associations, community development corporations, resident cooperatives, and local public agencies – there is not the constant tension between the social goals of government and the private goals of those who own and manage the housing. Such forms of ownership as community land trusts, mutual housing associations, and limited-equity cooperatives can keep costs to a minimum (although even for these housing providers costs will continue to rise faster than residents' incomes, creating a constant need for additional operating subsidies). They can create housing that is permanently available to those who need it, while providing a sense of commitment and "ownership" by residents that leads to improved property maintenance and a range of social and personal benefits (see Institute for Community Economics 1982; Institute for Policy Studies 1989).[2]

A basic *right* to decent, affordable housing, a right guaranteed by the government through appropriate expenditures and programs, must be established immediately. The importance of a decent home and suitable living environment as a supportive setting for decent family life is beyond question. If the nation truly cares about its children and youth, it must make sure they have that right.

Notes

1. For a more detailed analysis of the EHAP program, from which the following paragraphs are drawn, see Hartman 1983a and b and Abrams 1983.
2. The Institute for Policy Studies Program identifies credit (debt repayment) as the central housing cost, for renters (indirectly) as well as owners, and puts forth a series of specific proposals to substitute up-front capital grants for borrowing to build and renovate housing units and to permanently retire debt on large portions of the existing housing stock.

References

Abrams, P. 1983, Spring. "Comment on 'Housing Allowances: A Critical Look'." *Journal of Urban Affairs.*

Bratt, R. G. 1986. "Public Housing: The Controversy and Contribution." In *Critical Perspectives on Housing,* eds. R.G. Bratt, C. Hartman, and A. Meyerson, 335-61. Philadelphia: Temple University Press.

Congressional Budget Office. 1988, Dec. *Current Housing Problems and Possible Federal Responses,* 10-35, 46-7 . Washington, DC: Government Printing Office.

Dolbeare, C. 1989, 6 Feb. "Low Income Housing Needs." Washington, DC: Low Income Housing Information Service.

Hartman, C. 1983a, Spring. "Rejoinder." *Journal of Urban Affairs.*

Hartman, C. 1983b, Winter. "Housing Allowances: A Critical Look." *Journal of Urban Affairs.*

Institute for Community Economics. 1982. *The Community Land Trust Handbook.* Emmaus, PA: Rodale Press.

Institute for Policy Studies Working Group on Housing. 1989. "A Progressive Housing Program for America." In *Housing Issues of the 1990s,* eds. S. Rosenberry and C. Hartman. New York: Praeger.

Leonard, P.A., Dolbeare, C.N., and Lazere, E.B. 1989. *A Place to Call Home: The Crisis in Housing for the Poor*. Washington, DC: Center on Budget and Policy Priorities and Low Income Housing Information Service.

9

Remedies for Homelessness: An Analysis of Potential Housing Policy and Program Responses

Michael A. Stegman

This chapter discusses housing policy remedies for homeless families with children. It is intended to complement two other chapters that deal with the causes of homelessness and the inadequacies of previous and current policy responses. The chapter consists of six sections. First is a brief retrospective look at assisted housing budgets during the Reagan years. Whether or not there is a causal link between the dramatic declines that occurred in new commitments to assisted housing during the 1980s and the rise of homelessness, it is the final Reagan budget that set the framework for housing deliberations by the 101st Congress.

The second section summarizes the debate on the causes of homelessness among families with children. This debate centers around the growing income inequality in our society, tightening local housing markets, and multiple problems of young single mothers that significantly retard their economic and social opportunities. The third section discusses six major low-income housing initiatives under consideration by the Congress, including the House's bill to reauthorize current housing and community development programs at somewhat higher than currently funded levels; the Senate's attempt to redefine dramatically the way in which federal low-income housing assistance is delivered; supplements or modest add-ons to current programs that would heavily target the homeless; and more radical housing initiatives, one of which would be funded from national defense accounts. The third section also outlines the parameters for a rental entitlement program that would apply to all very low-income renters who currently receive no housing assistance, and outlines the policy proposals put forth by a network of advocates who are urging the Congress to make low-income housing a part of the federal bailout of the savings and loan industry.

The fourth section assesses the extent to which previous housing programs have served different segments of the low-income population and suggests that without explicit planning at the local level, an expansion of the federal low-income housing budget will not necessarily benefit homeless families. The author's conclusions and policy recommendations are contained in the last section. As this book was going to press, the Bush administration introduced its HOPE initiative – Home Ownership and Opportunity for People Everywhere. Therefore a brief summary of the legislation and its implications for homeless families and their children is included as an addendum.

A Retrospective Look at the Assisted Housing Budget

Concentrating on the potential remedies for homelessness leaves little room in this chapter for an historical analysis of the federal role in low-income housing. Nevertheless, it is important to document changes in the assisted housing budget during the Reagan administration – not just to see if there is a causal link between the federal retreat and the rise of homelessness, but to inject a measure of fiscal reality into our discussions of policy options. The review of federal housing budgets during the Reagan years shows how relative allocations changed in favor of rental assistance over new construction programs, on the one hand, while concurrently the number of newly assisted low-income households declined each year. Both critics and supporters of the Reagan policy support their respective views by citing different budget statistics.

Critics document the federal retreat by pointing to the significant reductions in new budget authority (BA) for low-income housing since 1980 and by pointing out that *even these drastically reduced levels of funding consistently exceeded Reagan Department of Housing and Urban Development (HUD) budget requests* (Table 9.1). New budget authority – multiyear subsidy commitments for additions to the nation's subsidized housing inventory – plummeted 60 percent during the

Reagan years, from nearly $25 billion to an estimated $10 billion (Table 9.2). During this period, the number of subsidized housing starts per year dropped by more than 88 percent, from 175,000 to less than 21,000 (Table 9.3).

TABLE 9.1

Comparison of HUD Requests for New Budget Authority of Assisted Housing and Congressional Appropriations, 1983-1989 ($ Million)

Fiscal year	HUD request	Appropriation	Percentage of difference
1983	$11,815	$8,651	173.2
1984	515	9,913	1,824.9
1985	5,336	10,759	101.6
1986	499	9,966	1,897.2
1987	4,413	7,806	276.9
1988	3,457	7,687	122.4
1989	6,887	7,539	9.5

Source: "Special Memorandum," Low Income Housing Information Service, March 1989.

Reagan supporters, on the other hand, point to the steady rise in the number of households receiving housing subsidies and the corresponding increase in total annual outlays over the Reagan years. Approximately 1 million more households are receiving housing assistance today than in 1979, while annual federal expenditures for assisted housing have nearly tripled, from $4.3 billion to more than $16 billion.

In a December, 1988, op-ed piece in the *Wall Street Journal*, economist Edgar Olsen attempted to lay to rest what he called the "persistent falsehood" that the Reagan administration contributed to the rise in homelessness by starving the low-income housing sector (1988).

TABLE 9.2
Budget Authority and Outlays for Subsidized Housing, 1979-1990 ($ Million)

Fiscal year	Budget authority	Percentage of change	Low-income housing outlays	Percentage of change
1979	$24,790	—	$ 4,367	—
1980	27,932	+12.7	5,632	29.0
1981	26,927	-3.6	7,752	37.6
1982	14,608	-45.7	8,738	12.7
1983	10,498	-28.1	9,998	14.4
1984	12,671	+20.7	11,270	12.7
1985	26,879	+112.1	25,263	124.2
1986	11,643	-56.7	12,383	-51.0
1987	9,864	-18.0	12,656	2.20
1988	9,698	+1.7	13,906	9.9
1989 est	9,963	+2.7	15,299	10.02
1990 est	10,207	+2.4	16,197	5.9
Percentage of Change 1979-1990		-58.8		270.9

Source: "Special Memorandum," Low Income Housing Information Service, March 1989, Table 7.

Although new annual budget authority has plunged over the past eight years, Olsen argues that total outlays have steadily risen. This is because of an increasing federal preference for rental assistance, and not because of a reduced federal commitment to housing. That is, even if there were no diminution in the number of additional households receiving housing aid each year, a switch-over from new construction to rental assistance would result in a dramatic reduction in new budget authority. Using hypothetical figures, Olsen elaborates on this point:

> Each year Congress authorizes additional multiyear subsidy commitments under HUD's housing programs. For example, public housing projects are typically financed by issuing bonds that are retired over 40 years. At the

TABLE 9.3

HUD Subsidized Housing Starts and Completions, 1979-1990

Year	Section 8	Public housing	Total starts	Percentage of change
1979	153,251	21,868	175,119	—
1980	132,721	40,528	173,249	-1.1
1981	60,428	45,607	106,035	-38.8
1982	87,831	25,100	112,931	+6.5
1983	42,573	27,060	69,633	-38.3
1984	17,646	22,443	40,089	-42.4
1985	9,238	11,133	20,371	-49.2
1986	8,410	6,385	14,795	-28.9
1987	6,383	5,861	12,244	-17.2
1988	5,301	4,679	9,980	-18.5
1989 est	13,000	7,688	20,688	+107.3
1990 est	13,000	7,609	20,609	-3.8
Total	549,782	225,961	775,743	—
Percentage of change 1979-1990				-88.2

Source: "Special Memorandum," Low Income Housing Information Service, March 1989, Table 3.

other extreme, the commitment on voucher-type programs the administration has preferred is five years. The budget authority in a year is the sum of these additional future obligations. So if we were to shift from a strategy relying exclusively on vouchers, if the per-unit subsidies were the same under the two types of programs, and if we were to provide subsidies to the same number of additional households, budget authority would immediately fall by 87.5 percent.

In theory, Olsen is correct, but in truth, the movement away from new construction in favor of rental assistance has not held constant the number of newly assisted households each year. Concurrent with the federal government's elimination of virtually all new low-income

TABLE 9.4

Incremental Section 8 Existing Housing Certificates and Housing Vouchers, 1979-1990

Year	Section 8 certificates	Housing vouchers	Total	Percentage of change
1979	107,025	0	107,025	—
1980	107,288	0	107,288	0.3
1981	62,324	0	62,324	-41.9
1982	96,408	0	96,408	54.7
1983	108,955	0	108,955	13.0
1984	77,625	0	77,625	-28.8
1985	58,251	11,063	69,314	-10.7
1986	65,013	9,625	104,638	51.0
1987	45,341	69,836	115,177	10.1
1988	3,713	62,915	66,628	-42.2
1988 est	18,500	27,600	46,100	-30.8
1990 est	13,700	42,500	56,200	21.9
Total	764,143	253,539	1,017,682	—
Percentage of Change 1979-1990				-47.5

Source: "Special Memorandum," Low Income Housing Information Service, March 1989, Table 3.

construction programs – which were funded just ten years ago at a level that supported more than 125,000 new housing units – net additions to the rental assistance/voucher rolls have averaged fewer than 85,000 households per year between FY1979 and FY1990 (Table 9.4). In fact, the final Reagan budget only provided for a net increase of 56,200 vouchers for FY1990.

Despite the alleged cost-effectiveness of vouchers over new construction, the recent conversion to a demand-side national low-income housing policy has neither maintained the same number of new households receiving assistance each year at a lower cost nor permitted substantially more households to be helped at a constant cost. The theoretical justifications for a demand-side housing policy by housing

TABLE 9.5

Section 8 Certificate and Voucher Expirations FY89-FY94 ($ Billion)

Year	Section 8 certificates	Housing vouchers	New budget authority needed for renewal
1989	1,437	0	$ 0.038
1990	12,581	1,063	0.667
1991	256,133	39,773	8.618
1992	180,726	71,127	7.535
1993	157,879	51,576	6.408
1994	112,061	73,617	5.782
Total	720,817	237,156	$29.048

Source: "Special Memorandum," Low Income Housing Information Service, March 1989, Table 3.

substantially more households to be helped at a constant cost. The theoretical justifications for a demand-side housing policy by housing economists like Edgar Olsen notwithstanding, *rather than simply representing a move toward greater efficiency, the lingering policy legacy of the Reagan era is the substantial decline in the incremental number of new federal low income housing commitments of any kind.*

Those who argue that there is a causal link between the rise of homelessness and an inadequate supply of permanently affordable housing (which is discussed in the next section) must not only convince the Bush administration and the Congress to resume funding new production programs, *but to dramatically expand federal rental assistance programs as well. New production is necessary to provide housing opportunities for very low-income families who suffer severe housing deprivations or are without permanent shelter. Rental assistance is also desperately needed to deal with the shrinking supply of affordable rental units in the private market and the imminent expiration of hundreds of thousands of Section 8 certificates and housing vouchers.* With respect to the latter, the cost just to renew all five-year rental assistance contracts that will expire between FY1989 and FY1994 exceeds $29 billion in new budget authority (Table 9.5).

Is Homelessness a Housing Problem?

Despite continuing debate about the causes of homelessness, there is a growing consensus that the scarcity of permanently affordable housing exacerbates the problems of families who are most vulnerable to losing their homes and, at worst, is a central cause of the problem. Though housing's role in *causing* homelessness is not a principal theme of this discussion, an overview of alternative perspectives on this issue can help the reader evaluate the various legislative proposals that are later discussed.

The growing inequality of income and opportunity in the United States ("New Study" 1989; Sege 1989) is an issue that must be addressed. Minority single-parent families, who compose the majority of all homeless families, are represented disproportionately in the bottom of the income distribution. This fact combined with the globalization of the American economy means that the rich can continue to prosper even as the fate of less competitive Americans declines (Reich 1989). If, as Reich suggests, these macroeconomic trends erode the "basis for a strong sense of interclass dependence" (1989), it will make it more difficult to create the political consensus necessary to elevate housing's role on the domestic policy agenda.

Growing price pressures in local housing markets are causing the supply of affordable rental housing to shrink, thus compounding the problems caused by stagnating incomes. Although "the percentage of homeless people who have lost their apartments through eviction is not known...one study in 1986 by the [New York] City Human Resources Administration estimated it was 26 percent" (Rimer 1989). The growing imbalance between the supply of and demand for affordable housing is discussed in this section. The section concludes with a discussion of the extent to which the problem of homelessness is both caused and compounded by other problems, such as health and related disabilities.

The Rich Get Richer

According to a recent study prepared for the House Ways and Means Committee, "taking inflation into account, the average family income of the poorest fifth of the population declined by 6.1 percent from 1979 to 1987, while the highest-paid Americans saw family income rise 11.1 percent" (Tolchin 1989). Tolchin reports, "The study found that the average family income of the poorest one-fifth of the population dropped from $5,439 in 1979 to $5,107 in 1987. In that same period, the family income of the top fifth increased to $68,775 from $61,917" (1989). Although this may be partially attributed to the feminization of poverty ("In 1960, .4 percent of all children under 18 lived with a never-married parent...in 1987 6.8 percent of children under 18 lived with a never-married parent" (Tolchin, 1989).), "almost 40 percent of the nation's 12 million poor children live with two parents, many in homes where at least one parent works" (Sege 1989).

Reich also questions the feminization-of-poverty hypothesis as an explanation of this income inequality:

> This widening gap can't be blamed on the growth in single-parent lower income families, which in fact slowed markedly after the late 1970s. Nor is it due mainly to the stingy social policy of the Reagan years. Granted Food Stamp benefits have dropped in real terms by about 13 percent since 1981, and many states have failed to raise benefits for the poor and unemployed to keep up with inflation. But this doesn't come close to accounting for the growing inequality. Rather, the trend is connected to a profound change in the American economy as it merges with the global economy. And because the merging is far from complete, this trend will not stop of its own accord anytime soon. (Reich 1989)

Because employed Americans are bearing the brunt of income inequality as a result of economic globalization over the past decade, Reich's policy proposals emphasize health care and education. By improving prenatal and postnatal health care, providing greater on-the-job learning opportunities, and improving the preparation and work skills of young people, American workers should have a better chance of being integrated into the new world economy (Reich 1989). In the meantime, housing problems will continue to filter up the socioeconomic ladder. The lagging incomes of millions of employed American households make it more difficult to accumulate enough savings for a down payment and to afford the carrying charges on a first house. Even rental housing expense burdens will only escalate for this population.

Whether this continued broadening of housing problems will increase the political support for a significantly larger federal housing presence or simply increase the competition for already-scarce housing subsidies cannot be predicted. According to Reich, however, "without the active support of the fortunate fifth, it will be difficult to muster the political will necessary for change" (1989).

The Growing Scarcity of Affordable Rental Housing

As real rents continue to increase more rapidly in the lower reaches than in the upper portion of local rent distributions, the argument that shrinking supplies of affordable rental housing have become a significant cause of homelessness is gaining more adherents. These price pressures seem to be a function of three things: the continued leaching from the inventory of some of the least competitive units; rising operating and maintenance costs; and, a filtering up of previously low-rent units in response to the demands of higher-income families for both rental and cooperative/condominium units in central locations.

Studies by the U. S. Conference of Mayors have supported the argument that "a diminishing number of low-income rental units and insufficient income are the driving forces behind much family homelessness" (Keyes 1988). This was also Wright and Lam's conclusion. In the 12 major metropolitan housing markets they examined during the period 1978-1983, the number of families in poverty rose by 36 percent, while the number of affordable rental units fell by around 30 percent (Wright and Lam 1988).

In New York City, where the poorest two-fifths of the population cannot afford to pay more than $250 a month in rent, there were 63 percent fewer apartments renting for under $200 a month and 56 percent fewer renting for under $300 a month in 1987 than in 1981. In 1987, the vacancy rate in New York City for apartments with asking rents under $300 was less than 1 percent, while it exceeded 4 percent for units with asking rents of $500 or more, and nearly 7 percent for apartments listed at $1,000 or more (Stegman 1988). While there is no systematic research on the relationship between homelessness and declining vacancy rates and rising rents, some anecdotal evidence is insightful:

> There was a time when eviction simply meant moving to another low-rent apartment – one with rats and broken pipes, but housing nonetheless. But now, in a city with an almost nonexistent vacancy rate, eviction can lead to homelessness.... Last year, 21,000 households were evicted in New York City, the overwhelming majority for nonpayment of rent....Thousands of other impoverished New Yorkers live perpetually on the brink of eviction. They are caught by a convergence of social and bureaucratic forces: the burdens of poverty, the inequities of the housing market, and welfare shelter allowances that fall far short of market rents.
>
> One tenant said she couldn't pay the rent because her husband had walked out. Another tenant was laid off. Still another can't get welfare benefits. One woman said she couldn't cover the rent because she had bought shoes for her children with the rent money; another had bought a color television. Someone else is chronically ill, or struggling with a death in the family, or addicted to crack. (Rimer 1989)

If a substantial portion of the privately held rental stock that is available to poverty-level families is in the process of being either abandoned to cut losses or upgraded in response to more positive market pressures, then the incidence of homelessness should not be expected to abate. The policy responses suggested by these market realities are a combination of demand-side and supply-side assistance. By increasing rent-paying abilities and cash flow possibilities, the former would act to prevent homelessness and improve the economics of the existing lower-rent stock, while the latter would expand the permanent supply of affordable housing.

The Causes of Homelessness

Jonathan Kozol is the most prominent proponent of the argument that the cause of homelessness is a lack of affordable housing. According to Kozol, homeless people "have no special claim, no intrinsic defect, that predisposes them to their condition" (Halpern 1989). "Would that it were that simple," say those less convinced that "housing per se can transform deeply troubled lives...." (Keyes 1988). The Institute of Medicine's Committee on Health Care for Homeless People found, for example:

These families have chronic economic, educational, vocational and social problems; have fragmented support networks; and have trouble accessing the traditional service delivery system....They also found that the prevalence rates for mental illness, alcoholism, and drug abuse are much lower among adults who are members of homeless families than among homeless adults who are not, but the fact remains that such health problems are more prevalent among homeless parents than among the general population. (Halpern 1989)

Although far from a representative sample, the conception that homeless families have multiple problems that must be dealt with comprehensively was given empirical support in a 1988 case study carried out by Catholic Charities Inc. In-depth interviews with thirty-seven homeless families with children who were illegally doubled up at Carey Gardens, a New York City public-housing project, determined that:

Carey Garden homeless families are for the most part single female headed households who belong to a minority group. The head of each household is single and never-married, has less than 4 years of high school and limited or no employment history. These individuals have multiple problems with primary emphasis on overcrowding, housing repair needs, employment, education/training and medical problems... Carey Gardens homeless families represent a client population that is in need of a variety of services that would include counseling, education/training and job placement. In addition, services should focus attention on strengthening the family unit with specific emphasis placed on helping the head of household not only cope with her particular situation but also aid in the development of necessary skills to complete their education and obtain adequate employment *prior to any attempt at finding suitable housing*. (Human Resources Administration 1988, 9, emphasis added)

Homeless families in Carey Gardens and elsewhere need a permanent home, but they also need much more than a roof over their heads. Unfortunately, with few exceptions, the major housing initiatives that are intended to address homelessness fail to treat the nonhousing problems discussed above. These initiatives are discussed in the following section.

The 101st Congress and Low-Income Housing

This section provides an overview of some of the more interesting bills that have been introduced in the 101st Congress, paying particular attention to how each of these measures would, if enacted, contribute to the provision of permanent housing for homeless families with children. Although it is not easy to distinguish a major initiative or precedent-setting legislation from a measure that would, more-or-less, carry on business as usual, six specific measures have been selected and rank-ordered as being particularly relevant to the issue of homeless families. These bills are listed, along with their principal sponsors and authorized funding levels, in the top portion of Table 9.6. Just above these proposed initiatives is the baseline budget authority the Congressional Budget Office (CBO) estimated would be required to maintain current levels of existing housing program activities over the next two years: $10.9 billion in FY1990 and $11.4 billion in FY1991. These figures are included to provide a comparison between the financial commitments embodied in the various initiatives and the current program mix.

The reader is reminded, however, that authorized funding levels can be misleading. Not only do authorizations mean nothing unless they are backed up by appropriations, but also some of the bills reauthorize current programs while others are intended to replace them; still others are being proposed as additions to current programs. Therefore, a direct comparison of authorization levels does not tell us all there is to know about the relative financial commitments embodied in the respective measures. Indeed, even CBO's baseline budget figures may be somewhat misleading because they do not reflect the cost of renewing the Section 8 certificates and housing vouchers that are due to expire over the next two years.

According to HUD, nearly 14,000 certificate/vouchers expire in FY1990, requiring nearly $700 million in new budget authority to renew for additional five-year terms. Another 290,000 will expire in FY1991, requiring nearly $9 billion in additional budget authority (Low Income Housing Information Services 1989). Thus, to the extent that these additional funds are required just to hold current Section 8 program levels constant, CBO's baseline budget numbers are substantially underestimated.

TABLE 9.6

The Legislative Landscape: Selected Low-Income Housing and Related Initiatives ($ Billion)

Bill number	Principal sponsor(s)	Major housing initiative	Funding authorization FY1990	FY1991
		CBO baseline BA to maintain current program levels	$10.9	$11.4
H.R. 1180	Gonzales	The Housing and Community Development Act of 1989	$22.9	$32.8
H.R. 140	Vento	Permanent Housing for Homeless Americans Act of 1989	$1.5	$1.5
S. 565	Cranston-O'Amato	The National Affordable Housing Act	$15.1	$15.7
H.R. 973	Frank/Kennedy	The Affordable Housing Act	$10.0	$10.0
H.R. 969	Conyers	The Jesse Gray Housing Act	$56.6	NA
H.R. 1122	Dellums	The National Comprehensive Housing Act	$35.0	NA
		CBO estimate of increased budget authority above baseline for Entitlement Voucher Program for very low-income renters[1]	$63.0	NA
		Related legislative initiatives		
S. 342	Sasser/Heinz	Liberalizes FHA down payment requirements for first-time buyers; authorizes insurance of ARMs.		
H.R. 582	Gallo	Makes eligible for Sec. 8 and gives preference to families in expiring use projects.		
H.R. 892	Kennedy-Gonzales	Strengthens and extends reporting requirements under the Home Mortgage Disclosure Act.		

TABLE 9.6 (Continued)

Related legislative initiatives (continued)

H.R. 363	Schumer	Demonstration to test cost-effectiveness of permanent housing over emergency assistance payment.
H.R. 1200	Donnelly	Extends Mortgage Revenue Bond/Mortgage Credit Certificates to 1992.
H.R. 258	Lent	Refundable federal income tax credit for owners and renters with high property taxes.
S. 355	Reigle	Authorizes tax-free withdrawals from IRAs/pensions for down payment on a home for first-time home buyers.
H.R. 1005	Dixon	Extends Low Income Housing Tax Credit (LIHTC) through 1991, and removes credit from passive loss restrictions of 1986 Tax Reform Act.
S. 405	Cranston	Extends until 1992 the VA's homeless Chronically Mentally III program.
S. 225	Moynihan	Provides mental health construction block grants to states.
S. 226	Moynihan	Safeguards mentally ill persons with episodic hospital stays from loss of SSI benefits, and extends types of mental health benefits covered by Medicaid.

Source: Congessional Budget Office, "Current Housing Problems and Possible Federal Responses," Washington, D.C., December 1988, p. 106.

The author's rationale for selecting the six major initiatives and deciding their order of importance is as follows. In first place is H.R. 1180, sponsored by Congressman Henry B. Gonzalez (D, Texas), who chairs the House Housing Subcommittee. Although it contains some new programs, H.R. 1180 is essentially a measure to reauthorize existing housing and community development programs at a slightly higher level than currently funded. In addition to containing two new initiatives, which are discussed below, another reason why the Gonzalez bill is authorized at twice the level of the CBO baseline is because it provides funds to replace expiring Section 8 certificates/vouchers.

H.R. 140, Congressman Bruce Vento's (D, Minnesota) Permanent Housing for the Homeless Act, is in second place because the potential impact of its modest authorization level ($1.5 billion for each of the next two years) only makes sense when these funds are understood to be increments to current program activity levels. In third place is S. 565, the National Affordable Housing Act, cosponsored by Senators Alan Cranston (D, California) and Alphonse D'Amato (R, New York), who are chairman and ranking minority member, respectively, of the Senate Housing Subcommittee. Authorized at a funding level that is 37 percent ($4 billion) higher than the CBO baseline, Cranston-D'Amato contains a dramatically new, more flexible approach to the funding and delivery of federal low-income housing assistance in the United States. This puts the Senate (via S. 565) in direct competition with the House (via H.R. 1180) to define the future framework of a national housing policy. Although the Gonzalez bill is authorized at a substantially higher level than Cranston-D'Amato, most of this difference is accounted for by the fact that H.R. 1180 reauthorizes community development and rural housing programs in addition to dealing with expiring Section 8 certificates. The Senate Housing Subcommittee plans to deal with Section 8 and related issues in a separate bill.

In fourth and fifth places are two measures that, if enacted, would dramatically alter the low-income housing landscape. H.R. 973, cosponsored by Congressmen Barney Frank (D, Massachusetts) and Joe Kennedy (D, Massachusetts), would provide $10 billion in additional low-income housing production funds per year for the next five years. The Jesse Gray Housing Act (H.R. 969), sponsored by Congressman John Conyers (D, Michigan), is even more expansive and costly. This measure authorizes the construction and preservation of 600,000 public housing units per year for the next 10 years.

The final major initiative is H.R. 1122, sponsored by Congressman Ronald Dellums (D, California). Authorized at an initial level of $35 billion in new spending authority, the bill would expand dramatically the social housing sector by providing funds for the public sector to buy out private landlords and other property owners for the benefit of the poor.

The Dellums bill is ranked at the bottom of the list of six major low-income housing proposals not because it lacks potential to aid families at risk. Quite the contrary, its potential is enormous. It is listed last because of the author's judgment that, unlike the Cranston-D'Amato measure, it does not have the necessary political support to engage the Congress in serious debate.

In addition to the six major proposals that will be discussed below, Table 9.6 lists other legislative proposals. Although they will not be discussed in detail, these proposals either are highly targeted on the homeless or are representative of broader housing concerns in the Congress. An example of the former is H.R. 363 sponsored by Congressman Schumer (D, New York) that authorizes HUD to undertake a demonstration comparing the relative costs of financing permanent housing for homeless families on welfare with the costs of emergency assistance payments that are used to house these same families in welfare hotels.

Among other low-income housing measures is a proposal to liberalize the passive loss and other restrictions relating to private investment in low-income housing that were contained in the 1986 Tax Reform Act (H.R. 1005). Another proposal would give families who live in government-assisted housing projects, where low-income use restrictions are due to expire, priority for Section 8 rental assistance (H.R. 582). Representative of efforts to assist first-time home buyers are the Sasser-Heinz bill (S. 342) to liberalize FHA down payment requirements; S. 355, which would permit tax-free withdrawals from Individual Retirement Accounts (IRA) and other retirement accounts for the purpose of making a down payment; and H.R. 1200, which would extend for another three years state and local authority to issue tax-exempt mortgage revenue bonds and mortgage credit certificates.

Curiously, despite the consensus that rising housing expense burdens keep countless thousands of low-income families at the brink of homelessness, only Congressman Vento's homeless assistance bill (H.R. 140) addresses the problem of rental assistance, and does so only modestly. Because of the importance of income support and the fact that rental assistance must compete for funds with the various production initiatives, CBO's estimate that it would cost $63 billion in new budget authority to extend rental assistance to every very low-income renter who does not now receive such assistance also has been noted in Table 9.6.

Following the discussion of the six major housing initiatives listed above is a summary of the affordable housing provisions of the Financial Institution Reform, Recovery, and Enforcement Act (the savings and loan bailout law) that was enacted by the Congress in the summer of 1989.

H.R. 1180: The Housing and Community Development Act of 1989 (Gonzalez)

This two-year $56 billion housing and community development measure, sponsored by the House Housing Subcommittee Chairman Henry B. Gonzalez, is important because it is the basis of the House of Representative's major housing legislation this year. Unlike the Senate's principal legislation (S. 565) that attempts to break new ground in the delivery of federal low-income housing resources, H.R. 1180 primarily reauthorizes existing housing and community development programs.

Of the measure's two new initiatives, one creates a housing trust fund that is aimed at reversing the recent decline in homeownership rates and the other attempts to increase the capacity of the nonprofit sector to produce permanently affordable housing. The latter, a program initially proposed by Congressman Joseph Kennedy, is also contained in H.R. 973, which is discussed later. The trust fund proposal authorizes $1 billion over the next two years to write down mortgages for first-time homebuyers to an interest rate no greater than 6 percent. Mortgage buydowns and other forms of assistance would be made available to families whose incomes do not exceed 115 percent of the area median income. The subsidies would be repayable with interest upon sale of the property.

In addition to reauthorizing HUD and Farmers Home Administration housing and community development programs at somewhat higher levels than they are currently funded, Title V – Homeless Prevention – authorizes approximately $15 billion for the continuation of rental subsidies in troubled assisted housing projects and renewal of expiring Section 8 rental certificates and vouchers. It also authorizes $250 million in each of the next two years for the Section 8 Moderate Rehabilitation Program that would be targeted specifically to the renovation of permanent housing for the homeless. These funds would be over and above those authorized for the same use under Section 441 of the McKinney Act.

Another element of the bill's homeless prevention provisions is a two-year extension of the moratorium on the prepayment of HUD-insured mortgages on privately owned low- and moderate-income rental projects that was initially enacted in the Housing and Community Development Act of 1987. As an incentive to owners not to convert their low-income properties to market-rate occupancy, the bill provides that up to 10 percent of the aggregate budget authority appropriated for the Section 8 Existing and Moderate Rehabilitation Programs shall be reserved for allocation to "expiring use" projects.

H.R. 140: Permanent Housing For Homeless Americans Act of 1989 (Vento)

Three distinguishing features of H.R. 140 are its near-term emphasis; the fact that it supplements rather than replaces existing federal housing assistance programs; and, its implicit belief that there are enough housing units in cities and towns across the country that, if renovated and made affordable to the poor, could make a significant dent in the homeless problem. The bill authorizes $1.5 billion for each of the next two years to be allocated across four program areas.

Section 8 certificates. Approximately 7,000 additional Section 8 certificates for allocation by public housing authorities to very low-income families or individuals, including the homeless, would be funded by $450 million in each of the next two years. What distinguishes these rental certificates from the mainstream Section 8 Existing Housing Program is their fifteen-year contract period. This is in contrast to the five-year term the Congress has set for newly authorized rental certificates and vouchers. This incremental allocation of rental assistance would be distributed using the Community

Development Block Grant formula. The formula would be modified to include a "homeless" variable derived from data included in Comprehensive Homeless Assistance Plans (CHAPs) submitted by localities under the McKinney Homeless Assistance Act.

Moderate rehabilitation certificates. The bill also authorizes $250 million per year in additional funds in FY1990 and FY1991 for the Section 8 Moderate Rehabilitation Program. These ten-year assistance contracts would support the renovation of up to 3,000 additional permanent housing units per year for homeless families and individuals.

Reclaiming vacant/abandoned public housing. Congressman Vento would add $500 million per year to the public housing modernization program over the CBO baseline level of $1.8 billion. This money would be targeted specifically to the thousands of vacant, derelict units that have fallen out of the usable inventory. At an average modernization cost of $25,000 per unit, this program could help reclaim around 20,000 public housing units for homeless families. Given the need to redesign and reconfigure many completely or partially vacant public-housing buildings, and the general complexity or of the modernization process, funds contained in this title of the bill probably would not bring additional housing units on line until late 1990 or 1991.

Reclaiming In Rem housing. H.R. 140 is the only proposed measure that would explicitly set aside funding for the renovation of city-owned housing units taken for failure of their private owners to pay property taxes. The bill provides $300 million in each of the next two years for individual grants of up to $10,000 for rehabilitating and converting these *In Rem* units. This section of the Vento bill alone eventually would create up to 60,000 additional housing units for homeless and other very low-income families.

S. 565: The National Affordable Housing Act (Cranston-D'Amato)[1]

According to its principal sponsors, the chairman and ranking minority member of the Senate Housing Subcommittee, the National Affordable Housing Act will define a new, cost-effective national housing policy. Building on the bipartisan recommendations of a two-year study by the National Housing Task Force, cochaired by noted developer James Rouse and Fannie Mae Chairman David Maxwell, S. 565 proposes a substantial reorganization of the Department of Housing and Urban Development. The bill calls for the creation of a new assistant secretary for supportive housing to administer programs serving elderly, handicapped, and homeless persons; a new Office of Affordable Housing Preservation responsible for retaining affordable privately owned and publicly assisted housing for low-income and moderate-income persons; and, a new corporate entity, the Government National Home Corporation (HOME), that would provide formula funding to states and localities for a range of housing activities. The HOME Corporation would help deliver various kinds of housing assistance, provide credit enhancements, and furnish technical assistance to program participants.

The Housing Opportunity Partnership (HOP) Program. In contrast to all previous project-specific production programs, housing aid under S. 565 would be delivered through a new Housing Opportunity Partnership (HOP) Program. Under this program HUD would allocate funds, partly by formula (80 percent) to states and large communities, and partly by national competition (20 percent), among those same participants, with half of the competitive fund going to states and half to localities. Jurisdictions would receive HOP funds from a revolving investment trust fund established in the HOME Corporation. They would be required to make a 25 percent match of the federal funds from other sources. HOP assistance would be targeted to low- and moderate-income persons. A jurisdiction would have to use at least 80 percent of its HOP funds for units occupied by lower-income persons, with at least 40 percent used for units occupied by very low-income persons. Rents in HOP-assisted units could not exceed the existing Section 8 fair market rent for comparable units.

Restrictions also would be applied to HOP-assisted homeownership. The housing purchase price could not exceed 95 percent of the area's median sales price; the housing must be the principal residence of a first-time home buyer who qualifies as moderate income at the time of purchase; and, further, the program must provide ownership opportunities to families with a broad range of incomes below the area median income.

Rental assistance. The bill also would create a single rent subsidy program incorporating both voucher and certificate programs. Called rental credits, the subsidies would have a five-year term, would require tenants to pay no more than 30 percent of their income on rent, and, in a

TABLE 9.7

National Affordable Housing Act (S.565)
FY1990 Authorization Levels ($000)

PROGRAM	CBO baseline Units	CBO baseline BA	S.565 Units	S.565 BA	Difference BA
HOME Corporation/HOP		$0	180,000	$3,000,000	3,000,000
Project Retrofit/CHSP		6,000		50,000	44,000
Subtotal new programs		6,000	180,000	3,050,000	3,044,000
Elderly:					
Advance[a]		441,000		829,400	388,400
Rental	7,077	1,009,322	12,000	481,608	(527,714)
Handicapped:					
Rental	2,359	370,065	5,000	328,705	(41,360)
Section 8:					
Rental assistance	70,395	2,311,443	100,000	3,155,500	844,057
Preservation:					
Prop disposition	3,136	320,083	3,136	320,083	0
Loan management	7,450	151,426	7,450	151,426	0
Public housing	331	31,313	331	31,313	0
SROs	1,260	46,845	1,345	50,000	3,155
Public housing:					
Operating costs		1,684,000		1,800,000	116,000
Modernization		1,714,473		1,900,000	185,527
Construction	4,967	357,422	5,000	359,825	2,403
Indian	1,235	92,973	1,250	94,125	1,152
Rural housing:					
Rental assistance		287,000		287,000	0
Grant programs		51,690		51,690	0
Loan authority	42,415	1,921,151	42,415	1,921,151	0
Homeless assistance		131,000		241,000	110,000
Total budget authority		$10,927,206		$15,052,826	$4,125,620
Total units	140,625		357,927		
Total units less estimated overlap and preservation	129,708		311,010		

Source: Senate Housing Subcommittee.

a. Includes advances on elderly and handicapped housing.

departure from current practices, would be allocated to states and localities, rather than directly to public housing authorities.

Homeless assistance. S. 565 provides that homeless assistance under the McKinney Act would be distributed by formula to states and localities in a way that gives grantees the flexibility to decide how to use the funds for various eligible activities.

Public housing. Although local public housing authorities are eligible to receive HOP funds, S. 565 also reauthorizes a separate public housing and Indian housing production program at a level of 6,250 units (Table 9.7) for each of the next two years and restricts the size of new projects to fewer than 100 units. It also would broaden the income groups served in public housing by permitting up to 25 percent of all new tenants in a single year to have an income between 50 percent and 80 percent of the local area median.

Authorization levels. For FY1990, the bill authorized $15.1 billion in new budget authority, including $3 billion for HOP, to create and support 311,010 incremental housing units (Table 9.7). This is approximately $4 billion more than the $10.9 billion CBO baseline authorization level for FY1990, which could support 130,000 incremental units at the current program mix.

H.R. 973: The Affordable Housing Act (Frank/Kennedy) (Also, Title III H.R. 1180)

This measure combines Congressman Barney Frank's proposal to create a $9 billion-a-year, five-year program to produce permanently affordable limited-equity cooperatives and mutual housing projects, with Joe Kennedy's nearly $1 billion-a-year Community Housing Partnership initiative. Although at a significantly reduced funding level, the Kennedy part of H.R. 973 is also contained in Title III of H.R. 1180, the Gonzalez reauthorization bill discussed earlier.

Presumably, both components of this bill are to be viewed as additions to the CBO baseline of current program activities. Title I, Assistance for Affordable Housing, authorizes capital grants (with a 20 percent local match) for new construction and substantial rehabilitation and acquisition of existing housing, including the modernization of public housing projects and housing owned by nonprofit entities. The title also authorizes the payment of continuing operating subsidies for the housing built under the measure. Construction funds would be allocated by formula to localities based upon the size of the low-income renter population, the number of very low-income families paying more than 30 percent of their income for rent, the vacancy rate in rental housing, and the size of waiting lists for federally assisted housing. Ninety percent of the funds would be reserved for families at or below 50 percent of the area median, and the remaining 10 percent for families between 50 percent and 80 percent of the median.

The Frank measure's direct tie to homelessness lies in its tight targeting requirements for those who will be eligible to live in the housing and those who will receive construction assistance. Priority for housing developed under the act is given to families, including homeless families with children, homeless elderly individuals, homeless individuals who are chronically mentally ill, homeless individuals with physical illnesses or disabilities, and other homeless single individuals. The bill also contains stringent requirements for potential grantees that will assure a long-term concern with the problems of the homeless. Each grantee organization must be established and controlled by residents of the community, must employ homeless individuals in the construction and rehabilitation or management of the project, must provide social services, and must be able to provide a 20 percent match of federal funds.

Title II of the bill, which provides both educational and technical assistance as well as capital funds to strengthen and expand the network of community housing partnerships, is based on the premise that "during the 1980s, the nonprofit sector has, despite severe obstacles caused by inadequate funding, played an increasingly important role in the production and rehabilitation of affordable housing in communities across the nation." H.R. 973 authorized $980.5 million per year for each of the fiscal years 1990 to 1994 to be allocated to community housing partnerships using the existing block grant (CDBG) formula, with 60 percent of the funds going to metropolitan areas and 30 percent to the states for use in nonmetropolitan communities, while 10 percent would be reserved for direct allocation to nonprofit organizations. As is the case with the Frank initiative, the Kennedy measure requires local contributions to affordable housing projects; in this case, however, it is a higher 25 percent match.

Unlike the housing that would be built under Title I of the bill, the community housing partnership projects of Title II would not necessarily be targeted to the homeless. They would, however, have to adhere to the occupancy requirements specified in the Internal Revenue Code relating to tax credit-eligible, low-income rental projects. Since the bill prohibits funds from being used to assist families with incomes above 80 percent of median, this means that up to 80 percent of the residents in units in community housing partnership projects may have incomes between 50 percent and 80 percent of the median.

H.R. 969: The Jesse Gray Housing Act (Conyers)

Named in honor of the late leader of the National Tenants Organization, H.R. 969 would mount a massive assault on homelessness and inadequate housing through the production of 500,000 new public housing units a year for the next ten years, plus the preservation of an additional 100,000 units per year. To appreciate the enormous commitment reflected in the Conyers bill, compare its production targets to the total size of the existing public housing inventory that took more than fifty years to create. Although it will not happen, if H.R. 969 were to be fully funded by the Congress – at an annual appropriation in excess of $34 billion excluding the cost of operating subsidies – the Jesse Gray Housing Act would double the size of the nation's public housing stock in less than three years.

In addition to an enormous production program, H.R. 969 would lower rents in public and other publicly assisted housing from 30 percent to 25 percent of income and create opportunities for tenants to learn productive jobs skills so that they eventually could move out of public housing. As a way of remedying racially discriminatory practices of construction trade unions, the bill would require each public housing authority to involve residents in the construction and preservation of the public housing stock. Up to 50 percent of construction workers would have to be public housing tenants or residents in the construction area.

H. R. 1122: The National Comprehensive Housing Act (Dellums)

This broad-based housing measure represents a radical departure from previous national housing policy for three reasons. First, its avowed purpose is to create a nonmarket social housing sector that, over time, would control an increasingly larger share of the nation's low- and moderate-income housing stock. Second, H.R. 1122, which is authorized at $55.8 billion for FY1990, is the first low-income housing bill that would tie future year authorizations to the level of tax expenditures on owner-occupied housing. Arguing that the present housing crisis threatens our national security, Congressman Dellums' bill directs that, whenever sufficient appropriations to fully fund his bill are not voted by the Congress, the difference would have to be provided from unnamed national security accounts. Third, the National Comprehensive Housing Act is the first housing bill that would condition local receipt of other entitlement and discretionary federal grant-in-aid funds – such as those for highway and sewer construction, CDBG, economic development, and small business programs – on local compliance with the act.

Creating a social housing sector. H.R. 1122 is based on five basic principles: (1) expand the amount of housing under social ownership; (2) expand social production and increase social control of the housing-production process; (3) expand direct public financing of housing production and ownership, thereby reducing the dependence on privately controlled debt and equity capital; (4) control speculative private use and disposition of land; and (5) increase resident control over housing and neighborhood decisions.

Of the four major titles, one authorizes a $33 billion program to expand the production of permanently affordable housing that would be owned and controlled by community-based nonprofits. A second mandates the local enactment of eviction and co-op conversion controls, a warranty of habitability, and standby authority for the implementation of rent controls and restrictions on housing demolitions of privately owned low- and moderate-income rental housing in the event of local emergencies. It also provides funds for local governments to acquire such housing from private owners who cannot or will not adequately maintain their properties. Once removed from the private market, the housing would be turned over to social owners or public housing authorities.

A third title of the bill would promote affordable homeownership through foreclosure protection by granting low- and moderate-income homeowners the option of deeding their dwelling units to a social entity in exchange for lifetime occupancy at an affordable monthly cost. The bill also would grant elderly homeowners a similar opportunity; rather than make monthly housing payments, however, the elderly would receive a lifetime annuity, based on the value of their equity, that would permit them to maintain an adequate standard of living.

Finally, the bill authorizes more than $6 billion for the purpose of protecting the federal government's enormous investment in government-assisted housing. Funds would be used to increase public housing operating subsidies; reduce rent in federally assisted housing to 25 percent of income; increase allowable deductions from income for child care and other expenses; restructure loan terms for government-held mortgages on nonprofit housing; and permit the same subsidies to be paid to private owners of subsidized housing if they agree to convert their projects to social ownership.

Expanding Rental Assistance to Prevent Homelessness

Paying too large a share of income for housing is the most widespread housing problem among very low-income renters. In 1985, about 80 percent faced this problem (CBO 1988). Despite the fact that an inability to pay the rent may be an important cause of homelessness, no major legislation has been introduced that would dramatically increase the amount of rental assistance for low-income families. Nor, for that matter, has any serious consideration been given to changing the welfare system to require that benefits to single-parent families and others receiving assistance be large enough to cover the basic costs of shelter. This is not only important for families struggling to maintain a decent home, but also for homeless families with children who are now living in emergency shelters or transitional housing because their welfare benefits are too small for them to find an affordable place to live.

According to Newman and Schnare, for example, "On average, neither AFDC, SSI nor GA provide shelter payments that equal the cost of standard quality housing as measured by HUD's Fair Market Rents (FMRs): AFDC shelter payments represent only 49 percent of the applicable FMR, whole SSI and GA allowances hover around 66 percent of FMR" (Table 9.8) (1988).

The politics of rental assistance. There are two main reasons why inadequate attention is being paid to the demand side of the housing equation. The first has to do with the politics of federal housing policy, and the second with the high costs of entitlement programs. Whether or not demand-side advocates are correct that rental assistance can help more low-income families per federal dollar than production subsidies, this efficiency argument has been used to do more than repeal costly new construction programs. As indicated in the section discussing the historical role of the government in low-income housing, rather than convert incremental budget authority that had been devoted to production subsidies to the expansion of the Section 8 Existing Housing Program, the Reagan administration shut off new production and simultaneously reduced the incremental number of low-income families receiving rental benefits each year.

Between FY1981 and FY1989, the combined number of Section 8 new construction, substantial rehabilitation, and public housing units approved for funding plummeted by more than 80 percent, from 110,000 to around 17,000. At the same time, more than 62,000 new Section 8 rental certificates (and vouchers) were funded in 1981, compared with just 46,000 in FY1989. Thus, with low-income housing issues regaining a prominent role on the nation's domestic agenda, there is good reason why most housing advocates would do anything to keep the policy debate from becoming unnecessarily polarized along new production versus rental assistance lines.

The high cost of entitlements. The second reason why there has been so little discussion of the role of rental assistance in preventing and remedying homelessness is its high cost. In this case, cost does not refer to the cost per new household assisted, but to the aggregate cost of closing the rental gap for the universe of very low-income renters. According to Newman and Schnare, for example, nationally, "shelter allowances under the major welfare programs would have to be raised by an average of between 50 and 100 percent to meet the Fair Market Rent standards employed by HUD," at a cost of about $10 billion a year in 1987 dollars (1988).

Long-time housing advocate Cushing Dolbeare, one of the few to promote a low-income entitlement program of rental assistance, has urged the Bush administration to boost federal spending on low-income housing by $30 billion a year in order to "provide housing allowances to all low income households who cannot obtain decent, affordable housing without it." According to Dolbeare:

TABLE 9.8
Comparison of Shelter Payment Adequacy under AFDC, SSI AND GA
(1984-85)

	Shelter payment	Fair market rent	Shelter payment: fair market rent
AFDC, 4-person family			
Northeast	$178	$301	59%
North Central	138	266	52
South	76	278	27
West	208	326	64
Weight average:	$144	$289	59%

Source: S. Newman and A. Schnare 1988, 6.

The program should be patterned on the present Section 8 existing or voucher programs, and cover the difference between the amount each household can afford and the monthly cost of housing of the size they need in the area or community where they live. Quality standards should be applied and enforced, but funds not used for allowances because decent housing is unavailable should be allocated to the local (or state) agency to be used to acquire, rehabilitate or build housing which will be permanently reserved for low income households. (Dolbeare 1989)

The Congressional Budget Office has carried out a more systematic analysis of the costs of a universal rental assistance program. Estimating that 2.2 million additional very low-income households would receive benefits under such an entitlement, CBO determined that:

If vouchers were used to provide all additional aid, an entitlement program would require an increase of $63 billion in Budget Authority in 1990, compared with current policy. It would add, when fully phased in, about

$11.1 billion per year (in 1990 dollars) to current outlays to serve all very low-income renters estimated to participate. (CBO 1988, 105)

The savings and loan bailout: a little room for low-income housing

According to syndicated columnist William Raspberry, "the savings and loan crisis is to economic theorists what the Bible is to religionists: There's something in it to justify practically any doctrine you care to name":

> It's either deregulation gone haywire or the result of too much reliance on government. It is the result of local economic conditions, or it is the inevitable outcome of merger-mania. It is caused by faltering confidence in the thrift institutions or else the overconfidence in the federal government's willingness to bail out the improvident. (Raspberry 1989)

Although a comprehensive assessment of the Bush administration's proposed $150 billion off-budget rescue of the Federal Savings and Loan Insurance Corporation (FSLIC) is beyond the scope of this chapter, there are several relevant low- and moderate-income housing provisions of the Financial Institution Reform, Recovery and Enforcement Act (H.R. 1278 – the Savings and Loan Bailout Bill) that was signed into law on 9 August 1989. Despite his inability to achieve consensus in the House on a major piece of housing legislation during the first session of the 101st Congress, House Banking Committee Chairman Gonzalez wanted to ensure that a restructured thrift industry contributes to "the real credit needs of local communities" by enacting stiffer antiredlining laws (Katz 1989). The Savings and Loan Bailout Law achieves this goal by expanding lenders' reporting requirements under the Home Mortgage Disclosure Act (HMDA) to include information not only on loans actually made, but also on the number and dollar amount of completed mortgage loan applications received by the lender, grouped by census tract. The bill also provides for the public release of lender reviews conducted by federal regulators under the Community Reinvestment Act (CRA), which requires financial institutions to meet the credit needs of their communities.

Financial Democracy Campaign proposals. Six months before the passage of the bailout bill, the Southern Finance Project, located in Charlotte, North Carolina, unveiled a radical plan to restructure the savings and loan system in a way that would dramatically increase the supply of low-and moderate-income housing. Endorsed by a loosely knit network of 150 community, labor, and consumer organizations under the name of the Financial Democracy Campaign (FDC), the plan would, among other things, "force the 12 regional Federal Home Loan Banks to require thrifts to invest at least 30 percent of the banks' cash advances in community development and housing for low- and moderate-income families" (Katz 1989). It would also establish a Housing Opportunities Fund that would be capitalized by a tax on the financial services industry to provide low-cost financing for first-time home buyers. Additionally, it would halt immediately the sale of any vacant residential properties held by FSLIC or other entities to which the properties may devolve, and establish a program to sell these properties at preferred rates to first-time home buyers and to local public housing authorities and community-based organizations for permanent use by low-income and homeless families. Finally, through a variant of the Depression-era Home Owner's Loan Corporation that refinanced the seriously delinquent mortgages of hundreds of thousands of families threatened with the loss of their homes, the Financial Democracy Campaign insists that a way be found to renegotiate loans with homeowners whose housing has been repossessed as a result of local or regional economic distress (Financial Democracy Campaign 1989). Although FDC did not get everything it was after, the bailout law does contain several affordable housing provisions that are variations of those it proposed.

The affordable housing program. The bill requires each of the regional federal home loan banks to create two new lending programs that will operate through local thrift institutions. The first is a cash advance program that will offer funds to thrifts at the FHLB's cost of borrowing to enable them to carry out community-oriented lending programs. Community-oriented loans can be used to finance home purchases, renovations, and economic development activities that benefit low- and moderate-income families. Though more modest than proposed by FDC, the bill also requires each FHLB to set up a second cash advance program with subsidized interest rates that would enable local thrifts to make low-interest loans for the purchase of low- and moderate-income housing. The Low Income Housing Information Service states:

The law does not specify the degree of subsidy that these cash advances are expected to provide. Between calendar years 1990 and 1993, each FHLB must contribute 5 percent of the previous year's earnings to subsidize the Affordable Housing Fund. In calendar year 1994 this goes up to 6 percent and in 1995 and beyond it rises to 10 percent. The aggregate contributions made by all FHLBs must equal at least $50 million per year in 1990-1994; at least $75 million in 1994; and at least $100 million in 1995 and beyond. (Low Income Housing Information Service 1989, 6)

Property disposition. As indicated above, the advocacy community fought to have included in the bailout bill a provision that would grant nonprofits priority status to acquire affordable residential properties held in portfolio by insolvent thrifts that could be used for permanent housing for low- and moderate-income families and homeless families. Specifically,

The law creates a new agency, The Resolution Trust Corporation (RTC) to acquire and dispose of the various assets held by insolvent institutions. The law requires that certain real estate assets be offered on a preferential basis to nonprofits and public agencies. The RTC may offer these properties with below-market rate financing and at prices below what might otherwise be possible to help these buyers maintain some of the units for low and very income use, at restricted rents, for the remaining useful life of the property.

For single family homes, the income limit is below 115 percent of the adjusted area median income. For multifamily properties, at least 80 percent of the units must be set aside for very low income people (below 50 percent of the adjusted median income) and at least another 15 percent for low income households (below 80 percent of the adjusted area median).

The single family properties must have an appraised value not exceeding $67,500. Multifamily properties must have a per unit appraised value not greater than $29,500 for studio apartments, $33,816 for one-bedrooms, $41,180 for two-bedrooms, $53,195 for three-bedrooms and $58,353 for four or more bedrooms. (Low Income Housing Information Service 1989, 2)

Despite this apparent victory for the low-income housing community, there are three reasons why this program is not likely to benefit very poor and homeless families with children. First, based upon the initial sales program announced by RTC, the federal government is not providing subsidized financing to potential buyers. Secondly, at best, there are just a few thousand properties that are potentially eligible to be sold under this affordable sales program, and, third, the properties are geographically concentrated in fewer than a dozen states.

Which of the Poor Shall Be Served?

Our housing assistance system is fraught with three kinds of inequities that impact homeless families with children and those threatened with homelessness. The first is that housing benefits are not universally available to all who meet the eligibility requirements, which means that there is a lottery effect to housing programs. Some needy households win big and receive large benefits, while other equally deserving families receive no help at all. This is even true for very low-income renters who, as a group, suffer from the most severe housing deprivations. According to the Congressional Budget Office, in 1988 no more than 38 percent of all very low-income renters could potentially be served by the 4.7 million rental assistance commitments available from past appropriations (CBO 1988).

The second inequity is the degree to which different household groups are served by new construction versus rental assistance programs. Despite the heavy supply-side emphasis of most legislative housing proposals dealing with the homeless, the fact is that "new [rental] construction programs have heavily benefited the elderly, while rental assistance programs have served a higher proportion of families with children" (CBO 1988). According to CBO:

> New construction programs traditionally have helped elderly renters at rates exceeding their share of the very-low-income renter population, which is estimated to be about 29 percent in 1988....This tendency is particularly strong in the Section 8 new construction program, under which more than two-thirds of all subsidies are received by the elderly, but is less pronounced in the older production programs such as public housing and Section 236. Moreover, while programs that assist renters living in existing dwellings are more likely than the production programs to serve families with children, they too aid the elderly disproportionately. (CBO 1988, 54)

More germane to this discussion, however, is the third inequity that considers the varying rates at which the different types of households are served by the assisted housing system and the kind of help they receive. For many reasons, including eligibility rules, differing subsidy levels, local management practices, and housing market dynamics, housing programs serve various types of households at different rates. CBO reports, "The roughly two million outstanding commitments available to the elderly can serve an estimated 51 percent to 57 percent of all very low-income elderly renters...[while] commitments available to households with children...can serve, at most, roughly 38 percent of those with very low income" (1988, xviii).

To quantify the extent to which very low-income families with children are underserved compared with the elderly, how many additional households would have to receive assistance to match the 51 percent service level of the elderly can be determined. According to CBO, it would take 850,000 new subsidy commitments to families with children while declaring a moratorium on new aid to the elderly just to equalize their respective service levels (CBO 1988).

The significance of this entire discussion to the future possibilities of homeless families with children can be summed up in a single sentence. Without explicit planning at all levels of government, neither a sizable increase in federal housing assistance, in general, nor a resumption of subsidized construction, in particular, would necessarily result in the provision of permanent housing for homeless families with children in a volume proportionate to the need.

Federal Selection Preferences

On 15 January 1988, HUD published a regulation in the Federal Register that will substantially increase the extent to which homeless families are given priority for assisted housing. The regulation, which all public housing authorities had to adopt by 15 July 1988, said, in part:

> In selecting applicants for admission to its projects, each PHA must give preference to applicants who are otherwise eligible for assistance and who, at the time they are seeking assistance, are involuntarily displaced, living in substandard housing, or paying more than 50 percent of family income for rent. (Code of Federal Regulations 1988)

Before enactment of the 1979 Housing and Community Development Amendments and the 1983 Housing and Urban-Rural Recovery Act, which mandated the above federal selection preferences, housing authorities were free to adopt their own tenant selection criteria (McCormick 1988). According to the National Association of Housing and Redevelopment Officials (NAHRO):

> PHAs took strong opposition to the federal preferences... They argued that nothing in the legislation creating the three preferences suggests that Congress intended to subordinate local discretion by granting primacy to the federal preferences. They also argued that local preferences are in the nature of a contract, and that communities agree to cooperate in the development of assisted housing in return for the assurance that their needy residents will be served. (McCormick 1988)

HUD responded to the opposition by permitting public housing authorities to select up to 10 percent of the applicants who initially receive assistance in any single year according to their own locally determined priorities. This same exception, however, was not granted to private owners involved in Section 8 programs, including certificates and vouchers. Thus, under current regulations, all new recipients of Section 8 certificates and vouchers and at least 90 percent of new public housing tenants each year must meet at least one of the three federal selection preferences.

Although the Congress does not rank various national housing goals, the introduction of mandatory federal tenant selection preferences has the clear effect of subordinating one federal housing goal – that of attaining a broad income mix in each public housing project – for the goal of providing scarce housing resources to the most needy. And, the most needy are those without a permanent place to live. The fact that HUD's definition of "involuntarily displaced" includes families and individuals who are "not living in standard, permanent replacement housing" (Code of Federal Regulations 1988) means that an increasing number of homeless families with children eventually will be rehoused in public housing. It should be mentioned, however, that HUD's definition of "family" includes single elderly persons and certain handicapped individuals. Thus, families with children might not always be favored by local public housing authorities (PHAs) (Code of Federal Regulations 1988). Moreover, under the new tenant selection system, local PHAs still retain the right to determine the relative weights to apply to each of the three federal preferences. If housing authorities wish to avoid placing high concentrations of homeless families in their projects,

PHAs could choose to weight substandard housing and excessive housing costs more heavily than the displacement criterion.

Do Federal Selection Preferences Apply To Other Programs?

The federal selection preferences will have a binding effect on housing authorities. More applicants per year on public housing waiting lists who meet at least one of the selection preferences – including homeless families with children – will receive permanent housing than would be the case without these federal preferences. It follows, therefore, that any low-income housing program to which the federal selection preferences apply is more likely to benefit homeless families with children.

For example, since H.R. 140, sponsored by Congressman Vento, would provide nearly $1.2 billion in each of the next two years to two programs subject to the federal preferences (Section 8 and public housing), dollar-for-dollar, the bill potentially would have a high impact on the homeless. The same can be said of H.R. 969, Representative Conyers' massive proposal to produce 500,000 new public housing units a year for the foreseeable future.

Because H.R. 1180, the House's principal low-income housing bill, reauthorizes a number of programs that are not directly related to homelessness, its impact may not be as great as the two-year, $56 billion price tag implies. A substantial proportion of the budget is for existing housing and community development programs that would be funded at only modest increases over current levels. Moreover, the bill also reauthorizes rural housing programs to which the federal selection preferences do not currently apply. Finally, the bill's trust fund for first-time home buyers would not benefit the homeless directly.

The two production initiatives contained in H.R. 973, the Frank-Kennedy initiative, will have a mixed impact. Although not subject to federal selection preferences, Congressman Frank's proposal to finance a large volume of limited equity co-ops and mutual housing projects would give funding priority to community-based organizations that agree to house homeless families, employ homeless individuals in the construction process, and provide social services to residents. However, Congressman Joe Kennedy's Community Housing Partnership, which would provide capital and operating subsidies to nonprofit housing developers, would leave tenant selection up to local sponsors. Although all rental housing produced under the bill would have to meet specified low-income limits, the federal selection preferences would not apply. Under this bill housing partnership projects would not necessarily provide permanent residences for homeless families.

Congressman Dellums' bill, H.R. 1122, is concerned more with the conversion of existing, privately owned housing to social ownership than it is in expanding the aggregate size of the housing stock. This bill to decommodify housing is more a prevention than a remedy for homelessness.

Of the six major legislative proposals described in the previous section of this paper, S. 565, the Cranston-D'Amato National Affordable Housing Act, has the most interesting potential for the homeless. As a condition for receiving HOP funds, states and localities must develop and update annually a five-year affordable housing strategy.

The major difference between the affordable housing strategy required under the Cranston-D'Amato bill and the Housing Assistance Plan (HAP) that communities used to file as part of their community development block grant programs is the extent to which the housing needs of different classes of "nonresidents" must be taken into consideration. The old HAP contained a federally mandated "expected-to-reside" element that, using local employment patterns, estimated the number of nonresident low- and moderate-income families who might choose to move into the community were an adequate supply of affordable housing available. The Cranston-D'Amato bill recognizes the realities of the 1980s by requiring communities to plan for the needs of their present homeless citizens rather than for a hypothetical population that, under more favorable circumstances, would live closer to their places of work. Under S. 565, each affordable housing strategy must:

> describe the nature and extent of homelessness within the jurisdiction, providing an estimate of the special needs of various categories of persons who are homeless or threatened with homelessness, a brief inventory of facilities and services to assist such persons, and a description of the jurisdiction's strategy for providing such persons with permanent housing.

In addition to forcing localities to consider homelessness in the development of their housing plans, the Cranston-D'Amato bill consolidates the Section 8 rental certificate and voucher programs into a single rental credit program to which the federal selection preferences would apply. Because, technically, homeless families in transitional housing may not meet any of the three federal selection preferences, S. 565 modifies them by adding the following exception that may be applied to 25 percent of the families who initially receive rental credits in any one year:

> A public housing agency may provide an exception to the preferences established above in order to assist very low income families who either reside in transitional housing assisted under Title IV of the McKinney Homeless Assistance Act or participate in a program designed to provide public assistance families with greater access to employment and educational opportunities. (*Congressional Record* 1989, p. S 2585)

Since all rental units that receive HOP funds must have rents that do not exceed the local fair market rent (FMR) for existing housing and homeless families receive priority for rental credits, some of them, undoubtedly, will end up living in housing built with HOP funds. However, since S. 565 does not extend federal selection preferences to all HOP housing, the Cranston-D'Amato measure will probably not serve homeless families with children proportionate to their need.

Conclusions

Whether calculated in terms of the dollars it takes to maintain a family with children in an emergency shelter, welfare hotel, or transitional housing, or in terms of the destruction of life opportunities for the individuals involved, the cost to society of ignoring the plight of homeless families is sure to exceed the cost of ending this hardship. Although preventing and ending homelessness may be cost effective in the long term, it does not mean that the Congress will enact a massive low-income housing construction program of the scale envisioned by either Representatives Conyers (H.R. 969) or Frank (H.R. 973). Nor, for that matter, should serious debate be anticipated on Representative Dellums' measure to spend billions of public dollars to create a social housing sector by acquiring distressed privately held properties and turning them over to public ownership. Before dismissing these legislative proposals as mere political rhetoric, however, there is much to be learned.

Legislative Principles Without Chance of Passage

Representative Dellums' bill H.R. 1122 is a reminder that community control of the housing stock is the only safeguard against speculative price increases in low-income neighborhoods that can force families to lose their homes. It also underscores the critical nature of the "expiring use" problem that could lead to the conversion of hundreds of thousands of privately owned, low-income units to market rate occupancy. The Dellums' bill also points out that long-term affordability cannot be assured with short-term subsidies: the Congress has been penny wise and pound foolish in reducing the term of new Section 8 rental assistance contracts from fifteen to five years. Finally, although the Congress is likely to pay no heed, the bill contains two provisions that emphasize the critical nature of the low-income housing problem. One provision says that local receipt of a variety of nonhousing federal grants-in-aid should be conditioned on compliance with the bill's antispeculation measures. The other seeks to establish the principle that annual funding for low-income housing should be no less than the federal cost of homeowner subsidies, which primarily benefit higher-income families.

What sets H.R. 969 apart from the other initiatives discussed in the section on Congress and the housing issue is not just its massive scale or cost. Rather, it is different because the measure recognizes the importance of building job skills for low-income residents. By requiring local housing authorities to involve project and neighborhood residents in the construction of public housing, the Jesse Gray Housing Act would create an enormous employment training program that would potentially help area residents in their move out of public housing. Its unrealistically large scale does not negate the value of using publicly financed low-income housing as a source of training local residents in the construction trades. Job training was an important component of many multifamily homesteading programs during the early 1970s. The experience gained from those local experiments ought to be assessed and applied to any new low-income housing construction programs the Congress might create.

Barney Frank's bill, H.R. 973, has unique targeting requirements that are of special interest. Although other legislative initiatives would provide construction loans and grants to nonprofits, only H.R. 973 limits eligibility to neighborhood-based entities that both employ homeless individuals in the construction and deliver a broad range of social services to their residents. Moreover, priority for housing built under the Frank bill is given to homeless families and individuals, including those with physical illnesses and other disabilities. The problem is whether there are a sufficient number of experienced community-based housing developers that have the capacity to serve the homeless to the extent required by the act. Although many social service-oriented organizations have recently become involved in construction through their sponsorship of emergency shelters and transitional housing for the homeless, few are highly skilled housing developers. H.R. 973 underscores the importance of local bridge-building – of bringing together the nonprofits that serve the emergency shelter and related needs of the homeless with other prevention and permanent rehousing programs.

Coordinating Housing and Homeless Programs

Because the McKinney Act was adopted by a Congress that had gone along with the Reagan administration's draconian cuts in low-income housing programs, federal spending on homelessness was limited to emergency shelters, transitional facilities, and related services. Because very limited McKinney Act funds could be spent on permanent housing or for homeless prevention measures, local housing and homeless programs tend to be delivered by separate agencies in a largely uncoordinated manner. Yet, the author's review of the relevant literature and proposed legislative initiatives suggests that there are two planning imperatives regarding the homeless. First, planning for the provision of permanent housing must go hand-in-hand with the development of prevention programs. Second, planning for the prevention of homelessness and permanent rehousing programs must not be separate activities carried out by unrelated agencies. The importance of integrating the provision of permanent housing for the homeless into the traditional housing delivery system is underscored in a recent evaluation of Massachusetts' special rental assistance program for the homeless.

The self-assessment found that, despite continued growth in the volume of dedicated rental assistance for homeless families, the number of people entering the emergency shelter system increased (Executive Offices of Communities and Development 1989). Although the special allocation of rental subsidies was effective in enabling homeless families to find permanent housing, the set-aside of rental certificates

> had the unintended consequence of encouraging some desperate families to become homeless and enter an emergency shelter in order to access scarce housing subsidies.... Since most families at risk of becoming homeless are not eligible for an emergency preference or set-aside of rental subsidies, their only opportunity to receive rental assistance is through the homeless set-aside programs.... Thus, even if an at-risk family can stay in their current housing situation for a longer period, they have no incentive to remain there without an assurance of timely availability of rental assistance. (Executive Office of Communities and Development 1989, 5)

Massachusetts plans to stop administering a separate set-aside for the homeless and to reintegrate its rental assistance program into the existing network of housing programs operated at the local level. The state hopes to convince local housing authorities to grant absolute preferences for federal Section 8 certificates to families who come out of the emergency shelter system, while dedicating state-funded rental certificates to families who are threatened with the loss of their housing due to nonpayment of rent.

With the close of the Reagan era, it is no longer necessary to continue the charade that the rise in homelessness in America is unrelated to the growing shortage of affordable housing. One component of a reinvigorated national low-income housing policy that would help prevent the continued rise of homelessness is a substantial expansion of rental assistance. Although not a rental entitlement of the kind advocated by Cushing Dolbeare, H.R. 140 is the only major homeless measure that seeks to attack the problem through a one-time increase in rental assistance funds as opposed to an expansion of the low-income housing supply. The Vento bill would distribute rental assistance funds using a CDBG distribution formula modified to include a "homeless" variable. Because it links distribution of Section 8 funds to local homeless plans, H.R. 140 presents an excellent opportunity for the Congress to reassert the link between housing and homelessness and to broaden the planning role of the McKinney Act to include the development of homeless prevention and permanent rehousing programs that would coordinate the activities of service providers working on behalf of the homeless with those who are engaged in the direct provision of low-income housing, including local housing authorities and community-based housing producers.

The Bush Administration's HOPE Initiative

On 13 March 1990, the Bush administration introduced its first major housing bill and authorizing legislation in the Congress. Although the President's proposed legislative agenda cannot be fully analyzed here, it is fair to say that the advocacy community has found it to be significantly wanting. According to the Low Income Housing Information Service, for example:

> The Fiscal Year 1991 budget request for HUD's low income housing assistance and community development programs is a major disappointment to housing advocates and community-based groups struggling against a rising tide of homelessness. Stripped of budgeting gimmicks, the Administration proposal actually requests substantially less new funding for low income assisted housing efforts than Congress appropriated in FY90... the new budget would provide low income housing assistance to a total of only 82,049 new households, the same number on average that were committed during the Reagan years. (Low Income Housing Information Service 1990, 1)

The dominant theme of the President's new legislative agenda, dubbed the HOPE initiative, which stands for Homeownership and Opportunity for People Everywhere, is the expansion of homeownership opportunities to residents of public- and other privately owned and assisted rental housing in order to increase self-sufficiency. Because it focuses primarily upon families who are already housed, many of whom are already receiving federal housing assistance, HOPE is not likely to have a major impact on homeless families in shelters or other temporary facilities.

In addition to the several initiatives intended to convert assisted renters to homeowners, the President's HOPE plan does contain a new homeless initiative. Unfortunately for homeless families, this new, $161 million program that will extend rental assistance in permanent housing to an additional 6,600 homeless, is targeted exclusively to homeless individuals with serious mental illness or chronic alcohol or other substance-abuse problems. Even more regrettably, in order to fund this new initiative, the administration proposes to cancel the present Supplemental Assistance for Facilities to Assist the Homeless (SAFAH) program that was created under the McKinney Homeless Assistance Act. SAFAH "has provided funds for comprehensive strategies (including prevention) to meet the needs of the homeless, and supplement other McKinney grants to help meet the special needs of homeless families with children, the elderly homeless, and handicapped homeless persons" (Low Income Housing Information Service 1990, 2). Thus while the HOPE bill makes good on the President's campaign promise to fully fund McKinney Act programs, because of its narrow focus on seriously troubled homeless individuals, it is not at all clear that the FY1991 budget will be kinder and gentler to homeless families with children.

Note

1. Major provisions of S. 565 are quoted from the *Housing Development Reporter*, March 20, 1989, 920–2.

References

Barbanel, J. 1989, 4 Jan. "Homeless New York Families to Get U.S. Rent Subsidies." *New York Times.*

Bureau of National Affairs. 1989, 6 Feb., 6 Mar., 20 Mar. *The Housing Development Reporter.* Washington, DC: Bureau of National Affairs.

Code of Federal Regulations. 1988, 15 Jan. "Federal Selection Preferences for Public Housing," 24CFR 960, Section 960. Washington, DC: Government Printing Office.

Congressional Budget Office. 1988, Dec. *Current Housing Problems and Possible Federal Responses,* pp. 18, 54, 105. Washington, DC: Government Printing Office.

U.S. Congress. 1989, 15 Mar. The National Affordable Housing Act. (101st Congress, 1st session, S.565). *Congressional Record,* p. 2572. Washington, DC: Government Printing Office.

Dolbeare, C. 1989. "Expanding on Section 8." *Shelterforce* 11, no. 4: 12.

Financial Democracy Campaign. 1989, 2 Mar. "Remedies for the S&L (and Housing) Crisis," pp. 4, 5. Mimeographed.

Executive Office of Communities and Development. 1989, 30 Jan. "Permanent Housing for the Homeless: Moving Towards Homeless Prevention," p. 5. Boston: By the author.

Halpern, S. 1989, 16 Feb. "The Rise of Homelessness." *The New York Review of Books* 36, no. 2: 26.

Human Resources Administration, Family and Children's Services Agency. 1988, 9 Feb. "Profile of Homeless Families Who Reside at Carey Gardens." New York City: By the author.

Institute of Medicine. 1988. *Homelessness, Health and Human Needs.* Washington, DC: National Academy Press.

Interagency Council on the Homeless. 1988. *A Nation Concerned: A Report to the President and the Congress on the Response to Homelessness in America,* pp. 1-2. Washington, DC: By the author.

Keyes, L. 1989, Mar. "Housing and the Homeless," HP #15. Cambridge: MIT Center for Real Estate Development.

Kriz, M. 1989, 18 Mar. "Broadening the S&L Bailout." *The National Journal* 21, no. 11: 682-3.

Kutner, R. 1989, 27 Feb. "Why Bush's S&L Bailout is Fundamentally Flawed." *Business Week,* No. 3093: 24.

Loth, R. 1988, 15 Dec. "Study Finds a Third of State 'Shelter Poor'." *The Boston Globe.*

Low Income Housing Information Service. 1989, Mar. "Special Memorandum." Washington, DC: National Low Income Housing Coalition.

—1990, Feb. "Special Memorandum, The Fiscal Year 1991 Budget and Low Income Housing." Washington, DC: National Low Income Housing Coalition.

McCormick, D. E. 1988, 15 June. "Implementation Date Arrives for Federal Tenant Preferences." *NAHRO MONITOR* 10, no. 11: 3.

Newman, S., and A. Schnare. 1988, Mar. "Integrating Housing and Welfare Assistance," HP #12. Cambridge: MIT Center for Real Estate Development.

"New Study Finds the Poor Getting Poorer, Younger and More Urban." 1989, 12 Mar. *New York Times,* p. 1.

"No Funds for Housing" (editorial). 1989, 4 Mar. *Washington Post.*

Olsen, E. O. 1988, 12 Dec. "Housing Subsidies Rise for the Needy." *Wall Street Journal.*

Raspberry, W. 1989, 20 Mar. "S&L: The Way to Bail Them Out." *The Washington Post.*

Reich, R. B. 1989. "As the World Turns." *The New Republic,* Issue 3,876: 28.

Rimer, S. 1989, 24 Mar. "The Rent's Due and for Many, It's Homelessness Knocking." *The New York Times*.

Sege, I. 1989, 12 Mar. "Poverty's Grip on Children Widens." *The Boston Globe*.

Stegman, M. A. 1988. "Housing and Vacancy Survey Report, New York City, 1987," p. 47. New York: New York Department of Housing Preservation and Development.

Tolchin, M. 1989, 23 Mar. "Richest Got Richer and Poorest Poorer in 1979-87." *The New York Times*, pp. A1, A23.

Wright, J. D., and J. Lam. 1988. "The Low-Income Housing Supply and the Problem of Homelessness." Unpublished manuscript.

U.S. Bureau of the Census. 1987. *1987 New York City Housing and Vacancy Survey*. Washington, DC: Government Printing Office.

10

The Welfare System's Response to Homelessness

Linda A. Wolf

Traditional welfare programs can do little to help the homeless with the basic problem of finding permanent, safe, affordable housing. Welfare benefits are not high enough to make poor people true competitors in the limited low-income housing market and welfare agencies cannot create new housing. Because of the growth of the homeless population, however, the system has been forced – sometimes under court order – to respond to the problem. These efforts often have caused as many problems as they have temporarily solved, and yet there seems only faint hope that the situation will improve. As a result, the welfare system is often the last resort for homeless people seeking help even though it may not be fully equipped to address their needs.

Since 1986, the nation's public welfare administrators have been working to create a national movement for welfare reform with the clear understanding that homelessness, like other social symptoms, has a root cause in poverty. Within their national organization, the American Public Welfare Association (APWA), these administrators have also been working to create a more useful and effective response to homelessness by seeking new relationships with their housing colleagues at the state and local levels.

The real response of the welfare system to homelessness rests in this interplay between rigid and underfunded programs and a leadership group determined to make a difference. Because the system response has been very ineffectual or, in some cases, perverse, the leadership of the welfare system determined that change must occur.

Defining the Programmatic Response

The first way to understand how the welfare system responds to the homeless is to examine its programs and how well they serve.

Aid to Families with Dependent Children

Aid to Families with Dependent Children (AFDC) is the core program of the welfare system and is designed to provide cash assistance and economic services to those who meet eligibility criteria. It is the only national program that exists to meet the cash assistance needs of families with dependent children. This program is financed by federal and state governments as an entitlement. State expenditures are matched by federal financial participation at a variable rate that averages around 50 percent. In 1987, the lack of a fixed current address was officially declared not to be a bar to eligibility. (It should be noted, however, that an Urban Institute Study reports that only 33 percent of eligible homeless families actually receive AFDC (Burt and Cohen 1989).)

AFDC program benefits vary from state to state, with a low of $118 per month for a family of three in Alabama and a high of $749 per month for a family of three in Alaska. The median national payment is roughly $354 per month for a family of three. The AFDC payment is meant to cover basic food, clothing, and shelter needs. The fact that the average monthly cost of a rental unit in this country is over $300 would seem to be proof enough of the inadequacy of current benefit levels. Unfortunately, considerably more proof is available.

The same AFDC grant that is insufficient to meet housing costs is also insufficient to meet any of the other basic needs of a poor family. The purchasing power of AFDC benefits has eroded by more than 30 percent over the past eighteen years (American Public Welfare Association 1989). No state AFDC benefits come close to the federally mandated poverty level. In short, AFDC benefits do not provide the support needed to cover basic needs. Shelter costs are often paid to the exclusion of other family needs. Poor families do without clothing and food and play a month-to-month round-robin with utility companies to avoid eviction.

Young adults with no children receive cash assistance at state or local option under a general relief or general assistance program available in forty jurisdictions on a very limited basis. Therefore, to be a young, homeless adult puts you at greater risk of having no public support for anything, let alone housing.

Special Needs Allowances

In order to compensate for the inadequacy and inflexibility of the basic economic assistance package provided by AFDC, thirty-three states use a small program called "special needs" for which other federal funds are available. The special needs program is designed to meet unique circumstances that may or may not reoccur. Special needs are determined on a case-by-case basis. They include allowances for such items as training, child care, special diets, and so forth. Some states cover shelter items such as allowances for utility deposits, and in at least three states, special needs funds are used to pay shelter costs in hotels or motels for homeless people.

Emergency Assistance Program

The Emergency Assistance (EA) program – authorized, like AFDC, under Title IV-A of the Social Security Act – was established in 1967 to help families with children meet emergency needs. Thirty state welfare agencies used EA funds in FY88 to supplement AFDC with immediate short-term assistance. Furthermore, certain families may be helped even if not eligible for AFDC. EA funds can be used to address a range of problems – including housing – in a variety of ways – including the costs of "welfare hotels." Some states also use EA funds to prevent eviction or to supply resources to forestall the loss of a family residence.

In 1987, the U.S. Department of Health and Human Services (HHS) proposed new regulations aimed at severely restricting the flexibility of the EA program. Human service administrators, through APWA, have lobbied effectively to place a moratorium on such restrictions (American Public Welfare Association 1987a). They argued that EA funds were one of the few tools available to the welfare system to prevent homelessness and address the problem once it occurs. Perhaps the most telling observation is that these program funds are still labeled as "special" and "emergency" while the nature of the problem they address is becoming much more the norm.

Beyond the cash assistance provided by AFDC, special needs allowances, and EA programs, there are other programs to help poor individuals, including those who are homeless.

Nutrition Programs

Food stamps. The Food Stamp program, which is federally funded but state administered, provides food coupons to families and to individuals who meet eligibility requirements. AFDC eligibility is not a prerequisite, and food stamp eligibility is not restricted by the lack of a permanent address. The program does not, however, provide the flexibility to purchase certain personal hygiene items especially needed by homeless people. Further, homeless people, with no access to stoves or refrigerators, are limited in the type of food they can purchase. Recent changes in federal regulations allowing food stamps to be used in certain congregate meal settings, such as group homes for the elderly or mentally handicapped, do little to address the situation of some homeless individuals and families. Human service administrators are recommending that further changes be implemented during the upcoming reauthorization of the Food Stamp program that would allow the homeless more options in using coupons to obtain prepared meals.

WIC. The Special Supplemental Food Program for Women, Infants, and Children (WIC) is available to certain portions of the homeless population. The food coupon or commodities distribution center service-delivery mechanism of the program create the same problems for the homeless as the Food Stamp program, without the flexibility of congregate meal possibilities. Recent changes in WIC made by the Hunger Prevention Act, however, include better tailoring of food products for homeless families.

School lunch program. The school lunch program, for which welfare departments can certify eligibility, provides another nutrition program. Homeless children, however, are rarely attached to a single school and frequently not to any school, so the opportunity is usually foregone.

TEFAP. Surplus commodities are also available to low-income families, including the homeless, through the federal Temporary Emergency Food Assistance Program (TEFAP).

LIHEAP. The Low-Income Energy Assistance Program (LIHEAP) is a federally funded program providing money or vouchers to help homeowners meet utility costs. It is administered by the welfare department in most states. These grants can be crucial in allowing low-income homeowners to keep their homes because they lessen the need to divert mortgage money to pay rising utility costs. LIHEAP funds also help to ensure that homes will be habitable during severe weather conditions. Funds available for LIHEAP have been cut 33 percent since 1985, and the program does not have enough funding to reach the entire eligible population. Although LIHEAP does not help homeless people, it can save others from becoming homeless by helping to pay utility bills and free scarce resources for other shelter costs.

Medicaid

Medicaid, the basic health insurance program for poor families, is funded by both federal and state governments. Eligibility is tied to AFDC eligibility, but exceptions are made for pregnant women and small children. A fixed address is not a prerequisite for eligibility. For single adults needing medical assistance, whether homeless or not, the only program available is a state-option medically needy program. Thirty-three states have such a program.

JOBS

The Job Opportunities and Basic Skills Training Program (JOBS) is intended to help needy families with children obtain the education, training, and employment they need to avoid long-term welfare dependence. It was established under Title IV-F of the Social Security Act by the Family Support Act of 1988 and will be implemented in all states by October 1, 1990. JOBS replaces, consolidates, and expands current welfare education, training, and work programs such as the Work Incentive (WIN) and WIN Demonstration programs. Child care, medical assistance, and other support services are available to JOBS participants. Homeless families, unless exempt for other reasons, will be eligible to participate in the JOBS program.

The Unintended Consequences of the Welfare System Response

Basic welfare benefits are clearly not adequate to meet the escalating housing costs in the open market, and to meet the other living costs of poor families with children. Many programs are simply ill-suited to the needs of homeless families, regardless of benefits. The widespread use of emergency and special needs monies to augment AFDC payments only underscores the seriousness of the problem. The current stop-gap approaches deal only with immediate crises and not the long-term problem. And if AFDC benefits are inadequate, at least they exist. In many states, poor men and women without families have no source of public funds at all with which to purchase shelter.

Welfare program responses, however inadequate, have also assumed that housing is, in fact, available. Increasingly, this is simply not the case. A great deal of moderate-cost housing stock is now occupied by middle-class families frozen out of the real estate market by rising prices and high interest rates. Other affordable units are gentrified to attract higher-income tenants, or torn down to accommodate urban renewal projects or commercial developments. Although this lack of affordable housing is most apparent in large urban areas, the problem is not confined to New York City or Los Angeles.

Inadequate public benefits offered by a welfare agency for often nonexistent housing have lead to some very unintended consequences. One "worst case" is that welfare-agency dollars become a mainstay in the survival of slum landlords. Clients and welfare agencies with few, if any, options pay too much rent for units that are often substandard. Newspaper stories abound about vermin-infested "welfare" apartments with broken windows and appliances, no heat, and lead paint chipping off the walls.

In addition to the difficulty of convincing code enforcement agencies that these problems merit attention, the welfare department and/or the client faces a classic double bind. If a rental unit is judged uninhabitable by other public authorities, the welfare department and the client – not those other authorities – are faced with the equally poor choice of life on the street or relocation to another undesirable unit.

In far too many of these cases, all parties tacitly approve the status quo. This laissez-faire approach to substandard housing simply guarantees that more of the same will occur. Incentives to rehabilitate old rental units are removed from the market because even the worst unit is rentable at a profit.

Welfare hotels are another result of inadequate benefits, inadequate housing stock, and a system forced to respond to a crisis beyond its capacity. There is no clear-cut, widely accepted definition of what constitutes a welfare hotel. In most people's minds, however, a welfare hotel is a commercially owned "hotel" with a clientele composed almost entirely of welfare recipients. The owners of these facilities are thought to be paid exorbitant sums to house homeless people in squalor for long periods of time. The welfare-hotel image is one of a high-rent, low-service warehouse for society's castoffs. Unfortunately, all of these perceptions or assumptions are true at some time, in some cities, for some populations.

The use of hotels or motels to shelter welfare families is a fairly widespread phenomenon. The U.S. Conference of Mayors reported in 1987 that fifteen major cities used hotel shelters (American Public Welfare Association 1987b). The Federal Emergency Management Administration (FEMA) reports that many local service providers use such alternatives for short-term problems (U.S. Congress 1989a). There is also evidence from a General Accounting Office survey that urban, suburban, and rural areas use the hotel/motel shelter alternative (U.S. General Accounting Office 1985).

As homelessness increases and court orders force more jurisdictions to provide shelter, the use of hotels and motels may well expand. In some jurisdictions the stay in a hotel or motel may be brief, but in some instances hotels are the only form of permanent housing that welfare clients know. New York City has a very large welfare-hotel population, and in that city the length of stay averages thirteen months. Many families spend two to three years in such a setting. New York has also announced plans to end hotel use by the mid-1990s, and is successfully pursuing a phase-out strategy.

Hotel costs can be exorbitant and, while conditions vary among hotels, overcrowding is common. When hotel rates are negotiated fairly, however, they may be cheaper than the cost of other forms of transitional housing – presuming, of course, that other forms exist.

It is a sad commentary on the state of public policy and practice that the payment authorized for a family under AFDC may be increased 500 percent if that family must be housed in a hotel. While states and communities accept the financial and political burden of sheltering the homeless when forced to do so by court order, in the absence of a judicial mandate there is no such political will. Welfare agencies are caught up in the expedience of welfare hotels without a great deal of control over any other political, fiscal, or physical resources to solve the problem of homelessness.

In addition to welfare-hotel populations and families living in inadequate substandard housing, thousands of families who currently live under another's roof are not counted among the homeless. These are families doubled or tripled up in rental units designed for single-family occupancy. At recent hearings held before the House Subcommittee on Housing and Community Development, former Representative Robert Garcia (D.- N.Y.) said that New York City estimates that 40 percent to 60 percent of its assisted housing units are occupied by more than one family (U.S. Congress 1989b). New York is not an isolated example.

Although there are many reasons to want an accurate count of these "stacked" families, once again both clients and welfare agencies are in a double bind. These "housing squatters" would probably become homeless if evicted, so their presence must be hidden from landlords. If discovered, they also might forfeit any benefits received while living with another family. Children in these families could be placed in foster care, since homelessness could be considered a form of neglect in some jurisdictions. These near-homeless people are invisible to many service systems that could give them assistance, but their anonymity may protect the roofs over their heads.

Changing the Response: The Challenge to Public Welfare

As noted earlier, the state and local leadership of the welfare system, namely, the nation's welfare administrators, have been actively engaged in transforming their own system. Under the rubric of welfare reform, they proposed sweeping changes in the philosophy, organization, delivery system, and benefit levels in public welfare. This blueprint for change, contained in the publication *One Child in Four*, became the touchstone for federal reform legislation known as the Family Support Act of 1988 (American Public Welfare Association 1986).

The administrators pushed beyond *One Child in Four*, however, in examining the kind of reform that would need to occur if welfare dependence were to be replaced by self-sufficiency. In 1988, the welfare administrators made the following observation as part of a larger housing policy statement.

A prerequisite for strong, self-sufficient families is the ability to live in safe, decent, affordable housing. Today steadily rising housing costs and steadily diminishing resources – both wages and the value of cash assistance – force many American families into housing that is neither safe nor decent. Where safe, decent housing is available it is often not affordable. Federal housing assistance for low-income families has dropped precipitously while the number of homeless individuals and families has grown, a circumstance that marks the urgent need for new policies to address the housing needs of poor Americans. (American Public Welfare Association 1989, p. 6)

In *One Child in Four,* the welfare administrators laid out a series of recommendations aimed at reducing poverty among families with children. In their 1988 policy document on housing and homelessness, they took a step beyond their traditional boundaries and into the world of housing policies and programs. On the issue of poverty, the human service administrators were in known territory even if the issue of servicing the homeless poor was still open for exploration. Responding to homelessness in terms of housing stock, housing alternatives, housing policies, and housing agencies was, and is, very new terrain to them. They needed and sought new colleagues to help them change the welfare system's response to homelessness.

Non-traditional Partnerships

Fostering and expanding cooperation among welfare agencies and counterparts in housing assistance programs or agencies is not a simple problem. Welfare agencies are not equipped or trained to assist indigent clients in securing decent, permanent housing. At the same time, public housing agencies do not possess adequate resources to assist poor families toward self-sufficiency.

A variety of factors currently inhibit coordination between housing and welfare agencies. In 1988, the welfare administrators joined with the National Association of Housing and Redevelopment Officials (NAHRO) to examine these factors in more detail as a preamble to making changes in their systems. A joint Advisory Panel of the NAHRO and APWA, funded by the Ford Foundation, cited the following as the five greatest barriers to a coordinated effort to promote family self-sufficiency (National Association of Housing and

Redevelopment Officers-American Public Welfare Association Advisory Panel 1989):

1. Welfare benefits are entitlements, which all households establishing eligibility receive, whereas housing assistance depends on the annual availability of federal funding. Consequently, housing assistance reaches only a small proportion of the low-income families who need it.
2. Most federal assistance for welfare programs is delivered through state governments, whereas assistance to housing programs goes primarily through local governments. While states are the primary welfare agencies for the federal government, social services are delivered through local offices.
3. AFDC cash grants allow flexibility for individuals to make household spending decisions, whereas housing assistance programs deal with specific housing structures.
4. Welfare programs support households individually, whereas the housing assistance system supports households only within the context of housing structures and neighborhoods.
5. Housing assistance is available to families who cannot meet the costs of available private housing in the local market, including families earning from 50 percent to 80 percent of median income. Welfare assistance is available only to poverty-level households, largely with incomes below 50 percent of median income.

These statements of differences reveal the very difficult realities of moving two public systems toward a common purpose. This collaborative exploration can be tedious and uncomfortable, but it is nothing compared to the real process of change. In the case of NAHRO and APWA, representing the leadership of the two systems, a new partnership has been formed and some real changes have been proposed.

In its September 1989 report, *Findings, Initiatives, and Recommendations,* the joint Advisory Panel issued a series of recommendations that include but are not limited to the following (National Association of Housing and Redevelopment Officers-American Public Welfare Association Advisory Panel 1989):

1. Full implementation of the Family Support Act.
2. Continuation and expansion of HUD's Project Self-Sufficiency.
3. Expanded use of Section 8 certificates.
4. Expanded support for family development programs in federally assisted housing.
5. Interim incentives for welfare families in transition.
6. Coordinated programs (welfare and housing) on all levels of government and within governmental structures.
7. Expansion of research on housing/welfare linkages.

Working together with NAHRO on these recommendations will change the welfare system's response to housing and homelessness issues, as will work that is currently underway with another new welfare partner, the Council of State Community Affairs Agencies (COSCAA).

APWA and COSCAA are currently involved in another joint project on welfare-housing linkages at the state level. Both organizations recognize the need for change within the systems they represent and cite the following as a rationale for their work:

1. A reformed welfare system will focus on self-sufficiency for poor families, and a major part of the transition to independence is securing decent housing. Shelter availability and costs are major barriers to self-sufficiency for low-income families.
2. Housing policy does not serve all those in need effectively. People who reside in public housing are, for example, covered by existing policy, but they are only part of the universe of low-income families to be served. The welfare department must meet the needs of all low-income families, regardless of where they live or whether they have a residence.
3. There are major gaps in the availability of decent, affordable, private housing stock and the availability of assisted housing. The inadequate and stop-gap solutions that have been wrought by using the welfare agency as a de facto housing agency must be dealt with jointly by housing and welfare agencies and in concert with the private sector.
4. Improving the linkages can decrease substantially the onset of family destabilization and homelessness by identifying the need

for a housing-related intervention prior to or immediately after an action that triggers an exit from housing.
5. Welfare recipients and other low-income individuals face problems with regard to code enforcement, tenant-landlord relationships, fair housing, and other issues. Welfare and housing agencies must focus on total communities, not just the population they assist or the housing units they oversee.

Neither the housing nor the welfare systems can effectively address these issues without the assistance of its counterpart. Only as the dialogue expands and each agency better understands the other's respective role and position in the community can the goal of self-sufficiency and equitable housing for poor families move beyond shared rhetoric.

Concluding Thoughts

Homeless people do not fit into the traditional programs or service delivery mechanisms of most public institutions, including the welfare system. The welfare system's attempts to deal with the homeless have been ineffectual or, in some cases, perverse. A forced fit confronts the system and the people who desperately need its services.

The commitment of the leaders of the welfare system to change their own system and challenge the root causes of poverty through new social legislation is a necessary prerequisite to changing the system's response to homelessness. Joined by their colleagues in housing and community development, this leadership cadre can change the system, but much more remains to be done.

No one system will be able to successfully affect the housing and homelessness crisis facing the nation. Collaboration and innovation will be necessary at the program, policy, and service delivery levels. Billions of dollars from the federal treasury must be made available now and for the foreseeable future. Public policy must support public/private partnerships in creating and maintaining affordable housing stock. The whole financing structure of public housing and supported housing must be re-examined.

In the cause of permanent, safe, affordable housing for poor Americans, there can be no disinterested public players. The welfare system is prepared to hold itself accountable for its role and is seeking opportunities to expand that role with professional colleagues in other systems and professional disciplines.

To quote from *One Child in Four:*

> Without the courage to face the risk inherent in change, real reform will be impossible. To improve practices we must be willing to confront the unknown, including the challenge of those who might be less interested in improving programs than in ending them. We must be willing to transcend the parochial boundaries that define our professional interests. We must be willing to integrate the expertise of various bureaucratic domains. Our commitment must be unequivocal. (p. 31)

References

American Public Welfare Association. 1986. *One Child in Four.* Washington, DC: By the author.

American Public Welfare Association. 1987a, 18 Dec. *This Week in Washington* VIII, no. 50.

American Public Welfare Association. 1987b, 18 Dec. "The Continuing Growth of Hunger, Homelessness, and Poverty in America's Cities: 1987," U.S. Conference of Mayors, cited in *This Week in Washington* VIII, no. 50.

American Public Welfare Association. 1989. "Housing the Poor." *Public Welfare* 47, no. 1: 5-12.

Burt, M., and B. Cohen. 1989. *America's Homeless: Numbers, Characteristics, and Programs That Serve Them.* Urban Institute Report 89-3. Washington, DC: The Urban Institute Press.

National Association of Housing and Redevelopment Officers-American Public Welfare Association Advisory Panel. 1989. *Findings, Initiatives, and Recommendations.* Washington, DC: By the author.

U.S. Congress. House. 1989a, 1 Mar. Committee on Banking, Finance, and Urban Affairs. Subcommittee on Housing and Community Development. Testimony from Hearings on the Federal Emergency Management Administration. U.S. Government Printing Office, Serial No. 101-9.

U.S. Congress. House. 1989b, 15 Mar. Committee on Banking, Finance, and Urban Affairs. Subcommittee on Housing and Community Development. Hearings. U.S. Government Printing Office, Serial No. 101-9.

U.S. General Accounting Office. 1985. *Homelessness: A Complex Problem and the Federal Response.* Washington, DC: U.S. Government Printing Office.

11

Child Welfare Services and Homelessness: Issues in Policy, Philosophy, and Programs

Carol W. Williams

The linkage between child welfare services and homelessness among families, children, and youth has become stronger and much more apparent in the last decade. For many children, the lack of adequate housing is a major factor in their entry into the public child welfare system. At the same time, the philosophy, decision-making, and operations of the child welfare system may have the unanticipated consequence of promoting homelessness among families and children.

Altering the experience of children and families at risk of homelessness requires that policymakers address two issues. First, the child welfare system is being used to respond to family crises that result from society's failure to adequately assist families with basic minimums: income and housing. Second, the approach to helping families is categorical and results in services that are often narrowly targeted and fragmented. As a result, services are not designed to meet the needs of families. Rather families must adapt to the services that are available.

To explore the linkages between child welfare services and homelessness, this discussion will examine the intent and purposes of child welfare intervention, the interaction between the child welfare system and homelessness, and the psychosocial consequence of homelessness for children and families. Policy recommendations will be offered at the conclusion.

Overview of the Child Welfare System

Narrowly defined, the child welfare system is that constellation of publicly administered services designed to meet the needs of children and families experiencing abuse and neglect. In 1987, over 2 million reports of abuse and neglect were received by the fifty state child welfare agencies serving America's children. Approximately 40 percent of the reports made to public agencies were substantiated (American Association for Protecting Children 1988). Among the substantiated reports, 26.3 percent were physical abuse, 15.7 percent were sexual abuse, 8.3 percent were emotional maltreatment, 54.9 percent were neglect, and 8 percent were other forms of maltreatment, including abandonment and lack of supervision. The major resources used to assist children in need of protection are supervision in the home and foster care. In 1985, approximately 265,000 children were in out-of-home care due to abuse or neglect (Tatara 1988).

The legislation for child welfare services is embodied in Title IV-B of the Social Security Act, which provides grants-in-aid to the states to make child welfare services available at the state level. State laws are enacted which provide for the implementation of federal policy by defining maltreatment, establishing reporting requirements, and authorizing the delivery of services.

The guiding framework for child welfare services, Public Law 96-272, the adoption assistance and child welfare amendments of 1980, was developed in response to concerns about the unanticipated outcomes of protective services intervention. During the 1970s, research documented foster care drift, multiple placement, lack of case plans, and limited work with parents to resolve problems. Children were growing up in foster care with no families of their own. Goals were established to reduce the unnecessary removal of children from their homes, reduce the length of time children spend in out-of-home care, and secure permanency for children (Allen, Golubock, and Olson 1983).

In an effort to prevent the unnecessary removal of children from their families, a "reasonable efforts" standard was established which required a judicial finding that placement prevention efforts had been undertaken before states could qualify for federal financial participation in the costs of foster care. Although Title IV-B of the Social Security Act clearly articulated a goal of *protection* for children, the 1980 amendments added *permanency* planning for children to the goals of public intervention.

In 1985, the independent living amendments were added. They focused on the issue of adolescents who "age out" of the foster care system with limited skills to assure their independence. The independent living initiative provided grants to the states to develop model programs to facilitate the emancipation of minors who were exiting the foster care system. This legislation added a *developmental* goal to child welfare services.

In assessing the impact of the recent amendments on the child welfare system, several issues are noteworthy. Shortly after the passage of Public Law 96-272, the number of children in foster care declined significantly. However, in the last five years the number of children in foster care has begun to escalate. The emphasis on permanency planning that was a part of the 1980 legislation has been effective in enabling large numbers of children in the child welfare system to find permanence. However, not all of the children in need of permanent substitute families have been able to secure them.

A major outgrowth of the implementation of Public Law 96-272 has been the increased emphasis on maintaining children within their own families and providing assistance to families to resolve the problems that led to abuse and neglect. The current interest in and expansion of intensive home-based services for children and families experiencing abuse and neglect are a reflection of a broad incorporation of this philosophy. However, for many children, the absence of affordable family housing has limited the placement preventive effort.

A current examination of the foster care system indicates that basically two populations of children are in care. The first population consists of younger children with moderate problems who tend to stay in the foster care system for periods of less than two years. These are the children for whom permanency planning is the most effective.

A second group of children, comprising 39 percent of the population in foster care, are youngsters over age thirteen (Tatara 1988). These adolescent children are more likely to have experienced multiple placements and attenuation of the ties to their families and to demonstrate emotional and behavioral problems. This is a population of children for whom it is difficult to secure family reunification and difficult to find permanent alternative families. This group of children ages out or drops out of the child welfare system with limited life skills and/or social support for emancipation and find themselves at risk of homelessness. The number of adolescents in foster care has grown as the child welfare system has become the system of last resort for many children who have not found effective remedies for their problems in the mental health or juvenile justice systems. These systems have focused on deinstitutionalization and/or diversion from restrictive settings. Although this policy has been effective for some youngsters in the absence of community-based services, it has also meant that there are youngsters for whom child welfare services are the only resource.

The Interaction Between Child Protection and Homelessness

Among the issues which reflect the interaction between child welfare services and homelessness are the philosophical basis of child welfare services, the definitions of abuse and neglect, the unanticipated consequences of placement decisions, and the effectiveness of work with adolescents.

Philosophical Issues

As noted in the brief overview of the policy context of child welfare, the philosophical principles underlying the delivery of child welfare services have been evolving. Initially the focus was on the *protection* of children. In the context of that goal, services tended to revolve around the removal of children from their own families and placement in foster care. This approach has been characterized retrospectively as a "child rescue" approach, and it dominated professional practice although there was a clear articulation of the need to help families resolve their problems so that children could be returned home.

Services which emphasize placement as a strategy came into question in the 1970s. Out of that questioning and challenging, the focus on *permanence,* the second philosophical base of child welfare, emerged. Initial efforts were directed at enabling children to secure permanence through adoption when they were unable to return to their own families. Also emerging from this quest for permanence was a commitment to strengthen and *preserve families* in order to minimize removal.

In the independent living initiatives, the beginning of a *developmental* focus in child welfare services is seen. Recognizing that many children "graduated" from the child welfare system without the necessary skills to function as young adults, the independent living initiative challenged child welfare agencies to develop services that would allow youngsters to have the social, vocational, and emotional competencies necessary to emancipate.

The focus on protection, family preservation, and permanency planning, without a strong developmental emphasis, has had unanticipated consequences. The failure to be certain that youngsters achieve certain knowledge and skill minimums has set the stage for many of our older children to age out of the system and to become part of the homeless population.

Definitions of Neglect

Given that child welfare services are designed to protect children, one of the major issues being debated today relates to whether homelessness is prima facia evidence of neglect. As early as the 1909 White House Conference on Children, there was consensus among child welfare professionals that no child should be removed from his or her family for "reasons of poverty alone." In recently developed *Guidelines for a Model System of Child Protective Services,* the National Association of Public Child Welfare Administrators has indicated that child abuse or neglect is any "recent act or failure to act on the part of parents which results in death, serious physical, sexual, or emotional harm; or presents an eminent risk of serious harm to a person under the age of 18" (1987).

The guidelines recommend that child protective services do not intervene if parents use the resources available to them but are still not able to support their children adequately. Given these guidelines, homelessness is not prima facia evidence of parental neglect and intervention is not recommended. Homelessness in the absence of a parental act of omission or commission that places the child in serious jeopardy would not warrant the intervention of child protective services.

The states of California, Texas, and Maryland have ruled out intervention and/or placement based on the fact of homelessness alone (Robison 1989). The exclusion of homeless families from the target population for child protective services assumes the availability of resources to meet the housing needs of families. The reality is that, in the absence of affordable housing for families, homeless youngsters come into the child welfare system. After a period of homelessness, the children frequently experience medical neglect, educational neglect, and/or a lack of supervision while parents look for work and housing. Given this, child protective services often intervene in situations of homelessness with a more intrusive intervention than would be required if families had access to appropriate housing resources.

The Placement Decision

Once a child has come to the attention of a child protection agency and abuse or neglect has been substantiated, the agency must decide about the level of risk that the child is experiencing and determine whether that child can safely remain in his or her home or must be placed in out-of-home care. For families who are the recipients of aid to families with dependent children (AFDC), one of the unanticipated outcomes of a decision to separate a child from his or her parents is the loss of benefits dependent upon the presence of the child in the family. And the loss of those benefits may, in fact, render the family homeless.

AFDC provides benefits to children based on the absence or unemployment of a parent. One-half of the families receiving child protective services are recipients of AFDC (American Association for Protecting Children 1988). When children are placed in out-of-home care, AFDC benefits are reduced if there are remaining children in the family. Benefits are terminated if there are no children left in the family. As a consequence, the family's ability to maintain its housing is threatened.

For those families who are living in public housing, the decision to place one or more of the children may change the size of the unit for which they are eligible. In the absence of children, low-income parents may find themselves ineligible for public housing and without a home.

For many parents for whom a placement decision is made, particularly those who are dependent upon AFDC for their income, the placement decision reduces family income to that available from general assistance. Some of these parents end up as unattached adults living in shelters. Once they move into the world of shelters, they are difficult to locate because the length of residence in each shelter is limited.

Visitation between parents and children is almost impossible (McIntosh 1989).

As families prepare for the return of their children, they also find themselves in a dilemma. They are not eligible for AFDC or housing benefits until the children reside with them, yet many agencies will not return the children until stable housing has been secured. The inability of the child welfare/income maintenance system to assist families with the cost of first- and last-month's rent and utilities creates an obstacle to securing adequate housing and a real obstacle to reunification. Massachusetts has responded to the limitations of AFDC by issuing an AFDC waiver which continues AFDC payments to parents of children in out-of-home care when the placement will be of short duration, allowing families to maintain their residence while protective issues are being resolved.

In response to the housing problem, some states have made flexible dollars available to child welfare workers which can be used in a variety of ways, including the payment of rent and utility bills. The monies are limited and are usually less than the initial amount needed to establish a household. In contrast, New York state recently passed a rent subsidy for the purpose of family reunification. The provisions of the law allow a cash grant to families whose lack of housing impedes the return of their children. Families may receive $300 a month for three years which can be applied to current rent as well as to rent that is in arrears (New York Statutes 1988, Chapter 542 Section 1). The funding for these grants comes from state general revenues. This initiative represents an institutional attempt to address housing barriers to family reunification, but it is not an adequate substitute for decent levels of income maintenance and affordable housing (Robison 1989).

Work with Adolescents

The final issue in the relationship between homelessness and child social services is the effectiveness of the work of the child welfare systems with adolescents. As definitions of abuse and neglect are delineated more clearly, administrators feel strongly that no adolescents should come into the system unless they have experienced abuse and neglect. Those children who are experiencing parent-child conflict, who are status offenders, or who are adolescent parents are no longer deemed appropriate for child protective services (National Association of Public Child Welfare Administrators 1988). Even with this narrowing of the target population, there continues to be a problem in the delivery of protective services to adolescents who are appropriate candidates for protective intervention. Problems are related to the adequacy of resources to meet both their in-home and placement needs.

Nationally, the out-of-home care resources available to these teen-agers are limited. For those children for whom an appropriate resource can be found, placements proceed smoothly. However, when adequate resources are absent, two other patterns emerge. In some instances, youth are screened out at the point of placement because there are no available resources. These youngsters are then left in their family situations although they are experiencing substantial risk.

In other instances, youngsters are placed in out-of-home settings that are not appropriate for their needs. As a result, their adjustments within these settings – whether in families, small group settings or institutional settings – are not good and they often require replacement. These youngsters are often subject to multiple placements and thus the out-of-home care plan, rather than providing stability for youngsters, presents further problems in terms of their development and maturation. Some of the children who are inappropriately placed or left in dangerous situations resolve the issue by running away. In 1985, 2.5 percent of the children exiting substitute care ran away (Tatara 1988).

Many of these children became homeless. Nine percent of the children who exited substitute care either had reached the age of majority or were emancipated (Tatara 1988). This is the group for whom there is the greatest concern because of their potential to become homeless persons. Funding for foster care ends at age eighteen unless a child is in school.

Many youngsters emancipating from the child welfare system find themselves turning eighteen without job skills and/or the social skills necessary for daily living. In a recent study of the independent living experiences of youngsters who had been out of foster care for a minimum of two years, one in three spent their first night on the streets, one in three lacked a high school degree or its equivalency, and many had problems with depression. The average number of living situations these young people experienced was six, and 29 percent had periods of homelessness and/or weekly moves. These youngsters spoke of the need for support, for nurturance, and for help with the practicalities of emancipation. These included securing housing, furniture, and money for first- and last-month's rent, and having the things that were necessary to start a new job (Barth 1988).

The Title IV-E independent living initiative provided grants to states for independent living programs for those minors eligible for AFDC. The initiative has been targeted at youngsters sixteen to eighteen years of age. (It is noteworthy that the average age of children leaving home is twenty-three years for the general population (U.S. Department of Commerce 1986). Foster children are asked to move toward independence at age eighteen even though they have had extremely difficult and traumatic backgrounds.)

The states were given a great deal of flexibility in developing pilot programs to foster independent living. Grants have been used to pay subsidies after age eighteen, provide preparation and skills development opportunities for youth, conduct support groups before, during, and after emancipation, and assist in securing transitional housing. In addition, some young adults are provided with mental health and counseling services. When the independent living initiatives are done well they help avoid homelessness by creating a transition from the dependency of out-of-home care to semi-independent living.

There are several major issues affecting the independent living strategy. The first challenge is to institutionalize the programs so that they encompass all children who will age out of foster care. The strategy needs to be expanded so that the process of building independence in youngsters starts earlier than age sixteen.

A second issue concerns the targeting of independent living services. In some situations, those youngsters who are the most likely to succeed are targeted for independent living programs, leaving the more difficult youngsters with greater educational, vocational, and emotional needs unserved. In other situations, there are so few resources for adolescents that the independent living programs and the transitional living facilities are used to meet the needs of youngsters in crisis rather than as a resource to facilitate emancipation.

For independent living to be successful, foster parents must be trained to promote the development of independence in youngsters rather than maintain inappropriate dependence. Initiatives in this area need to be developed. Given these constraints, the independent living strategy has potential for becoming a powerful policy tool to reduce the incidence of homelessness among children emancipating from the public child welfare system.

Emerging Issues

All of the challenges confronting the child welfare system are complicated by the increasing incidence of drug dependency and AIDS among both parents and children who are served by the child welfare system (National Commission to Prevent Infant Mortality 1988).

Addiction to drugs is one of the major factors contributing to the escalating numbers of substantiated cases of abuse and neglect. Some agencies report drug involvement in as high as 70 percent of their cases (Weber 1988). With addictions to cocaine and other street drugs, effective substance-abuse treatment is necessary to reunify parents and children. Of the children with family reunification as the case plan, 72 percent had parents with alcohol or drug problems (Henley 1988). In cocaine abuse, parents' obsession with the narcotic supercedes their concern for their children (Lynch 1987). One urban administrator described the addicted families as "families with no parent" (Carter 1989).

Without substance-abuse intervention strategies that focus not only on the individual but also on the family and family issues, it is difficult to make progress with many of these families. The major linkages between child welfare and substance abuse are referral mechanisms. While these are useful in some instances, services continue to be limited, and many parents wait a substantial period of time before being served.

Out of the interaction between AIDS and substance abuse comes a new population of homeless children, the "boarder babies." These youngsters are being abandoned in the hospital by their parents out of fear that they are either drug dependent or have the AIDS virus. The child welfare system is struggling to respond to the need for care of these youngsters. However, the boarder babies problem is only the tip of the iceberg. As parents become ill, they will lose income, housing, and the ability to care for their children. As parents die from AIDS and drugs, leaving youngsters who test positive for the human immunodeficiency virus (HIV), the challenges of providing care for these children will escalate.

The Psychosocial Consequences

It is possible to discuss the problem of homelessness from a policy and program perspective, using the best analytic tools, and lose sight of the impact of this issue on the lives of families and children. An examination of the consequences raises these questions: What is the social cost of homelessness? Is a generation of children being lost because of social neglect? In the child welfare system, is social neglect being treated as parental neglect?

In Westchester County, New York, half of the 900 homeless families are women under the age of twenty-one with more than one child. These young women have been rejected by their families of origin either because of the birth of the child or intrafamilial conflict, or because the economic burden has become too great. Many of these women have attempted to share households with others – their mates, other women, and relatives. These arrangements are generally short term or have not been successful. They find themselves without a place to live, and without adequate income to secure housing. These young women become high risk for drugs and prostitution. Their children often come into care because they are incarcerated (Allen 1989).

One shelter operator in Richmond, Virginia, reports that many of the parents in shelters seem to have experienced neglect during their own development. They function as "isolates," showing limited ability to nurture their own children. The children lack the kind of caring that would enable them to become whole people (Purnell 1989).

Social workers in Los Angeles County have discussed the dilemma of serving children who have been placed in foster care because their families lack housing. Workers were struck by the level of rage that children expressed toward their parents. The rage was shaped by the children's perception of the parents' lack of power and their own sense of vulnerability. The parents were viewed by their children as unable to help themselves, unable to help their children, and unable to manage their world. When these youngsters compared their experiences with foster parents to those with their biological parents, they often accused their own parents of not loving them (McIntosh 1989).

Children growing up in families without a stable home often move from shelter to shelter, living with parents in single-occupancy rooms. Their health is in jeopardy; their education is in jeopardy; their self esteem is in jeopardy (Kozol 1988).

Conclusion

The effectiveness of the child welfare system in meeting the productive and family preservation goals is compromised in several ways. Inadequate provision for income maintenance and housing contributes to the level of risk that many children experience and results in intervention which is unnecessarily intrusive. Children are placed in out-of-home care when they might have been cared for in their own homes by their own families had housing been available. A supply of adequate housing would enable agencies to make reasonable efforts to prevent placement.

As resources for children's services have declined, agencies have begun to limit the target population by narrowing the definitions of abuse and neglect, making services more residual. Families must demonstrate very serious problems in order to be served. As a result, early intervention and preventive services have diminished, often providing families with "too little too late."

Once those children and families come into the child welfare system, the services response is limited. Placement prevention services are inadequate; out-of-home care resources are sometimes inappropriate; and independent living resources are not institutionalized and are narrowly targeted.

Given this context and experience, the following recommendations are made:

1. Federal, state, and local governments should work together to assure that an adequate supply of low-income housing is available for families with children.
2. States should take advantage of AFDC waivers, which allow the parents of children in placement to continue to receive AFDC when the placement will be time-limited and family stability can be maintained.

3. Federal, state, and local governments should collaborate to assure the funding for housing when its absence is a barrier to the reunification of children with their families.
4. The Title IV-E independent living program should be institutionalized, and the development of employment and living skills should begin prior to age sixteen.
5. Transitional living programs should be developed for youth emancipating from the child welfare, juvenile justice, and mental health system. They should provide comprehensive health education and support to young adults through age twenty-one.
6. Given that substance abuse is a major cause of loss of housing among families, family-focused substance-abuse treatment resources need to be developed.

Homeless families and their children are often the most difficult families to serve. Schorr's recent work on effective programs for troubled families identified the characteristics of successful programs. Among them were the provision of a broad range of services, a multisystem approach, a focus on families in the context of community, and coherence and accessibility in the way services are organized (1988). As policy alternatives to meet the housing needs of families, children, and youth are thought through, consideration must be given to developing approaches that embody these principles.

A family which cannot stabilize itself has difficulty nurturing its children. It is from a family's home, its base, that safety and security, self-assurance, and the ability to master the world are learned. Families who are homeless, children who are homeless, youth who are homeless cannot achieve this.

References

Allen, M. L., C. Golubock, and L. Olson. 1983. "A Guide to the Adoption Assistance and Child Welfare Act of 1980." In *Foster Children in the Courts,* ed. M. Hardin. Boston: Butterworth Legal Publishers.

American Association for Protecting Children. 1988. *Highlights of Official Abuse and Neglect Report - 1986.* Denver: American Humane Association.

Barth, R. P. 1988, Dec. *On Their Own: The Experiences of Youth After Foster Care.* Berkeley, CA: Family Research Group, University of California Berkeley, School of Social Welfare.

Children's Defense Fund. 1989. *A Vision for America's Children: Agenda for the 1990's.* Washington, DC: By the author.

Hope, M., and J. Young. 1988. *The Faces of Homelessness.* Lexington: D. C. Heath Company.

Kozol, J. 1988. *Rachel and Her Children: Homeless Families in America.* New York: Fawcett Columbia.

"Housing The Poor." 1989. *Public Welfare* 47, no. 1: 5-12.

Lynch, T. 1987. "Growing Substance Abuse in Cities and Its Impact on Families and Children." In *Summary of Second National Symposium on Urban Child Welfare.* Washington, DC: American Public Welfare Association.

Nance, L. G. 1988. "Homelessness." Master's Essay, University of North Carolina, School of Social Work. Draft.

National Association of Public Child Welfare Administration. 1988. *Guidelines for a Model System of Child Protective Services for Abused and Neglected Children and Their Families.* Washington, DC: American Public Welfare Association.

National Commission to Prevent Infant Mortality. 1988. "Perinatal AIDS." Washington, DC: By the author.

New York Statutes. 1988. Chap. 542, sect. 1.

Schorr, L. B. 1988. *Within Our Reach.* New York: Anchor Press.

Tatara, T. 1988, July. *Characteristics of Children in Substitute Care.* Washington, DC: American Public Welfare Association.

U.S. Department of Commerce. 1986. *Statistical Abstract of the United States - 1986.* Washington, DC: Government Printing Office.

United States Code. U.S. Public Law 96-272, Child Welfare and Adoption Assistance Amendment of 1980.

Weber, M. 1988. Testimony on child welfare reform before the House Select Committee for Children, Youth and Families. Washington, DC: Government Printing Office.

William T. Grant Foundation Commission on Work, Family and Citizenship. 1988. "The Forgotten Half: Path Ways to Success for America's Youth and Young Families." Washington, DC: By the author.

Telephone Interviews

(No drafts available)

Allen, J. Commissioner, Westchester County Department of Social Services, White Plains, NY. 1989.

Carter, G. Executive Director, Survival Skills Incorporated. Minneapolis, MN. 1989.

Henley, C. Associate Professor, University of North Carolina, School of Social Work, Chapel Hill, NC. 1988.

McIntosh, J. Western Regional Director Child Welfare League of America, San Dimas, CA. 1989.

Purnell, J. C., Jr. Friends Association for Children, Richmond, VA. 1989.

Robison, S. Director Child Welfare Program National Council of State Legislators, Denver, CO. 1989.

Contributors

Chester Hartman, Ph.D., is a fellow at the Institute for Policy Studies in Washington, D.C.. Hartman is also chair of The Planners Network, a national organization of progressive urban and rural planners and community organizers, and has been active in housing and neighborhood preservation issues in Boston, San Francisco, and Washington.

Julee H. Kryder-Coe, M.S.W., is coordinator of special programs and a senior policy specialist at the Johns Hopkins University Institute for Policy Studies in Baltimore, Maryland. Kryder-Coe served as coordinator of the National Conference on Homeless Children and Youth.

Kay Young McChesney, Ph.D., is assistant professor of sociology and a fellow in the James T. Busch Center for Leadership and Social Policy at the University of Missouri-St. Louis. McChesney has published widely in the field of family and child poverty.

Lisa Mihaly is a senior program associate in the Child Welfare and Mental Health Division at the Children's Defense Fund in Washington, D.C. Mihaly is an expert in national policy affecting homeless children, youth and families.

George Miller is congressman for the Seventh District of California and chairman of the U.S. House Select Committee on Children, Youth and Families. Congressman Miller is considered to be a leading spokesman for children in the United States Congress.

Janice M. Molnar, Ph.D., is a research scientist in the Research Division at the Bank Street College of Education in New York City. Molnar is author of *Home is Where the Heart Is: The Crisis of Homeless Children and Families in New York City.*

Yvonne Rafferty, Ph.D., is director of research at Advocates for Children of New York in Long Island City, New York. Rafferty is co-author of *Learning in Limbo: The Educational Deprivation of Homeless Children.*

Marjorie J. Robertson, Ph.D., is an associate scientist at the Alcohol Research Group, Medical Research Institute of San Francisco in Berkeley, California and director of a longitudinal study of homeless adults and children in Alameda County. Robertson is also co-editor of the book *Homelessness: The National Perspective.*

Lester M. Salamon, Ph.D., is director of the Johns Hopkins Institute for Policy Studies in Baltimore, Maryland and author of a wide variety of works ranging from social welfare policy to national studies of the nonprofit sector. Salamon is a former deputy associate director of the U.S. Office of Management and Budget.

Michael A. Stegman, Ph.D., is chairman and professor at the Department of City and Regional Planning and chairman of the Ph.D. curriculum in Public Policy Analysis, University of North Carolina, Chapel Hill. Stegman is a former deputy assistant secretary for research in the U.S. Department of Housing and Urban Development.

Carol W. Williams, D.S.W., is senior research associate in the Center for the Study of Social Policy in Washington, D.C. Williams is the immediate past director of the National Child Welfare Leadership Center at the University of North Carolina, Chapel Hill.

Linda A. Wolf, D.P.A., is deputy director of the American Public Welfare Association in Washington, D.C. Wolf formerly served on the graduate faculty of Virginia Tech's Center for Public Administration and Policy and as a local director of human services.

James D. Wright, Ph.D., is Favrot Professor of Human Relations in the Department of Sociology at Tulane University in New Orleans, Louisiana. Wright is author af *Address Unknown: Homelessness in Contemporary America.*

Barry Zigas is president of the National Low-Income Housing Coalition in Washington, D.C. and executive secretary of the Low-Income Housing Information Service. Zigas was formerly assistant executive director for the U.S. Conference of Mayors.

Name Index

Abrahamson, M., 158, 169
Accardo, P., 107, 139
Achenbach, T., 108, 131
Adams, G. R., 34, 36, 58, 63, 68
Aday, L., 77, 99
Aiken, L. H., 77, 100
Aker, P. J., 131
Allen, J., 295, 298
Allen, M. L., 286, 297
Allen, W., 76, 100
Alperstein, G., 74, 80, 99, 131, 132, 133
Alstrom, C. H., 76, 99
American Association for Protecting Children, 286, 290, 297
American Public Welfare Association, 271, 272, 273, 277, 278, 279, 283
Anderson, R., 77, 99
Angel, R., 132
Apgar, W. C., Jr., 186, 193
Armstein, E., 131
Association of the Bar of the City of New York, 132
Atlanta Task Force for the Homeless, 21, 29

Bach, V., 132
Barbanel, J., 132, 267
Barden, J. C., 36, 41, 63
Bartelt, D., 19, 32, 37, 57, 67
Barth, R. P., 54, 64, 293, 297
Bassuk, E., 22, 23, 24, 29, 80, 81, 88, 99, 106, 107, 108, 109, 110, 111, 132
Bax, M. J., 137
Baxter, E., 132
Beaty, A., 27, 30
Benker, K., 132, 134
Berezin, J., 106, 133
Bergmann, B. R., 158, 170
Bernstein, A. B., 133
Bingham, R. D., 133
Blank, R. M., 147, 148, 170
Blau, F. D., 158, 170

Blendon, R. J., 77, 100
Blewett, C. D., 138
Blinder, A. S., 147, 148, 170
Bluestone, B., 155, 166, 170
Board of Education, New York City, 123, 124, 125, 126, 127, 128, 130, 133
Bogue, D., 75, 99
Boxhill, N., 27, 30
Boyert, M., 107, 139
Bratt, R. G., 202, 223
Breakey, W. R., 13, 30
Brennan, T., 34, 36, 64
Brickner, P. W., 74, 99, 103, 133
Brinner, R., 150, 171
Bronfenbrenner, U., 133
Brown, H. J., 186, 193
Brown, J. H., 21, 30
Bucy, J., viii, 36, 41, 58, 64
Bureau of National Affairs, 267
Burgess, A. W., 44, 65
Burt, M., 14, 30, 272, 283

Camp, P., 106, 135
Caper, A., 133
Carter, G., 294, 298
Carter, Jimmy, 217, 219
Caton, C. L. M., 33, 43, 47, 48, 49, 59, 64, 67, 110, 133, 138
Cautley, E., 76, 102
Center for Law and Education, 133
Chavkin, W., 76, 99, 133
Chelimsky, E., 34, 36, 38, 40, 44, 52, 64
Chen, C. H., 79, 103
Chicago Coalition for the Homeless, 33, 40, 44, 45, 52, 53, 58, 64
Children's Defense Fund, 15, 30, 133, 150, 170, 298
Christenson, B. A., 76, 102
Christofides, A., 139
Citizen's Committee for the Children of New York, 22, 24, 30, 43, 53, 55, 58, 64, 109, 133, 134
Clancy, M. A., 34, 63
Cobb, S., 134
Cohen, B., 14, 30, 272, 283
Cohen, E., 33, 47, 48, 49, 50, 51, 54, 60, 68, 74, 80, 103
Colson, P., 62, 67
Community Food Resource Center, 134
Conanan, B., 74, 99

Congressional Budget Office, 177, 182, 184, 193, 209, 216, 218, 219, 220, 223, 239, 251, 253, 254, 257, 258, 267
Conover, S., 62, 67, 135
ConServe (Washington, D.C.), 29
Consortium for Longitudinal Studies, 106, 134
Corcoran, M., 157, 170
Corey, C. R., 77, 100
Council of Community Services, 38, 41, 52, 58, 59, 64
Council of the City of New York Select Committee on the Homeless, 134
Cowan, C. D., 13, 30
Croft, C. J., 64
Crystal, S., 64
Culp, J., 152, 170
Cuomo, M. M., 134

Daley, S., 64
Dalton, A., viii
Damrosch, S. P., 46, 67, 138
Danziger, S., 160, 161, 170
David, T., 33, 36, 38, 39, 40, 41, 42, 43, 45, 49, 53, 54, 57, 58, 59, 66, 67
Davis, K., 77, 99
DeChillo, N., 137
Decker, E., 78, 101
Dehavenon, A. L., 134
DeLeon, M., 79, 103
Dennis, D. L., 64
Department of Health, New York City, 134
Deykin, E. Y., 64
Dickman, J., 57, 66
Diesenhouse, S., 64
Dinkins, D. N., 134
Doeringer, P. B., 151, 170
Dolbeare, C. N., 20, 21, 30, 176, 187, 188, 192, 193, 209, 222, 223, 224, 252, 253, 265, 267
Dott, A. B., 76, 100
Dreyer, B. P., 131
Drucker, E., 61, 65
Duggan, R., 35, 38, 39, 40, 42, 49, 50, 59, 66
Dumpson, J. R., 134
Duncan, G. J., 75, 100, 157, 170
Dunson, B. H., 152, 170

Eckstein, O., 147, 170

Edelbrock, C., 108, 131
Edelman, M. W., viii, 9
Egbuonu, L., 77, 88, 100
Ehrenreich, B., 75, 100
Elliot, D. S., 34, 36, 64
Ellwood, D. T., 147, 149, 150, 155, 159, 160, 167, 170
Elvy, A., 74, 77, 99
Emergency Services Network, 17, 20, 22, 30
Executive Office of Communities and Development, 265, 268

Farber, E. D., 40, 65
Farber, S. S., 135
Farley, R., 76, 100
Faulkner, D., 40, 65
Felner, R. D., 134, 135
Felton, E., 67
Ferber, M. A., 158, 170
Ferguson, L., 42, 47, 49, 50, 53, 54, 66, 137
Fierman, A. H., 131, 133
Financial Democracy Campaign, 255, 267
Fisher, G., 75, 101, 138
Fisher, P. J., 13, 30
Flanigan, J. M., 74, 80, 99, 132
Fleming, G. V., 77, 99
Fodor, I., 135
Fort, A. T., 76, 100
Fox, E. R., 138
Frankenburg, W. K., 106, 135
Freeman, H., 77, 100
Freeman, R. B., 14, 30, 155, 170

Gallagher, E.,   135
Garmezy, N., 135
Gault, N., 150, 171
General Accounting Office, 15, 16, 17, 30
Geronimo, M., 139
Gewirtzman, R., 135
Ginter, D. W., 48, 67
Godfrey, W., 36, 58, 68
Gold, M., 77, 99
Goldstein, A., 106, 135
Goldstein, I., 19, 32, 37, 57, 67
Golembiewski, G., 38, 42, 49, 62, 68

Golubock, C., 286, 297
Gordon, I. S., 44, 65
Gortmaker, S. L., 77, 100
Gottschalk, P., 160, 161, 170
Gracey, C. A., 109, 137
Graham, G. C., 78, 100
Granovetter, M., 171
Greater Boston Emergency Network, 34, 37, 40, 41, 42, 43, 65
Green, R. E., 133
Greenblatt, M., 33, 48, 59, 66, 137
Grella, C., 42, 47, 54, 61, 66
Grinker, W., 135
Gross, T. P., 74, 100, 135
Grossman, S., 62, 67
Guigli, P. E., 76, 99, 133
Gulotta, T., 34, 63
Gutierres, S. E., 41, 65

Halfon, N., 77, 101
Hall, B., 14, 30
Hall, J. A., 111, 136
Halpern, S., 235, 236, 268
Hamberg, J., 176, 193
Hansen, W. L., 158, 171
Hardoy, J. E., 76, 100
Harris, C. C., 156, 171
Harris, C. S., 155, 171
Harrison, B., 155, 166, 170
Hartman, C., v, vi, viii, 6, 9, 44, 65, 135, 175, 197
Haskins, R., 106, 135
Health Care for the Homeless Coalition of Greater St. Louis, 77, 100
Hein, K., 61, 65
Helton, J. R., 48, 67
Hemmens, K. C., 37, 46, 57, 65
Henley, C., 294, 299
Hernandez, C. E., 76, 102
Hersch, P., 47, 65
Hevesi, D., 33, 34, 65
Hill, M. S., 157, 170
Hinds, M. W., 76, 102
Hingson, M. J., 62, 67
Hirschman, C., 154, 171
Hoch, C., 135
Hodes, B., 135

Hoffman, F., 35, 38, 39, 40, 42, 49, 50, 59, 66
Holden, K. C., 158, 171
Holzer, H. J., 152, 155, 170, 171
Hope, M., 298
Hopper, K., 132, 135, 176, 193
Horton, G., 135
Huizinga, D., 34, 36, 64
Human Nutrition Information Service, 79, 100
Human Resources Administration, New York City,   135, 136, 236, 268

Institute for Community Economics, 223
Institute for Policy Studies Working Group on Housing, 192, 193, 223
Institute of Medicine, 15, 30, 33, 38, 42, 65, 74
Interagency Council on the Homeless, 268
Irvine, J., 79, 102

Jahiel, R. I., 109, 136
Janus, M., 44, 65
Johnson, C. M., 19, 30
Johnston, W. B., 165, 171
Jolly, M. K., 64
Jonas, S., 136

Kahan, M., 77, 78, 101
Kamerman, S., 159, 171
Karp, R., 78, 101
Kasarda, J. D., 155, 156, 171
Kay, K., 137
Kelly, J. T., 98, 100
Kendagor, R., 107, 139
Kennedy, J. T., 47, 61, 67
Keyes, L., 234, 235, 268
Kilduff, M., 138
Kinast, C., 40, 65
Knickman, J. R., 17, 30
Knight, J. D., 82, 98, 103, 139
Knight, J. W., 95, 98, 100, 101
Koegel, P., 42, 47, 48, 49, 50, 53, 54, 61, 66, 137
Kovacs, M., 107, 136
Kozol, J., viii, 136, 235, 296, 298
Krasniewski, D., 15, 20, 31
Krauser, J., 77, 78, 101

Kristal, A., 76, 99, 133
Kriz, M., 268
Kronenfeld, D., 137
Kufeldt, K., 45, 65
Kutner, R., 268

Lam, J., 82, 98, 101, 103, 139, 234, 269
Lam, J. A., 139
Landers, S., 49, 65
Lang, A. R., 47, 65
Lattin, D., 65
Lauriat, A., 22, 24, 29, 80, 99, 106, 107, 111, 132
Lazere, E. B., 20, 21, 30, 176, 187, 188, 193, 209, 223, 224
Leavitt, R., 136
Leland, P., 15, 19, 31
Lemieux, D., 76, 101
Leonard, P. A., 20, 21, 30, 176, 187, 188, 193, 209, 223, 224
Levey, L. A., 77, 101
Levey, S., 77, 101
Leviton, A., 137
Levy, F., 161, 165, 171
Levy, J. C., 64
Lin, E. H. B., 80, 101, 136
Lindelius, R., 76, 99
Litan, R. E., 147, 163, 166, 172
Lloyd, C. B., 151, 172
Loth, R., 268
Low Income Housing Information Service, 20, 30, 227, 228, 229, 230, 231, 237, 255, 266, 267, 268, 269
Lowther, L., 45, 65
Luecke, M. R., 37, 46, 57, 65
Lynch, T., 294, 298

MacDowell, M., 77, 101
MacKenzie, R., 33, 47, 48, 49, 50, 51, 54, 60, 68, 74, 80, 103
Main, T., 136
Makuc, D., 77, 99
Manov, A., 45, 65
Matthews, B., 36, 58, 68
Maza, P. L., 111, 136
McCoard, W. D., 40, 65
McChesney, K. Y., v, viii, 5, 9, 17, 23, 24, 31, 62, 66, 136, 143, 172
McClure, D., 57, 66

McCormick, D. E., 259, 268
McIntosh, J., 291, 295, 299
McKinney, S., xvii, 26, 97, 138
McKormack, A., 44, 65
Mellor, E. F., 158, 172
Michigan Network of Runaway and Youth Services, 38, 58, 66
Middleton-Jeter, V., 137
Mihaly, L., v, viii, 3, 4, 11
Miller, C. A., 75, 101
Miller, D., S., 35, 38, 39, 40, 42, 49, 50, 59, 66, 80, 101, 136
Miller, G., xviii
Minnesota Coalition for the Homeless, 23, 31
Moen, P., 148, 154, 172
Molnar, J., v, viii, 3, 107, 136
Moreno, S., 136
Moullinix, C. F., 77, 100
Mundy, P., 33, 44, 59, 66, 137

Nance, L. G., 298
Nann, R., 136
Naor, E., 76, 101
National Alliance to End Homelessness, 13, 14, 31
National Association of Housing and Redevelopment Officers – American
    Public Welfare Association Advisory Panel, 279, 280, 283
National Association of Public Child Welfare Administrators, 289, 292, 298
National Black Child Development Institute, 18, 31
National Coalition for the Homeless, 13, 110, 136, 137
National Commission to Prevent Infant Mortality, 294, 298
National Housing Task Force, 20, 31
National Network of Runaway and Youth Services, 34, 37, 39, 40, 41, 42,
    44, 47, 51, 53, 54, 57, 59, 66
Neckerman, K. M., 156, 173
Neeleman, H. L., 137
Nersesian, W. S., 76, 101
Newacheck, P. W., 77, 88, 101, 137
Newburger, C., 77, 101
Newburger, E., 77, 101
Newman, S., 251, 252, 253, 268
Newman, S. J., 20, 31
New York State Council on Children and Families, 38, 42, 44, 52, 53, 54,
    55, 56, 66, 137
New York State Rules and Regulations, 137
New York Statutes, 291, 298
Niemi, B. T., 151, 172

Nimmo, M., 45, 65
Nix, C., 137
Novick, L. F., 47, 61, 67

Oberg, C., 97, 101
Olsen, E. O., 227, 228, 229, 231, 268
Olsen, L., 286, 297
Owen, G., 21, 22, 31

Packer, A. H., 165, 171
Paone, D., 137
Partnership for the Homeless, 137
Parvensky, J., 15, 20, 31
Patton, L. T., 16, 19, 31
Pennbridge, J., 33, 47, 48, 49, 50, 51, 54, 60, 66, 68, 74, 80, 103
Petit, M., 76, 101
Peuquet, S., 15, 19, 31
Phillips, M., 137
Piliavin, I., 62, 66
Piore, M. J., 151, 170
Piven, F., 75, 100
Powell, J., 67
Primavera, J., 135
Purnell, J. C., Jr., 295, 299

Rafferty, Y., v, 5, 105, 137
Rappaport, C., 74, 80, 99, 132
Raspberry, W., 254, 268
Reagan, Ronald, 188, 217, 225-232, 252
Redlener, I. E., 96, 101, 137
Reich, J. W., 41, 65
Reich, M., 152, 172
Reich, R. B., 232, 233, 234, 268
Reinherz, H., 109, 137
Reuben, N., 61, 65
Reuler, J. B., 137
Reyes, L. M., 15, 16, 18, 19, 26, 31
Reynolds, C. R., 108, 137
Richmond, B. O., 108, 137
Richmond, J., 77, 101
Rimer, S., 232, 235, 269
Robertson, J. M., 48, 59, 66, 137

Robertson, J. R., 137
Robertson, M. J., v, 4, 33, 35, 38, 39, 40, 41, 42, 43, 45, 46, 47, 48, 49,
    50, 51, 52, 53, 54, 58, 59, 60, 61, 62, 66
Robertson, P., 79, 103
Robins, L. N., 67
Robison, S., 289, 291, 299
Rollins, N., 105, 137
Rosenberg, L., 23, 29, 107, 111, 132
Rosenberg, M. L., 74, 100, 135
Rossi, P. H., 75, 97, 98, 101, 138, 139
Roth, L., 138
Rothman, J., 33, 36, 38, 39, 40, 41, 42, 43, 45, 49, 53, 54, 57, 58, 59, 67
Rowe, A., 16, 31
Rubin, L., 22, 24, 29, 80, 88, 99, 106, 107, 108, 109, 110, 111, 132
Ruddick, S., 67
Ryan, P., 19, 32, 37, 57, 67
Ryan, W., 138

Salamon, L. M., v, ix, 3
Salum, I., 76, 99
Sampson, J. H., 137
Savarese, M., 74, 99
Scharer, L. K., 74, 99
Schlesinger, D. P., 76, 102
Schnare, A., 20, 31, 251, 252, 253, 268
Scholl, T. O., 78, 101
Schorr, L. B., 8, 9, 297, 298
Seabron, C., 76, 99, 133
Sege, I., 232, 233, 269
Shaffer, D., 33, 43, 47, 48, 49, 59, 67, 110, 138
Shah, C. P., 77, 78, 101
Shaper, R., 76, 101
Shapiro, D., 154, 172
Sidel, R., 75, 101
Sigelman, L., 158, 169
Simpson, J., 138
Sinai, A., 147, 170
Singell, L. D., 151, 172
Singer, J. D., 78, 102
Skaggs, J. W., 76, 102
Smith, J. P., 157, 172
Smith, S. J., 138
Sogunro, G. O., 76, 102
Solarz, A. L., 33, 37, 67

Sosin, M., 62, 66, 67
Speck, N. B., 48, 67
Spurlock, C. W., 76, 102
Starfield, B., 77, 88, 100, 101, 137
Stark, L., 138
State Education Department, New York State, 138
Status Reports, 16, 24, 32
Stegman, M. A., vi, 7, 9, 225, 234, 269
Steinhagen, R., 132
Stewart, C. E., 139
Stone, M., 190, 191, 192, 193
Streuning, E., 62, 67
Stricof, R. L., 47, 61, 67
Strunan, L., 62, 67
Sudman, S., 77, 100
Sullivan, C., 33, 67
Sullivan, P. A., 46, 67, 138
Sum, A. M., 19, 30
Summers, L. H., 147, 149, 150, 170
Susser, E., 62, 67, 135
Sutermeister, O., 185, 193

Tatara, T., 286, 287, 292, 298
Taylor, M., 138
Tessler, R. C., 139
Theophano, J., 78, 101
Thurow, L. C., 165, 166, 172
Tilly, C., 171
Tolchin, M., 233, 269
Tomaszewicz, M., 18, 32
Towber, R. I., 37, 67, 68

Upshur, C. C., 38, 40, 48, 49, 54, 68
U. S. Bureau of Census, 144, 145, 146, 153, 154, 157, 161, 162, 169, 172, 269
U. S. Conference of Mayors, 105, 138
U. S. Congress, House, 25, 32, 68, 267, 277, 278, 283
U. S. Congress, Senate, 34, 38, 68
U. S. Department of Commerce, 75, 102, 293, 298
U. S. Department of Education, 109, 139
U. S. Department of Health and Human Services, 40, 68
U. S. General Accounting Office, 277, 283

Vanderbourg, K., 139
Vander Kooi, R. C., 38, 58, 62, 68
Van Dusen, K. T., 49, 68
van Houten, T., 38, 42, 49, 62, 68
Vermund, S., 61, 65

Wadsworth, M. E., 77, 102
Ward, M., 157, 172
Warren, C. A. B., 49, 68
Waxman, L. D., viii, 15, 16, 18, 19, 26, 31
Weber-Burdin, E., 82, 98, 103, 139
Weber, E., 74, 76, 95, 98, 103, 139
Weber, M., 294, 298
Weill, J. D., 19, 30
Weisfuse, I. B., 47, 61, 67
Weitzman, B. C., 17, 30
Wells, V., 64
Westerfelt, H., 62, 66
Westoff, C., 76, 102
White, S. B., 133
Whitman, B., 107, 139
William T. Grant Foundation, Commission on Work, Family and
    Citizenship, 298
Williams, C. W., vi, 8, 285
Williams, J. A., 21, 22, 31
Willis, G., 75, 101, 138
Wilson, W. J., 156, 172, 173
Wilton, K. M., 79, 102
Winick, M., 79, 102, 139
Wolf, L., vi, 7, 271
Worobey, J., 132
Wright, J. D., v, 4, 71, 72, 74, 75, 76, 80, 81, 82, 95, 96, 97, 98, 101, 102,
    103, 138, 139, 234, 269

Yates, G. L., 33, 36, 39, 41, 46, 47, 48, 49, 50, 54, 57, 58, 60, 66, 68, 74,
    80, 103
Yinger, J., 21, 30
Young, J., 298
Young, R. L., 36, 58, 68

Zee, P., 79, 103
Zigas, B. v, vi, vii, 6, 9, 175, 197

Subject Index

Abandonment (property), 179
"Accessory units," 181
Acute disorders, 77, 87-88, 89
Adolescents:
    child welfare services and, 291-294
    foster care and, 287-288
    physical health problems, 45-47, 89-95
    See also Homeless youth
AFDC (Aid to Families with Dependent Children), 20-22, 96-97, 159-160,
    167, 272-273, 276, 290-291
Affordable housing, 168, 234-236
Affordable Housing Act, 247-249
Aftercare and discharge planning, 55
AIDS, 47, 294-295
AIDS prevention programs, 54
Alcohol use and abuse, 49-50, 94
Anxiety, 108
Asia, 165
Assisted housing budget, 226-232

"Baby-bust," 167
Barracks-style shelters, 26-28
Behavioral disturbances, 108-109
Birth control, 46
Blacks:
    labor market discrimination, 152-155
    male joblessness, 155-156, 176
    single-mother families, 145
"Boarder babies," 294
Building codes, 181
Bush, George, 226, 266-267
Business cycle, 146-147, 150-151

Census of Population, 14
Child care, 159

Children:
    developmental delays, 106-107
    educational problems, 109-111, 123-128
    effects of homelessness on, 105-131
    foster care placement, 18
    health problems and poverty, 74-98
    psychological problems, 107-109, 295
Child support, 159-160
Child welfare services, 285, 296-297
    adolescents in system, 291-294
    emerging issues, 294-295
    neglect defined, 289-290
    overview of, 286-288
    philosophical issues, 288-289
    placement decision, 290-291
    social cost of homelessness, 295-296
Chronic physical disorders, 88, 89
Comparable worth, 158
Comprehensive services, 53
Condominium conversions, 178
Congregate living, 28
Credit shock, 166
Current Population Survey, 144

Deindustrialization, 155-156
Density bonuses, 181
Depression, 107-108
Developmental delays, 106-107
Disability, 146
Disability insurance, 149-150
Discouraged worker rate, 147, 149, 159
Doubled-up households, 16-17, 185
Drug use and abuse, 50-51, 94, 294
Dual labor market, 151-152
Dysfunctional families, 40

Educational attainment, 22, 38
Educational problems, 109-111, 123-128
Eligibility rules, tenants, 257-262
Emancipation, 292
Emergency Assistance (EA) program, 273-274
Emergency services, 52
Emergency shelter, 25-29

Europe, 165
European Economic Community (EEC), 165
Experimental housing-allowance program (EHAP), 206

Family poverty. *See* Poverty
Family problems, 39-42
Family Support Act of 1988, 278
Family violence, 24
Farmers Home Administration (FmHA), 209, 217
Federal deficit, 165-168
Federal Housing Administration (FHA), 199
Federal housing assistance, 20, 200-223, 226-232
Female-headed families, 19, 145, 156-164
Financial Democracy Campaign (FDC), 254-255
Financial Institution Reform, Recovery, and Enforcement Act (Savings and
    Loan Bailout Bill), 254-257
Food Stamp Program, 274
Foster care, 18, 42, 287

Gentrification, 178
Germany, 165
Global economy, 155-156, 165, 233
GNP, 164
Grace Hill Consolidated Services (Missouri), 29

Health Care for the Homeless (HCH), 71-98
Health services, 77
Hidden homeless, 13
Hispanics:
    single-mother families, 145
Holdover rates, students, 125-127
Homeless child syndrome, 96
Homeless families:
    female-headed, 19, 145, 156-164
    hidden, 16-18
    number of with children, 14-16
    single-parent, 19, 186
    young, 19-20
Homelessness rate, 12
Homeless youth, 33, 55-56
    alcohol use and abuse, 49-50

characteristics of, 37-38
drug use and abuse, 50-51
family problems of, 39-42
groups at risk, 52
history of homelessness among, 38-39
mental health problems, 47-49
as next generation of homeless adults, 51
physical health problems, 45-47, 89-95
population estimates of, 36-37
residential instability among, 42-44
services, gaps in, 52-55
survival while homeless, 44-45
terminology, 34-35
See also Adolescents
Homeowners:
   shelter-poor, 191
   tax deductions of, 197-198
HOPE initiative, 226, 266-267
Housing Act (1968), 180
Housing and Community Development Act (1974), 203
Housing and Community Development Act of 1989, 242-243
Housing cost-to-income gap, 186
Housing market, 175-192
Housing policy, 225-226, 232-234, 262-267
   affordable rental housing and, 234-235
   assisted housing budget and, 226-232
   causes of homelessness and, 235-236
   eligibility rules and, 257-262
   housing legislation, 237-251
   rental assistance and, 251-254
   savings and loan bailout and, 254-257
Housing programs:
   federal mortgage market support, 199-200
   homeowner tax deductions, 197-198
   public housing programs, 200-223
Housing starts, 179-180
HUD (Department of Housing and Urban Development), 201, 203-204, 209,
   217, 221, 259
"Human capital" thesis, 151, 152

Illegal activities, 45
Illness, 146
Improvised shelter, 44
Income:

distribution of, 177
distribution of during Reagan administration, 233
relationship of to housing problems, 185, 187-189
Independent living initiative (Title IV-E), 293
Infant mortality, 75-76
Institutional contact, 43
Intervention programs and sites, 54
Involuntary part-time worker rate, 147
Iron-deficiency anemias, 78

Japan, 165
Jesse Gray Housing Act, 249
Job Opportunities and Basic Skills Training Program (JOBS), 275
Job segregation, 158

Labor market, 151-152, 158
Labor shortage, 167
Living wage, 146
Long-term services, 54-55
Low-Income Energy Assistance Program (LIHEAP), 274-275
Low-income housing ratio, 143, 168

Male children, 26
Malnutrition, 78
Married-couple households, 145-146
Mathematics achievement, 125, 126
Median family income, 160-161, 177
Medicaid, 275
Mental health problems, 47-49, 80-81, 94-95
Mental health treatment history, 48-49
Mental illness, 24
Minimum wage, 150
Morbidity, 77
Mortgage-interest deductions, 197-198
Motels, 27, 276-278

National Affordable Housing Act, 244-247, 261-262
National Ambulatory Medical Care Survey (NAMCS), 80, 83
National Comprehensive Housing Act, 249-251
Neglect, 40-41, 289-290

Nixon, Richard, 203, 205
Nutrition, 78-81
Nutritional deficiency disorders, 78-80, 89
Nutrition programs, 274

Oil shock, 161, 166
One Child in Four, 278-279, 283
Our House (Atlanta), 29

Parent alcohol/drug use, 42
Parental roles, 27
Permanent Housing for Homeless Americans Act of 1989, 243-244
Physical abuse, 40-41
Physical health problems, 73
    homeless adolescents, 45-47, 89-95
    homeless children, 83-88
"Pink collar" occupations, 156, 158
Placement, out-of-home, 290-291
Population:
    homeless youth, 36-37
Poverty, 74-75, 143-145
    business cycle and, 146-147, 150-151
    causes of, 145-160
    deindustrialization and, 155-156
    dual labor market and, 151-152
    feminization of, 233
    and infant mortality, 75-76
    and morbidity, 77
    and nutrition, 78-81
    policy implications for families, 164-168
    racial discrimination and, 152-155
    safety net programs and, 147-151
    in single-mother families, 156-160
    trends in, 160-164
Poverty line, 143, 168
Poverty rates:
    children, 71
    families, 144-145
    single-mother families, 163-164
Pregnancy, 46-47, 76, 89
Primary labor market, 152
Privacy, 27
Private housing market, 178

Problem behaviors, 45
Property taxes, 197-198
Psychological problems, 107-109, 295-296
Public housing programs, 200-223

Race, 185-186
Racial discrimination, 152-155
Reading achievement, 123-124
Recession, 147, 166
Recommended daily allowances (RDA), 79
Rental assistance, 251-254
Rental housing, 234-235
Renters, 198
Rent-to-income ratio, 187-189
Residential instability, 42-43
Residential options, 54
Rickets, 78
Runaways:
    defined, 34-35
Rural homeless population, 16
Rust-belt, 155

"Safety net" programs, 147-150, 177-178
Savings and loan bailout, 254-257
School attendance, 127-128
School lunch program, 274
School performance:
    holdover rates, 125-127
    mathematics achievement, 125, 126
    reading achievement, 123-124
    school attendance, 127-128
Secondary labor market, 152
Section 236 (mortgage-insurance program), 202-203
Section 8 program, 203-208, 252
Services:
    AIDS education, 54
    comprehensive, 53
    emergency, 52
    health, 77
    intervention programs and sites, 54
    long-term, 54-55
    special, 53

    tailored, 52-53
    treatment, 53-54
Sex discrimination, 157-159
Sexual abuse, 40-41
Sexual history, 46
Sexuality, 89
Sexual orientation, 46
Shared housing, 17
Single-mother families, 145, 162
    causes of poverty in, 156-160
    child care and child support in, 159-160
    poverty rate of, 163-164
    sex discrimination and, 157-159
Single-parent families, 19, 186
Single-room-occupancy hotels (SROs), 178-179
Socioeconomic pressures, 44
Special education and training services, 53
Special needs allowances, 273
Squatters, 278
Stuart B. McKinney Homeless Assistance Act, 81, 264
Subsidized housing, 180, 221-222
Substance abuse, 24, 49-51, 94, 294
Substandard housing, 184-185
Suicide, 48
Support networks, 23-24

Tailored services, 52-53
Taxes:
    mortgage-interest deductions, 197
    property taxes, 197-198
Teen pregnancy, 46-47, 89
Temporary Emergency Food Assistance Program (TEFAP), 274
Tenant selection, 257-262
Throwaways, 41
Title IV-E (independent living initiative), 293
Treatment services, 53-54

Undermaintenance, 179
Unemployment, 146
    black males, 176
Unemployment insurance, 147-148
Unemployment rate, 147, 148, 154, 156, 159

Vouchers (housing), 208, 230

Wage gap, 157-158
Welfare hotels, 27, 276-278
Welfare system, 271, 282-283
    AFDC, 272-273
    challenge to, 278-279
    consequences of response of, 275-278
    Emergency Assistance program, 273-274
    JOBS program, 275
    Low-Income Energy Assistance Program, 274-275
    Medicaid, 275
    non-traditional partnerships and, 279-282
    nutrition programs, 274
    special needs allowances, 273
Whites:
    single mother families, 145
WIC (Special Supplemental Food Program for Women, Infants, and
    Children), 274
Women:
    child care and child support issues, 159-160
    labor force participation, 161
    sex discrimination and, 157-159
Worker's Compensation, 149
Work Incentive program (WIN), 275
World War II, 146, 160, 161, 165, 175

Young families, 19-20
Youth alcohol/drug use, 41

Zoning, 181

362.708 H765

Homeless children and
youth : a new American
c1991.

DATE DUE

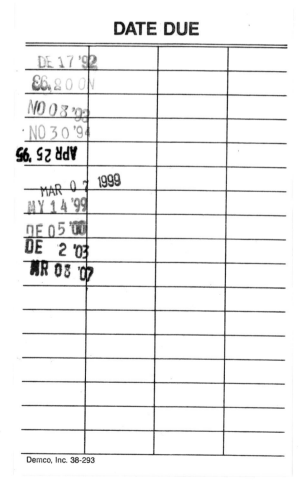

DE 17 '92		
NO 8 '00		
NO 03 '93		
NO 30 '94		
APR 25 '95		
MAR 07 1999		
MY 14 '99		
DE 05 '00		
DE 2 '03		
MR 08 '07		

Demco, Inc. 38-293